WHO WOULD EVER HAVE THOUGHT

NANCY GOUDIE

First edition 2020

ISBN 9-781916-299511

Graphic design by Chris Mathison

Published by The NGM Trust
Caedmon Complex, Bristol Road, Thornbury, Bristol BS35 3JA, UK

www.ngm.org.uk

Printed and bound in Great Britain by TJ Books Limited, Padstow, Cornwall.

DEDICATION

I want to dedicate this book first of all to the one whose presence I absolutely love and adore. **Lord** thank you that you called Ray and myself to leave everything behind in order to take us on a great and wonderful adventure. What an incredible journey! I could never have imagined that you could do so much through two ordinary human beings like us. I can never thank you enough for all you have done and all you continue to do. You are my everything!

Secondly this book is dedicated to my two sons. **Daniel and Aidan** this book is part of your history and part of your inheritance. It's a record of what God did when two people decided to do what God told us to do and to go where he told us to go. This book will help you and your beautiful wives to know your spiritual inheritance as you continue to follow the call of God. Your dad and I are so proud of you both. We love you so much and my prayer is that you will both accomplish so much more than your dad and I have ever done.

Thirdly this book is dedicated to my best friend and husband of 43 years, **Ray**, the one who walked all these years and more with me. We were a brilliant double act who shared the same heart and vision. We encouraged and built each other up to continue to pursue the heart of God. I am so amazed and so grateful for all we saw and accomplished together through the love and power of God. I miss you so much!

CONTENTS

ENDORSEMENTS FOR WHO WOULD EVER HAVE THOUGHT

This book by my friend Nancy Goudie is a fascinating account of the steps of trust and obedience she and Ray took on their remarkable walk of faith that has blessed so many over so many years. It's not just a history; it's a tremendous encouragement for us to take our God at his word and step out in faith and then marvel at all the fruit. I applaud and salute you Nancy and your dear husband Ray, who has already been promoted to glory.

J.John, Minister
Speaker & Author

Today, when even many Christians view simple trust in God through a filter of suspicion and scepticism, Nancy's candid account of her and Ray's adventures on the raw edge of faith is a bright shaft of sunlight. If you are hungry for adventures of faith with God and wonder where to begin, this book is for you.

Graham Kendrick
Songwriter

It has been our privilege to have travelled with Ray and Nancy over most of their 40 years and have seen first-hand the results from their ministry and from their lives.

Their friendship and love have affected our own family personally. We are so glad that Nancy has written this book as our world is crying out for answers right now.

Delve into Who Would Ever Have Thought - an inspirational story written for such a time as this, by an amazing and inspiring lady.

Dr John Lancaster MBE and Rosemary Lancaster MBE

Usually a biographical book coincides with either the incredible high point or the final conclusion of the story. Nancy has chosen neither ending - for hers is a story still being written. And that is what makes this an amazing book, and one that is so well-worth reading. For success and loss, spiritual triumph and suffering are interwoven in a story of new beginnings, with only the final chapters awaiting the sequel. Here is a story of happiness briefly coupled with despair, of shattered dreams intermingled with outstanding fulfilment, linked together by the bravery and faith of an incredible lady. Do not miss this book, for knowing Nancy has indelibly impacted the lives of so many of us. And now it's your turn!

Clive Calver, Preacher
Pastor and former President of World Relief

Jesus promises a bumper harvest to those with a good heart who keep going. These two things perfectly describe my friend Nancy Goudie. I love everything she stands for and know that this book will be yet another blessing and bearer of much fruit. Read on and be encouraged.

Andy Hawthorne OBE
CEO and founder The Message Trust

Here's a book that's very difficult to put down! What a story of faith, courage & adventure! But if you're thinking, "All these stories full of positive things are not what I experience," stop right there, pick the book up and read it because it has more than its fair share of tears and discouragements as well. You and I can identify with that, so let's be open to learn from the raw honesty of Nancy's writing. Thanks, Nancy, for letting us in on your and Ray's journey through life; I for one have been greatly challenged and encouraged.

Rob White
Former National Director of YFC, Church-planter and Author

Ray and Nancy's unwavering faithfulness to God's calling, their humility and integrity are qualities we have always admired. They worked as a team, striving to be faithful not famous until Ray went on to be with the Lord. Ray's legacy and Nancy's continued work has impacted generations and continues to do so today. This book will encourage and inspire anyone who seeks to fulfil the call of God on their life. 'All things are possible to them that believe.'

Pastors Kofi & Jayne Banful
Praise Christian Centre, London

I am so pleased that Nancy has taken time out to write this story. If you enjoy reading about life's challenges, in times of risk, adventure, faith, disappointment, heartache and pain, then you will appreciate this account. It is penned with passion for God's purposes.

But it's more than a story. It's an insight into how God uses ordinary people to accomplish what's on His heart and pours out His blessing in return for faithfulness and obedience – often in very difficult circumstances and along life's tough terrain.

Invest some time in absorbing all that Nancy learned on her journey and be blessed.

Dave Pope B.Sc. (Hons)
CEO: Flame Trust

I have only known Nancy for a few years and, sadly, never had the pleasure of meeting Ray. However, this outstanding book will introduce you to them both and by the last chapter you will feel like you know them so well, as you will have shared the incredible adventure of their lives. You will have grieved with them in the trials and rejoiced in the blessings. You will have learnt more about the amazing God they serve and delight in.

Who Would Ever Have Thought will introduce you to the King of kings. This book will encourage you in your life and walk with God. It will inspire you to trust and serve him throughout your life. It will disciple you in how to navigate through life's ups and downs. This book is a must have for young, old and all of us in between. I love this book!

Sue Eldridge
Director of Presence Ministries International

It was always fun and exciting to be with Ray and Nancy at ngm - a ministry that they founded and led. They equipped and trained their students to bring healing and Jesus' love to the world through the arts. This was unique and done with passion, faith, love and a lot of energy which was so worth it!

As you read this book you will be inspired by Ray and Nancy's awesome journey of adventure. You will learn how to have faith in difficult times and how to hear God's voice and to know the persistent love of our Father for you and me.

Are you looking for more? Do you have dreams yet to be fulfilled? Read on! This is your time!

Ian and Rosemary Andrews
citadelministries.com

Nancy and Ray have had a profound effect on our nation, our continent and in fact our world. They have given their whole lives to see God's Kingdom advance and we get to reap the benefits of their sacrifice.

Who Would Ever Have Thought takes the reader on a rollercoaster ride of faith, delight, problems, promise and provision. Their story is a discipleship tool to help us navigate a life of trusting in God that will change the way we live, if we let it.

Tim Eldridge
Director of Presence Ministries International

ACKNOWLEDGEMENTS

I am hugely grateful to the following people who have assisted me in the publication of this book and also to those who have journeyed with me during these 40 years.

Jill Kemp – Jill thank you so much for your wonderful proofreading skills and also for the many encouragements you sent my way. You are a brilliant proofreader and your comments were so helpful. I have always loved working with you and it was my joy to do so again as you worked your way through this book. Thank you, Jill, you are truly amazing!

Derek Tiffany – Thank you Derek for offering to do a second proofread through this book in your spare time. Thank you so very much. Your comments and observations on the book were so helpful. It was my joy to work with you again. Thank you to you and Ruth for your love and friendship down through the years.

Zoe Wickham – There's so much that you have done behind the scenes to make this book come into being. I want to thank you for that and also for the massive encouragement you gave me after you read the first draft. I love our special friendship and the fact that we have the joy of working beside each other every day. I cannot fully express what it means to have you walk beside me in life and in ministry. If anyone is superwoman – it's you!

Chris Mathison – It is always a joy to work with you Chris. Many years ago you were in ngm and now we get to spend a number of days working together every time we put my annual Spiritual Health Magazine together. This is the first time we have worked on the graphics of a book together and it has been a great joy to do so. You have a massive talent and a great heart and it's my privilege to know you. Thank you for all you have done.

All my special friends who have given endorsements for this book – wow! All you have said is so encouraging and special. Thank you for sending words to endorse this book, but also thank you for standing with Ray and myself during all or some of these 40 years.

All who have been in Heartbeat, ngm and Inspire – What a privilege it has been for Ray and myself to work with so many wonderful and talented people. To see you grow and develop has been an amazing joy. Many of you have gone on to make a huge impact in your own way in our world whether it's been in the West End, London or Broadway, in the theatre world, in the music industry, in clubland or in the media. Others have gone on to work in the church in this country and also abroad. Ray and I have always been so proud of you and love to champion all you do.

John and Rose Lancaster – Thank you for your friendship and your partnership in the gospel with us. You two have been born for such a time as this and we thank God for your generous and wonderful hearts. What wonderful and incredible memories we have of knowing you both for almost all these 40 years. We loved and continue to love your special and incredible friendship.

Thank you too for all who have stood with us financially throughout the Heartbeat and ngm days – every donation to our work does not go unnoticed. We praise God for every person and every donation given as you have partnered with us.

Thank you to our Trustees down through the years. Our present Trustees are **Richard Collier-Keywood** – Richard you have been with us almost from the very start of our ministry. You are amazing and I value your love and friendship so much. **Doug McGinn** – Doug your friendship with us goes beyond these 40 years – we knew you in Scotland when you were just a young teenager and now you and your incredible wife, Ellen are so faithful and supportive. Thank you for always being there for us/me. **Hazel McGreavy** – You and Ken have stood with us through all the ups and downs of the last 40 years. I am so grateful for your friendship and your prayers. You are a very special lady! **Jayne Banful** – I have known you and your wonderful husband, Kofi since we met after our luv esther performance at The Shaw Theatre in the centre of London in 2008. It was then that we became friends. Your friendship is so special to me. I value you immensely. I will never forget how you and Kofi immediately travelled two hours to come and see me when Ray went to be with Jesus. What an incredible couple you are! **Sean Cavanagh** – you only joined our Trustee board in 2014 but we have known you too since the 80's. Ray always valued your incredible wisdom and your friendship has been so special to us both. Thank you Sean.

To my two sons, **Daniel and Aidan**, and my beautiful and kind daughters-in-law, **Veronica and Leanne** – I cannot put into words how much I love you. Daniel you have been with us during 33 years of this amazing 40-year journey and Aidan you have been with us for 23 years. Both of you carry our DNA – not just our physical DNA, but our spiritual DNA too (of course it's not really our DNA, its God's). Throughout the years, you never fought against what we were doing, instead you took what we were doing and valued it as precious. There is no doubt that you are the sons of your mum and dad. You carry our heart and vison and I want to say to you both that I am so proud of you and your special wives too. Leanne, it's wonderful to have you in ngm and Veronica it was so good to have you on the team at the Spiritual Health Weekend this year.

To Ray – my amazing husband of 43 years. You encouraged me into writing my first book and through you, I discovered a love for writing within me. I didn't think I could write one book, but you believed in me. This is my 17th book. I can hardly believe it. It has been a real joy writing this book and recalling the many memories, but it has been a far greater joy living the adventures of this book with you.

To the friend who sticks closer than a brother – this book would not have been written if it hadn't been for you. You go before me and are behind me you surround me and are in me. It's your presence I love and could not live without, thank you for caring for me like no other and for helping me not only to write this book but to live my whole life. My prayer is that you would take what I have written and deeply impact those who not just read it, but take steps to go on their own faith journey. What an adventure it has been Lord and thank you that the truth is that the best is yet to come!

PREFACE

Who would ever have thought that God could do so much through two ordinary, young people from Ayr in Scotland? Who would ever have thought that they would leave their beloved Scotland and follow God wherever he wanted them to go? Who would ever have thought that this decision to go where God said to go and do what God said to do would make waves so huge that it would affect many thousands of lives and bring what seemed like a tsunami of salvation to many at various points throughout the journey? Who would ever have thought that they would see so many lives transformed? Who would ever have thought that they would see not only people saved, but also see people physically and emotionally healed? Who would ever have thought that God would do so much through ordinary people like us?

Who would have thought that we would learn to live by faith and depend on God for our finances, not only for ourselves but also for the whole ministry for over 40 years? Who would have thought that God would provide us with a £3 million mission and arts building, custom made for the work we do? I certainly would never have thought that God would do so much with two very ordinary individuals who dared to trust him. This truly is a story of God's amazing grace!

As Ray and I left Ayr on 1st June 1980, I can honestly say as we sat on the train taking us to Wolverhampton, England with tears in our eyes at what we were leaving behind, but excitement in our hearts at what we were going to experience, that we didn't realise how relevant the verse from 1 Corinthians 2:9 was going to be for us. No eye has seen, no ear has heard, no mind has imagined the things that God has prepared for those who love him (God's Word). We had no idea that God would do so much. We were at the beginning of a great adventure where we felt in a small way like Abraham and Sarah being called by God to leave their country, their friends and their relatives to go to a land that God would show them. They had never been that way before. They left with the promises of God on their lives and with trust in God in their hearts and so too did my husband and I. It was a scary yet wonderful adventure of faith. This is the story of that adventure. It's an open and honest account of the last 40 years taken from memory, from others who shared the journey, from our newsletters and from my diary. This is a story of H.O.T. faith – hearing, obeying, trusting and seeing God do so much more than we could ever ask or imagine. Who would ever have thought?

1

THE BEGINNING

On 12th January 1951 and on 27th February 1953 two beautiful and beloved babies were born to two families in Thornyflat Maternity Hospital in Ayr, Scotland, but it was not until both of them were in their teens that they met and fell in love. Ray was the last son born to Jim and Cath Goudie. He had two older brothers, Durward and Derek. They thought about calling him David (then all the boys' names would have started with the letter D), but instead they called him Raymond James Goudie. Raymond because they liked the name and James after his dad. Ray's dad and the three brothers were all very musical. Durward played guitar, Derek played the piano and Ray played the drums. From the age of 14, Ray started to play the drums in a well-known band in Scotland called The Chordials. His brother, Durward was also in that band; they travelled extensively across Scotland during the 1960's and made an album that sold really well. Ray ended up playing in bands with both of his brothers as time went on. Before he learned to play the drums, friends of his parents, after discovering that Ray's brothers played instruments, used to ask Ray what instrument he played. His answer was always that he played records! He absolutely loved music, therefore collecting and playing records of well-known bands was one of his favourite things to do.

I was the third out of four children born to Jack and Mary McVicar. My mum and dad already had two sons, Jim and Tom, who had been born very quickly one after the other. There is only just over a year between them, but it was after a further eight years of praying for a girl when my parents had me. I have always said as a joke, "And, what an amazing answer to prayer!" When my brother Jack was born just over three years later, this completed our family. Because there were a quite a number of years between my older brothers and my younger brother and I, it seemed to me like there were two families within the one family. I have memories of Jim and Tom working with my dad in his shop and borrowing his car to go out with some girls and crashing it, as well as Tom stealing my Bunty and Judy magazines when I was asleep! However, most of my memories as I grew up were with my brother Jack. We were always very close, well mostly anyhow. We used to fight occasionally, until the day when Jack won, after that day, I never fought him again! I learn quickly!

I do remember being told by Elaine, Tom's girlfriend at the time, now his wife, about a time when she had to sleep in the same bed as me. Seemingly, I sat up in bed in the middle of the night and said, "Shut up Jack" and promptly slapped her across the face! Then lay down on the bed with an angelic look on my face and continued to sleep. Of course, I had no recollection of this in the morning! I remember as Jack and I were growing up that we used to entertain ourselves by pretending we were doing church. Jack would act out the role of the presenter, whilst I would be the preacher. We would do everything that we had seen the leaders of our church do and then when the preach and the appeal were over, we would change it around and I would be the presenter and he would be the preacher. Who would ever have thought that we would both in later life be pastors, preachers and presenters?

Jack and I loved sports and I remember Jack being great at football. He was scouted by Celtic Football club to join their boys' team. This was something that at that time seemed like a dream come true, but my mum wouldn't allow him to join Celtic because they sometimes had to play on a Sunday. The music teacher at my school led an interschool, area wide choir. This choir was quite famous in our locality and travelled widely. In order to join the choir, you had to audition and only if accepted were you allowed to join. One day in our music lesson, a friend and I were asked to stay behind after the class had finished. The music teacher told us that he would love us both to join his choir. He said that neither of us needed to go through an audition, but that we would automatically join the choir. No one else in the school could believe it. This had never happened before. I went home ecstatic and told my mum, but she gently told me I couldn't join the choir as the choir often travelled to faraway places such as Canada. In both these situations, my mum was trying to protect us and make sure we didn't get distracted from our faith by having other secular activities in our lives. I had to go to school the next day and turn the invitation down. It's only in retrospect that you understand a mother's concern for her children.

2

THE ROMANCE

I remember the first time I heard the name Raymond Goudie (as he was called by all his Scottish family and friends – it was only many years later when we moved to England that his name was shortened to Ray). I was a young teenager on a bus travelling through Prestwick, Ray's hometown, when my friend exclaimed, "Look, there's Raymond Goudie!" I thought this must be a good-looking guy for my friend to bring him to my attention, but as I looked out of the bus window, I couldn't see him in the midst of the crowds. Who would ever have thought that this was the guy I would eventually marry? At that time, this thought certainly never entered my mind.

A few months after this, my dad told me that he had bought some tickets for a gospel concert which was on at the Usher Hall in Edinburgh. He asked me to sell as many tickets as I could and he would organise a bus to take us from our hometown of Ayr on the west coast of Scotland to the capital, Edinburgh on the east coast. I sold so many tickets to all my friends that dad had to hire two buses! I was very fortunate in that I had a huge crowd of friends who attended the local Christian Brethren churches in Ayr, Prestwick, Kilmarnock, Troon and Irvine. We all hung around together each weekend after we attended various church events.

One of my friends, Gordon Mutch, sold a ticket to Ray and that was how I found myself sitting on the back seat of a bus next to Raymond Goudie on our way to the Usher Hall in Edinburgh. I was only 14 years of age and Ray was 16. I had been told that he was a good-looking guy and when I saw him, I knew my friends had not lied. He had almost black hair and was a very cool, trendy dude. He had been told by his friends that there was a beautiful blonde girl that he needed to look out for and when he met me, he thought it was me! It wasn't me; it was another girl in the crowd, but Ray only had eyes for me. For some reason, however, although both of us clocked each other, we didn't go out with each other until a couple of years later. I remember, however, telling my best friend at school, Catherine Clark, when she asked me if there was anyone in Ayrshire that I could ever consider marrying, that the only person I could see myself marrying was Raymond Goudie.

However, that was before at the young age of 15, I met and fell in love with a boy called Campbell. As our friendship developed, to be honest, I really thought I would end up marrying him. Ray was not even in the picture. Campbell was training to be a lawyer and my mother loved him! He would often travel from his home in Irvine to see me and when he did, he would bring both my mum and me chocolates or flowers. He won my mother's heart and I thought he was incredible. He was tall, handsome and very kind. I remember when I was ill at the same time as my mum, he came for the day and looked after us and cooked our meals. We had a very close friendship, but after a year I felt I was too young to settle down and with sadness in my heart I ended the relationship. I thought I had met him too early in life and convinced myself that after a couple of years that he and I would eventually marry, but it wasn't to be. I ended up marrying Ray and he ended up marrying 'the beautiful blonde'.

At the end of every church youth group Ray, who had a car, would ask if he could drive me home. I took the lift as it was much more preferable to walking and I found in the many conversations we had that Ray and I could talk about anything. We would talk for quite some time outside my home in the car and looking back now I realise that it was in those times when our friendship grew, long before we held hands or kissed each other. On 31st July 1969, Ray asked me to be his girlfriend. I was sixteen and he was eighteen. On that night, I discovered something about Ray that I hadn't known before. He told me he had a problem with jealousy and would not put up with me even looking at another guy. I didn't mind this at all, as I only had eyes for him!

It was a Friday night when our relationship started and the following day we were both going on holiday. We discovered that night that we just happened to be going to the same place, but not the same hotel. We were both going with a couple of friends to a beautiful island off the coast of France called

Jersey. We couldn't believe it. Ray was travelling by train and boat, whilst I was flying for the very first time with my two friends. The only reason Ray went by train and boat was because his friend, Cowan, was travelling that way and Ray didn't want him to be on his own. So, Ray chose to go with him to keep him company whilst his other friend, Gordon, flew with his parents and Ray's parents to Jersey. We all met Ray and Cowan as the ferry docked and as they walked off the boat, we couldn't help but see that they looked green! Both of them looked so ill. Seemingly, they were almost sick a number of times during the crossing. Ray told me that he would never again travel like that, but at the end of the holiday they had to go back the same way they came.

During the holiday the two lots of friends met up and went out together so I got to see Ray quite a bit. However, when we arrived back home, Ray seemed to lose interest in me. He didn't call or invite me out and so I decided to do something about it. I called Ray and told him that a cousin of my good friend, Frances, was coming to stay with her and he wanted to take me out. I asked him, as he hadn't been in touch, if our friendship was no longer happening and therefore, was I free to date this guy? Looking back now, I realise I appealed to his jealousy although this didn't occur to me at the time. He immediately told me that he still wanted me to be his girlfriend. He told me at a later stage that when he came back from Jersey another local girl who wasn't a Christian had turned her attention to Ray and he had been tempted to ask her out, but when I presented my friend's cousin scenario, he immediately made up his mind he wanted me rather than her.

What happened next was hilarious! After a number of weeks during which our friendship became much more secure, the cousin of my friend arrived. He was not my type at all and well, let me put it like this, he was not the most good-looking person I had ever seen! When I eventually told Ray what I had done, he and I laughed so much.

I remember when Ray first kissed me. We were at Ayr Railway Station sitting in his car in a small car park. The station car park was on a slight hill and as Ray leaned over to kiss me, he took his foot off the brake and the car gently rolled down the hill and crashed into another parked car! I should have known from that moment that our relationship was always going to be filled with crazy adventures!!

Campbell, however, did not give up easily. One night he arrived at my house unannounced! I was out on a date with Ray and so he spent some time with my parents. Later on, they heard the front door open and my parents and Campbell thought it was me coming home. He hid in our home so he could give me a surprise, but it was him who got the surprise as it was my brother, Jack, who came in through the front door! By the time I arrived home, Campbell was long gone as he had to get a bus back to Irvine where he lived.

My mum loved Campbell and at that time she didn't really know Ray. Campbell was always the perfect gentleman. He always picked me up by arriving at my front door usually with presents for me and my mum. Ray on the other hand never knocked on the door, instead he would only peep the horn of his car and wait in the car for me to come out. My mum compared them both and Ray was sadly lacking! However, eventually, he definitely won her over.

When I was introduced to Ray's parents, his mum gave me a picture of Ray that displayed his brilliant sense of humour. He was standing outside his house in a kilt, but the kilt was a mini-kilt. For some reason, Ray's parents had a kilt at their home for a page boy to wear at a wedding they had recently attended. Ray decided to try it on! The kilt was so short it hardly covered him, but I did notice what great legs he had. His mum and I laughed so much about this photo but I loved the fact that Ray was someone who was always up for a laugh.

After we had been going out for a number of months, Ray asked me what I would like for my birthday. I was a shy sixteen-year-old and was embarrassed by his question so I answered him this way, "Oh Ray, don't get me anything." But inside my head, I was shouting, "Oh get me something really nice." He kept persisting with his question and I kept answering, "Honestly Ray I'm fine with nothing!" Eventually the questions stopped and I thought he must have decided what he was going to buy me.

The night before my birthday arrived, the doorbell went and I opened the front door to discover Ray carrying a huge box. It was covered in beautiful paper and tied with ribbons. My eyes nearly popped out of my head! I thought, "What has he got me?" I was so excited. He took it into my bedroom and then told me that I wasn't to open it until the next morning. I said, "Ray, there is no way I can have that present sitting in my room overnight. I won't sleep!" He eventually said that if I waited up until after midnight then I could open it, because by then it would be my birthday.

I cannot tell you how excited I was. I was trying to imagine what on earth could be in this box. My mother, who was almost as excited as I was, decided to wait up with me. The last hour of the night seemed to go by so slowly. At a second past midnight, I tore into the box. I removed the ribbons and the paper and put my hand into the box to discover......nothing except a note which said, "When I asked you what you wanted for your birthday you said, "Nothing", so here it is, NOTHING!" My mother laughed so much. She thought it was hilarious and ran to tell my dad. I was stunned into silence. I could not believe it. I didn't know what to say! He really did have a wicked sense of humour! Throughout the night I kept chuckling to myself, however I did wonder if he would bring me some sort of present in the morning. I was hoping he would. The following day, he turned up at my home with a big smile on his face and a present of a gorgeous watch. I think he won my mother over with this one ruse! She loved his sense of humour.

3

THE PROPOSAL

After two years, on 31st July 1971, Ray and I got engaged and by then I knew that this was the right decision to make. I remember going with Ray to pick my ring at a jeweller's shop in Glasgow. We were there as you can imagine for some time looking at various rings. When the lady assistant was called away, Ray began to slouch over the counter. I told him to stand up as I was concerned about how he might be perceived by the lady who was attending us, but right at that moment, I felt faint and immediately said to Ray, "I'm going to faint!" He immediately stood up straight, and said, "Oh don't do that!" However, it was too late as I had already fainted. He was so embarrassed. Several men carried me out of the shop into the fresh air and placed me on a chair where eventually I recovered. I thought it was me who was going to be embarrassed by Ray slouching over the counter, but in the end, it was him who was embarrassed that his girlfriend passed out when he went to buy her an engagement ring. I wasn't laughing at the time, but later we both thought it was so funny. I could not believe I had fainted whilst choosing my ring!

Ray never asked me properly to marry him until our 40th wedding anniversary (this story will come later), he only said, "If I asked you to marry me, what would you say?" I used to tease him every time he asked that question by saying, "I would say, yes" and when he said with real excitement in his eyes, "Would you really?" I would say, "No I'm only joking." I didn't tell him at the time, but inside I knew I could not say yes until I knew from God that it was the right thing to do. I kept asking the Lord, but never felt a release in my heart. I was only around 17 years of age, but even then, I knew that I didn't want a broken engagement. In my church, a broken engagement was almost as bad as a broken marriage. I wanted to be sure that it was right before I told Ray that I would love to marry him, because for me it was a lifelong commitment. He asked me many times and my answer was always the same. I would say "Yes" and then laugh as I told him I was only joking! It became a standard reply, until one day, when he asked me, I said, "Yes." When he asked me if I was joking, I said, "No I'm not joking, I mean it", but he wouldn't believe me! I had joked too many times and he couldn't believe that I really meant yes.

I had felt a release from God that Ray was the right one and I never changed my mind. Even when we argued, I knew he was the one for me. It's so important that we bring God into every decision of our lives, whether it is a BIG decision like getting married or a smaller one like asking God to help you with a piece of clothing you want to purchase. Bring God into everything; he is interested in every area of our lives. I didn't realise it fully then, but from an early age I had made up my mind to do what the Lord told me to do and to go where he told me to go and to say what the Lord had told me to say. I wanted God's plan for my life rather than just my own.

We wanted to get married a year after we got engaged, but because Ray's eldest brother was already planning to get married that year, we were advised to wait until the following year which we agreed to do. However, it really would have been good to have been married the year before as our second year of engagement was tough. We had so many arguments. Some of them had to do with Ray's jealousy and me 'looking' at any other boy. I remember one argument on my birthday a few months before we got engaged when I received a card from Campbell and in it he had written some words in Latin. I knew what the words meant because it was something that Campbell had told me often when we were dating. It said that I was his beautiful one and that the card came from *the* one for me. Ray insisted that I tell him what the Latin words meant and when I did, he was so furious with jealousy that he tore the card into pieces in front of me. It was only years later when God began to work in Ray's life that his jealousy disappeared totally and never appeared again. During our two engagement years, Ray would often give his engagement ring back to me and tell me the engagement was off. I used to respond to him saying that I was not giving him my ring back, but instead I was going to keep it and sell it! Neither of us really meant what we said, because we loved each other so much, but the arguments were tough. When we eventually got married on 25th June 1973, all the arguments stopped. It seemed that we got all the usual first year of marriage arguments over and done with during our engagement years! We absolutely loved being married to each other.

I was attending a Christian Brethren church in Ayr and had done since my youth. Ray had been brought up attending a Baptist church in Prestwick and we had decided that rather than going to either of our own churches, we would attend another Christian Brethren church in Ayr called Riverside Evangelical church when we were married. We didn't want to get married in any of those church buildings and so we approached my mum and dad and asked if we could get married in a beautiful Church of Scotland building at the top of the street where I lived. At first, it was like a bomb going off in our home as no one else seemed to get married outside of the Brethren church. My mum wondered what everyone would think and if they would even attend the wedding, as our church thought if you attended a Baptist church it was regarded as you backsliding!

I grew up believing that only those who attended our denomination would be in Heaven. I had been taught that Church of Scotland people were not real Christians and Baptists were people who had fallen away from their faith and would only get into Heaven by the skin of their teeth. It was only when Ray took me to some of his gigs with his band, The Chordials, that I realised there were Christians in other denominations. They had gigs in various churches, including some in the well-known Tron Church of Scotland in Glasgow. It opened my eyes to the truth as I went with Ray to various wonderful godly events around Scotland.

My parents took time to think and pray about our bombshell request and eventually decided we could get married in the Church of Scotland building at the top of our street. We then told them that we would like a Baptist church minister, Rev Bill Freel, who was a close friend of the Goudie family, to marry us. We had been to Bill's church and home in Dunfermline many times and had grown very fond of him. I was very thankful that my parents were so different about their faith than others within our church. My mum knew nothing about the gifts of the Spirit, but moved in them so easily. She often had very accurate words of knowledge which scared me a little when I tried, at times in my youth, to stretch the truth!! She also believed in healing and often would lay hands on my dad to pray for him. At one point he developed glaucoma in his eye and he was told it would get worse. My mum got a word from God that said, "The eye that sees will not be blinded" and although the eye was never healed, my dad never went blind.

My parents were lovers of Jesus and they taught me so much in my youth about faith and trust in God. My dad had a grocers' shop in a rough area of Ayr. He worked so hard; getting up early in the morning before the family was awake and didn't finish until after 8pm every day apart from Sunday. He took Sundays off so that we could all go to church together. One night he came home and suddenly realised that when he locked the doors of the shop, he had left the cash tin with all his earnings on the step outside by mistake. Dad immediately got back in his car and drove back to the shop. My mum started to pray and beseech God to shut the eyes of the many people who used to wait for the bus to arrive on the very step on which he had left the cash tin. When Dad arrived at the shop, he was so thankful to see the cash tin still sitting there untouched. Their prayers were answered. To be honest there were so many stories of God answering their prayers and this was just one of them.

I remember my mum lost her rings one day. She and dad hunted everywhere for her rings but could not find them. Later that night when the search had proved fruitless, she prayed and asked God to send an angel to show her where they were. The next morning, she opened her eyes to discover her rings sitting in a prominent place on her dressing table. She and dad had searched the dressing table many times the previous day but there was nothing there. She could only thank God for answering her prayers and sending an angel to put them somewhere where she would see them.

My mum was also an avid gossiper of the Gospel. I have never known anyone with such an amazing gift of evangelism. She never had the opportunity of speaking from a platform, but her gift from God was used every day. It didn't matter who came to the door of her house, she would talk with them about the Lord so naturally and more often than not would lead them to Jesus. Her chats and phone calls to me were always filled with stories of people becoming Christians through her. My parents' lives were filled with miraculous stories of faith. My brothers and I are so thankful to God for our mum and dad and the spiritual inheritance they imparted to us. They prayed for us every day. When mum was young, her father stopped her from speaking in public in church because she was a woman. Her father, along with the Christian Brethren church at the time, believed it was wrong for a woman to speak in public when a man was present. However, despite the fact that she would never become a public preacher, she prayed that her children, whatever their gender, would be able to speak in public and do what she was not allowed to do. She never told me about that prayer until all four of us were preachers/pastors in full time Christian work. What a wonderful inheritance! My mum and dad were not perfect, none of us are, but my siblings and I are so grateful for the parents we had and the example they gave us.

Ray and I ended up being married in a beautiful red stoned Church of Scotland building by a Baptist minister when both Ray and I were at that time attending a Christian Brethren church. This was very unusual in those days! We also went on honeymoon to where the romance had begun – to the island of Jersey. Who would ever have thought?

4

THE PROMISE

When we got married, I was working as a Chief Cashier of a building society which meant that I got a low-cost mortgage for our newly bought home. We bought a three bedroomed home in Ayr and it cost us £7,500. Ray's parents kindly gave us a gift as our deposit and then we got a mortgage for the rest through my work. It's amazing to remember that you could buy a home for that amount of money in those days!

Ray worked as the manager in his parents' shoe retail business and at one point they were struggling for admin help, so Ray suggested that I could give up my job and come and work as an admin/accounts assistant for them. I wasn't sure if this was the right thing to do as I loved my job, but the decision was made for me. Ray's mum didn't think it was wise that Ray and I, as husband and wife, should ever work together. On reflection it was the right decision at the time as I loved my job, but today I find Ray's mum's conclusions really funny, because eventually Ray and I were to work together in joint leadership for 36 years! We absolutely loved working together.

I had a close relationship with Ray's parents and really loved them. Ray's mum was an amazing lady with such a generous heart. I don't think I have ever met someone as generous as she was – except perhaps Ray! She loved having all her family close at hand, so when it came to Ray and I leaving Ayr after being married for seven years and going to live and work for God in England, she and Ray's dad found this extremely difficult to accept. However, I'm jumping ahead of myself here – let me fill you in on what happened before this.

In 1978, after about five years of marriage, Ray went through a very difficult period of his life when he decided to give up Christianity. As you can imagine this was a complete shock to me. I had no idea he was struggling with his faith apart from the fact that I knew he found it difficult to believe he was loved by God. You see, at the age of 9 he followed his brother to the front of his church to give their lives to Christ, but he remembered laughing, probably because they were nervous, but that memory suggested to him years later that he didn't really mean his decision. He, of course, knew how I had become a Christian at the age of six. He had heard me talk about that many times, but each time, without me knowing, it seemed to emphasise to him just how 'weak' his salvation was. No matter what I said to him, it didn't change his mind.

I was brought up in a home where my mum and dad taught me that Jesus was very real. My parents were truly amazing and as I said earlier in this book, they had a living relationship with God that was so real. I was encouraged to talk with God and to expect that God would talk back to me, after all, that's what prayer is all about. Prayer is not a one-way conversation, rather it is a two-way conversation. There are many ways God speaks to us – let me list a few:

God speaks through the Bible. There have been many times throughout my life when I've been asking God for an answer to something and God brings a reference or a portion of scripture to my mind. But the problem is if you are not reading the Bible, how can God speak to you this way? It's so important for us to be reading his written word - the Bible. You see the Bible is like a love letter from God to us all. Have you ever received a love letter from someone? It's a precious thing to experience.

At one point during our marriage I received a number of love letters from Ray. This happened when Ray was on tour with a band and he was away three weeks out of four. The full story comes later on in this book, but I missed him hugely and so when his letters arrived (this is many years before mobile phone technology!) I would devour them. I wouldn't just read them once and discard them, I would read them again and again to get as much as possible out of them. I still have those love letters from Ray and I still read them from time to time. Letters from the one you love are important, they not only bring you closer, but they make you long for their presence even more. It's the same with the Bible. Reading the Bible not only helps us get to know the Lord more, but it also stimulates our love and passion for him. Through reading the Bible we fall in love with the one who loves us unconditionally and it makes us long to experience his presence even more.

I used to wonder how to read the Bible. Should I read a particular book first or what? I would consider Leviticus, Ecclesiastes and other books of the Bible like Lamentations and decide that today was not the day to start to read them! Inevitably, I would read my favourite passage once again until Ray introduced me to a Bible reading planner. In 1979, I started reading the Bible using a one-year Bible reading planner and it changed me completely. I have read through the Bible each year since 1979 and still do today!

A number of other ways that God speaks to us is through visions, pictures, dreams, through people, sermons, prophetic words, an audible voice and a still small voice. The latter one I mentioned is the way God often speaks to me. A still small voice that sometimes seems louder than all the other voices out there. God's spoken and written word have often directed by path. However, when I was only six years of age, before I really knew any of this, God broke into my life in a supernatural way.

Back in my early years as a child, my mum and dad had told me the gospel story so many times and of course I heard it when I attended my church every Sunday. Our whole family attended the local Christian Brethren church in James Street in Ayr. It was a hell fire preaching church, so you certainly knew what was at stake if you didn't give your life to Jesus. One Sunday night, my dad stayed at home to put me and my younger brother, Jack, to bed. I was the big sister and I was allowed up a little longer than my three-year-old brother, Jack. I had asked my dad a few weeks previously if I could give my life to Jesus and become a Christian, but as he looked at his 6-year-old daughter he wondered if I really understood the big step I was taking. Giving your life to the Lord is not something you should do without some thought. It is just a simple prayer, but at the same time it's much more than that. It's giving your whole life into the hands of God; it's telling him that you are putting him in control of your life. My dad gently suggested that I wait until I was older.

I accepted what my dad said, but the Lord must have thought differently as on that Sunday night whilst my dad was putting my little brother to bed, I had an amazing experience of God. I was in our lounge not thinking about God or Christianity, when all of a sudden I lost the power to stand and I fell to my knees in front of our couch. I didn't know what was happening to me, but I wasn't frightened at all, just bewildered. I tried with all the strength I had to stand up again but couldn't, so I laid my head down on the couch and thought to myself, "I'll have a little rest and then I'll try again." After a few moments I tried to lift my head, but I couldn't lift it from the couch. It was as if there was a huge hand over the back of my neck and a huge hand over the back of my legs. Suddenly, I knew that it was God. You see this is the way I prayed every night. My mum and dad taught me to kneel before God every night to say my prayers. They would say a few words and I would repeat it whilst kneeling at my bed. So, when I realised I was in a praying position, I knew God was speaking. I also heard a little whisper in my ear saying, "Nancy" and immediately knew he wanted me to become a Christian, but I didn't know how to do that. So, I said my first ever 'real' prayer which was, "Dear God, I'll tell my daddy." When I said those words, the pressure lifted from my neck and my legs and I stood up. Before another second went by, my dad entered the room and I told him what had just happened. He immediately said, "Come and I will tell you how to become a Christian." He led me through a small prayer, but that prayer and that decision changed my life. I was only six, but something happened that night inside of me that changed me forever. I was filled with an incredible joy. I knew that God had saved me.

Even though I had become a Christian, I still had to go to bed, but there was no way I could sleep. I kept jumping up and down on my bed, I was so full of joy. Earlier that evening, my mum and two friends, Hugh and Dawn had gone to church. Dawn was a Christian but Hugh was not. When I heard them arriving back, I immediately ran to the top of the stairs and shouted, "Mummy, mummy, mummy, come up here quick!" My mum and her two friends ran up the stairs into my bedroom. I'm not sure what they thought as they headed up the stairs, as my cries were so urgent.

What they discovered was me dancing and jumping on my bed. I said, "Mummy, I've become a Christian tonight and I'm so happy about it. Even the bed is happy about it as it's jumping up and down." I laugh now at the fact that I didn't realise at the time it was me who was jumping up and down. I immediately turned to Hugh, who wasn't a Christian and said, "Hugh, that's my mummy and daddy Christians, my two big brothers are Christians, I'm a Christian and Dawn's a Christian – wouldn't you like to give your life to Jesus?" Unbeknown to me at the time, because I was so busy dancing, Hugh's eyes filled with tears as he walked out of my bedroom.

However, I decided that night that Hugh was going to be my first prayer target. I was going to pray for him and every Sunday I would go to church and make sure I was sitting next to him. I wanted to give the Holy Spirit a helping hand and so every time the preacher would say: "If you leave this church without giving your life to Christ and you get run over by a bus, then you are going to Hell," I would make sure Hugh knew that the preacher was talking to him by sticking my elbow into his side. I have to say the preachers in those days would say that and many more similar 'encouragements' many times throughout the service, and so he must have gone home black and blue! But my strategy seemed to work, as he lasted two weeks before giving his life to the Lord Jesus!

I then turned my attention to my little brother. I used to share a room with Jack sometimes, and so at night before my little brother went to sleep, I would 'preach' at him. The only preach I knew was hell fire preaching and so that is what he got. I told Jack the Lord loved him, but that if he was not 'saved' he was going to hell. Poor child – he had me in his ear every night! He too didn't last long before he asked our mum at the age of 4 if he could become a Christian.

There were others after him – my cousin, Anne, came to stay and again, encouraged that my 'preaching' had produced results, I gave Anne the same sermons. She too asked my mum if she could give her life to the Lord and so it went on. My heart of passion for the Lord and my desire to make him known, through the only means I knew at the time, is something that has never left me. My understanding of my faith and how to share it has developed over the years but my joy at seeing people give their lives to the Lord has always been my passion and my desire. The joy of knowing and loving the Lord has only increased as I matured. I got baptised when I had just turned eleven years old, the youngest person ever to get baptised in our church. I was thrilled to hear that at my baptism a friend of mine decided to give her life to the Lord Jesus.

I remember when I was in secondary school, as I walked to school one day, my best friend asked me what I did the previous day. I told her I went to church and she looked at me as though I was an alien. There and then I shared my faith with her and I thought she was taking it all in, but then she told me she was an atheist and she didn't believe in God at all. I thought she was enjoying the conversation and I was very encouraged, but when I got to school, she immediately announced to all our mutual friends, "Hey everyone, listen to this, Nancy believes in God!" I could have died. She was making fun of me and encouraging others to do the same. However, what the enemy meant for harm, God turned it around for good, because I then had some wonderful and incredible conversations with a number of my school mates. A couple of days later, I led someone to Jesus there and then in the school playground. I invited my best friend to come to church with me, never imagining she would come, but she did, even though she had to wear a hat! In my church all the females had to wear head coverings. When I say head coverings, I mean we had to wear huge hats that would have looked great at Ascot but I'm sure looked absolutely ridiculous on us! Despite the fact that she had to wear one of my hats, she still said she would come with me. However, as she sat in our Brethren Assembly listening to the usual hell fire preach, I could see she was not enjoying what she heard. She would shout out, "No" when she disagreed with what he was saying. The first time she did it, I almost died with fright and embarrassment. I had never heard anyone shout out in church before and certainly not a woman! Women were not allowed to speak publicly in our church. She often disagreed with what was said and so it became quite interesting. I thought she would never give her life to the Lord, but one day she came into our house and asked to speak to my mum. I couldn't understand why she would want to talk to my mum on her own, but a few minutes later she came back transformed. My friend had given her life to Jesus.

Ray and I discussed our faith many times, but he often felt my testimony and the way I knew the Lord was a real challenge to him. What I didn't know at the time was that Ray was struggling with pornography and he felt that he was failing God every time he looked at a magazine. He didn't tell me about his problem because at that time it was a secret that he could not share with anyone. (Years later he not only shared it with me but also shared it very openly on many national platforms.) However, because of this secret, he decided one day to give up his faith. I could not understand his decision. He told me that he knew God was real, but from the Bible he understood that God chooses people. He said that God had obviously chosen me, but he felt that God had not chosen him so he no longer wished to live his life as a hypocrite, instead he was walking away from his faith. He told me that I could still go to church, but that he no longer wanted to be involved. I was devastated.

I started quoting the Bible to him, but then realised he knew the scriptures just as well as me. I could see that if Ray went in one direction and I went in another then it could lead us away from one another and our marriage could be in trouble. By this time, we had been married for five years and although I loved Ray with every fibre of my being, I knew I loved God too. I knew I had a decision to make. I could either give up my relationship with God and go with Ray, thus saving my marriage, or I could trust God for Ray and put this whole situation in his hands. I had always wondered if I loved Ray more than I loved the Lord, but when this decision had to be made, I chose God. I made up my mind, I was going to trust God for Ray and not stop praying until he answered me.

With many tears, I interceded and asked God to do something, but to me it seemed as though God was not listening. Have you ever gone through times in your prayer life when you felt as though Heaven was closed? To me, that day, it seemed like the heavens were like brass! My prayers seemed to hit the ceiling! After crying myself to sleep that night, I started again the next morning to pray for Ray after he had gone to work. At that time in our lives, I was only working for three hours each day and so I spent all morning bombarding heaven with my prayers and tears. I told God I would not stop praying until he answered, but there was no answer at all. When I went to work in the afternoon, I could hardly disguise my distress. I kept having to go out of the main office to the bathroom to wipe away my tears. The first thing I did when I arrived home was to get down on my knees again and plead with God to do something in Ray.

During my prayers, a verse came to mind, "Simon, Simon, Satan has asked to sift you as wheat, but I have prayed for you." Jesus said this to Simon Peter not long before he would deny knowing Jesus three times. Jesus encouraged him by telling him he was praying for him. I decided to keep praying and keep storming the heavens despite the lack of response from God. I told the Lord again I would not give up until he spoke. And speak he did.

Suddenly around five o'clock that afternoon, God answered. If he had spoken in an audible voice, I could not have heard him more clearly. He told me, "Nancy, I have heard your prayers and I have seen your tears. Don't cry anymore because if you could see what I am going to do in Ray, you would not believe it. Instead of praying for Ray, begin to praise me for what I am about to do." My tears and prayers were suddenly transformed into praise. I danced up and down our lounge knowing without a doubt that God had spoken and all would be okay. Hearing from God is of huge importance in our lives. This is the first step to living an exciting faith-filled life. When God speaks, true faith is kindled in our hearts. That day, God showed me again just how important it is to listen to him through his written word and also through his still small voice.

My tears were gone. God had spoken. He had promised. It was going to happen. I knew that in the Bible it says that not one of God's good promises ever falls to the ground, so as far as I was concerned, there was no way it was not going to happen. As I danced, I was like that small child of six bouncing on her bed but instead of bouncing on a bed, I bounced around our large lounge. Before I had a chance to leave the lounge, Ray arrived home. He walked into the lounge unaware of what God had said and told me that he was sorry he had been so hard of heart the night before. In my excitement, I told him everything the Lord had said. A cold look came across his face. He said, "Well, if God has said that, then *he* is going to have to do it, because I still feel exactly the same way!"

Unknown to Ray, I started to praise God daily for what God was going to do in him and I have to say through reading the Bible and praising daily, I changed too. I discovered a deeper walk with God. There were times throughout the next number of months when I got impatient and even angry with God. Why was nothing happening? Why was I not seeing a change in Ray? I remember one night, whilst Ray was sound asleep beside me, hitting my pillow in frustration and shouting inside my head at God, "When Lord? When are you going to do what you have said you would do?" It was only in retrospect that I realised that from the moment God spoke he had started to work behind the scenes. I could not see him working, but that did not mean God was being idle.

As I punched the pillow, I suddenly realised what I was doing. I was extremely angry with God Almighty, the creator of the Universe and in my heart I knew that this anger and frustration came from not trusting him. What right had I to be questioning his timing? I told the Lord I was sorry and that I would trust him. Peace once again came to reign in my heart and I went to sleep trusting that God would do it in his own time. About seven months after God spoke, I saw a glimmer of hope. Ray was invited to be the drummer for Dave Pope (a popular singer and speaker in the Christian world) for a six- month tour.

I learned through this time that hearing from the Lord is the first step to having a vibrant faith, but I could not afford to stop there. I had to move on to obeying and then trusting in God. What has he told me to do? He had told me to praise him for what he was about to do and this I had done and was continuing to do. However, I was in danger of not trusting that God would do what he had said he would do.

Trust is something that is important for all of us to learn. I've discovered as the years have gone by that trusting in God is something that people often find so difficult. It means not being in control. It means handing over the reins of our lives to God and often we find that so difficult to do. I had heard God speak and I had obeyed, but the third part of trusting him was proving to be a little difficult. Could I trust him when I couldn't see him working in Ray's life? Could I trust him despite the lack of evidence of change in the circumstances? I decided to do just that. This is an important lesson for us all to learn. I was to discover just how important it was to trust God as my life went on.

5

THE CHALLENGE AND THE CHANGE

As I said at the end of the 1970's Dave Pope and his musical director, John Daniels, asked Ray to be his drummer for a six-month tour of the UK, Canada and USA. Ray had been a drummer in a number of bands in his spare time and so he was thrilled to be invited, but as he was working in his parents' shoe retail business, it meant him asking if he could have six months leave of absence. At first, the answer was negative and although Ray was deeply disappointed, he went back to Dave and John and told them that it was impossible for him to have the time off his work and therefore he could not drum in the band. I was so disappointed for Ray, but as I prayed about it, I felt that it was right for him to be involved, so I prayed that somehow God would open up the way for that to happen.

A few weeks later, we received another phone call from John and Dave saying that each time they prayed about a drummer for the band, God kept bringing Ray's name to their mind. They asked if Ray would go back to his parents and ask again. We prayed that if it was right that Ray's parents would change their minds and allow Ray to have the time off work. Thankfully, Ray's parents loved the Lord Jesus and said they would pray and ask God about it. Whilst praying, they felt if three certain conditions were met then they would give a positive answer. The first condition was that Ray should only go for five months and come home after the USA/Canadian part of the tour. The second condition was that one of the ladies who worked part-time in the shop would have to be prepared to work full-time during those five months. The third was that I was happy that Ray would be away from home for three weeks out of every four. I would possibly only see him one week in four. We were so excited when every single condition was met! I knew I would miss him hugely, but I was positive that it was the right thing for Ray to do. The shop assistant agreed to do the extra hours and John and Dave said they would bring in another drummer for the last month of the tour.

Before we knew it, Ray was off on tour with what turned out to be a great bunch of people. The keyboard player in the band was Chris Eaton who is a singer/songwriter in his own right. He has penned thousands of fantastic songs, many of which have been sung by people such as Cliff Richard and Amy Grant. The most well-known song was the number one Christmas hit by Cliff Richard, Saviour's Day. The acoustic guitarist was Ian White who was another Scot and is now widely known for leading worship and for his Psalms recordings. On lead guitar was Rob Marshall who for some time was in the Mark Williamson band in the '80s. His wife, Liz, was also there to help with the admin and stock. We were already close friends with singer/songwriter, John Daniels who was on bass guitar. Davy Kidd, and at times his brother, Andy, was the sound engineer. Each person in the band became a very precious and special friend and our friendships have lasted down the years.

Very occasionally when I was able to take some time off work, I joined Ray on tour. These times were so special. I helped Liz on the stock table, helped Ray with setting up and taking down his drums and generally helped wherever I could. Rob Marshall, who has a wicked sense of humour played a trick on Ray one night. He put talcum powder on Ray's hi-hat cymbals and so you can imagine what happened when Ray played them. At another time it was Dave who was on the receiving end of the fun. Dave always had a handkerchief in his stage trousers, and so the guys in the band replaced the handkerchief with a pair of tights. When he pulled out the supposed handkerchief to wipe his brow, out came a pair of ladies' tights!

Throughout the tour Dave had three girl fans who came to see him every night no matter where the tour went. We decided to play a trick on Dave. We bought a Valentines card and wrote on it as though it was from these three girls. We told Dave he had a Valentines card and when he opened it, he told us it was from the girls. We smiled, but didn't let the secret out of the bag. That evening, we were astonished to see him thank the girls in the audience for the Valentines card before the concert began. We didn't expect him to do that! Of course, the girls didn't know a thing about it and told him that they wished they had sent the Valentines card. It was then that he noticed that we were all laughing so much! I still can't believe we got up to so much mischief. One day, when I was washing my hair, Dave told me I had a phone call. I told him that I was in the middle of washing my hair, but Dave insisted that it was urgent. I rushed out of the dressing room into the main auditorium with water and suds running down my face and neck, to discover that it was another joke – this time on me! Besides the fun, God did so much in each of the band members during those six months and we are so grateful to God and to Dave Pope for bringing us all together. It was during those six months that God called Ray and myself to leave our jobs and become missionaries for him in the UK and beyond.

When Ray had been invited to be part of Dave's tour, this was exactly what I needed to help encourage me in my prayers. Ray was still struggling with his faith, but he had reckoned he was okay going on Dave's tour because he could 'hide behind the drums' as he put it. Dave had explained that this would be an evangelistic tour, however after a couple of nights, Dave suddenly changed his message from evangelism to begin to challenge the Christians in the audience to live a vibrant life in Christ. Each night, Ray heard God speak directly into his heart. He began to read his Bible again and even to study the Bible with Rob and Liz. I noticed the tone of his letters and postcards in the first few weeks of going away beginning to change as God was working in his life, but it really came to a head when the tour took him to the very first Spring Harvest. Spring Harvest was the brainchild of two incredible people – Clive Calver who was, at that time, the head of British Youth for Christ and Peter Meadows who was, at that time, the editor of a national Christian magazine called Buzz. This festival became a yearly date in the Christian calendar in the UK and has affected many thousands of lives over the years.

When Ray and the band arrived at Spring Harvest, they discovered they were to be the band who led the worship with Dave Pope and Graham Kendrick at all the main meetings. One night, Luis Palau (the Argentinean evangelist) spoke from the following verse in 2 Corinthians 4:10: *We always carry around the death of Jesus in our bodies so that the life of Jesus is also shown in our bodies (God's Word).*

Luis told his personal story of how he would pray and dedicate his life to Christ every Sunday but then by the following Friday he would blow it. He would then rededicate his life to God again on the Sunday and again on the Friday he would blow it. This continued to happen until someone took him aside and explained 2 Corinthians 4:10 and asked him if he wanted to be victorious in his Christian life and no longer keep swaying from victory to defeat. Luis told us that he then had revelation of what it meant to be obedient to Christ. He said that every time God's will crossed his will, he would choose to go God's way and not his own way. He would do this in the big areas of life but also in the small areas. This decision to follow God's will changed his life. Ray was challenged by what Luis had said and reckoned, "If it is good enough for Luis Palau, then it is good enough for me." I remember Ray, with tears in his eyes, telling me that God had spoken to him as he sat on the drums and he was now going to live for Jesus. I was ecstatic! God was indeed moving in Ray's life.

Just after Spring Harvest, Ray went to Canada on a six-week trip that was supposed to take in a tour of the States as well. Just before they left for Canada, the American part of the tour fell through which left Ray and the rest of the band in Canada with nothing to do for four weeks. However, it was during those four weeks that God cemented the change in Ray. Each day, Ray put into practice what he learned from Luis. Ray would say to God, "What do you want me to do today?" And whatever God said, Ray had already made up his mind that he would do it.

In the Bible, when the Israelites were building Jerusalem, we read in Nehemiah that Ezra gathered all the people to hear the Law (the Bible of their day) being read. In Nehemiah 8:6, it tells us that the people said, "Amen! Amen!" (Amen means so, let it be) before they knew what God was going to say. In other words, they were saying, "Whatever you say, Lord, whatever you ask us to do, we will obey you." It's so important in our lives to determine to be obedient to the will of God. It's as we obey that God releases his power to help us to do his will.

Similar to the Israelites, Ray had made up his mind beforehand to obey God in the small things in life as well as in the big decisions he had to make. Each day he would be obedient and read his Bible and pray. One morning, when he read in the Bible that he needed to be filled with the Holy Spirit, he went down on his knees and asked the Lord to fill him with his Spirit. There were no flashes from the sky, but Ray knew within himself that God had done what he had asked him to do. Certainly, when I saw Ray several weeks later, I saw the difference in him for myself. I went over to Canada to be with Ray for two weeks, more of this story later in the book, but when I saw him and spoke with him, it was as though I had a new husband.

In the second week of his free time in Canada, shortly after praying and asking God what he wanted him to do that day, Ray received a phone call from someone who asked him if he would be a volunteer to help build a ranch for a Christian organisation. Although Ray's natural reaction would have been to say no, he felt it was right to say yes. In order to get to the ranch, he had to travel several miles on a bus. During his journey, he noticed that a young teenage girl sitting in the seat in front of him was crying. He felt God nudge him to speak to her. Again, choosing to go God's way, he nervously asked her if she was okay. She told Ray that she had run away from a children's home and a social worker was taking her back. Ray spoke to her and told her about the love of God. She listened to all that he had to say and before leaving the bus, she agreed to meet with some Christians that Ray knew who just happened to live in her town. We never did find out what happened to the girl, but Ray was really encouraged that God had used him in some small way.

When he arrived at the ranch, Ray was given the job of digging the sewers! He could not believe it. His complaints to God went something like this: "Lord, I am a drummer! Drummers don't dig sewers!" But because he had said he would always put God's will first, he said he would do it. The next morning, Ray was thrilled to see that it was pouring with rain. He reckoned he would not have to dig the sewers that day because it was so wet and he didn't even have a raincoat! He was wrong! They provided him with boots, a coat and a hat that were all too big for him and sent him out in the pouring rain. As he dug the sewers, I am sure God must have smiled from Heaven. Ray discovered, however, that even when he was soaked through to the skin there was a joy in doing what God had told him to do. Who would ever have thought?

6

THE BEGINNINGS OF A SIX-MONTH CALL OF GOD

During the first couple of months of the UK tour, whilst Ray was drumming for Dave, Ray met a young singer called Graham Kendrick at an event in Norwich. As Graham chatted to Ray, Ray was amazed to hear Graham ask him if he had ever thought of going into full-time Christian work. When Ray said that the thought had never entered his mind, Graham then encouraged him to pray about it. He revealed that he had a feeling from God that God's call was on Ray's life.

As the weeks went by more and more people kept asking Ray and myself if we had ever considered working for God. Although I realised that it would take a miracle to get Ray to move from Scotland, when I prayed about our future, I felt God confirm to me that we would, at some point, be in full-time work for God. At the very first Spring Harvest, Eric Delve, who was the national evangelist with British Youth for Christ at the time, took time out of his busy schedule to chat with Ray and myself and tell us that he believed God was calling us. So, when God broke into my husband's life at Spring Harvest, God was not only totally transforming my husband's life but was also beginning to change our direction.

When Ray got back to Toronto after his 'digging the sewers experience', he, Rob and Liz and a couple of friends, Terry and Ginny Bridle, went to People's Church to a meeting where Brother Andrew was speaking. Brother Andrew is a well-known missionary who smuggled Bibles into countries where you can be imprisoned for having a Bible in your possession. At the appeal, there was a word of knowledge given that there was someone in the audience who was under 30 years of age who thought God *could* be calling him to work for him, but did not know *where* God was calling him. Ray knew he was that person. The thought of having to stand in a meeting where 2,000 people were gathered was very intimidating, however because he had made up his mind to obey, he nervously stood. They called him to the front with hundreds of others who had responded to Brother Andrew's message.

Later, on his way out of the church, a man approached Ray and asked him if he felt called to full-time Christian work. When Ray confirmed that God could be calling him, the man went on to say, "I felt God ask me to speak to you. Many years ago, God called me to give up my job and work for him, but because I was involved in my family business and I didn't want to let my parents down, I gave in to family pressure and didn't respond to God's calling. Now, twenty-five years later, I realise I disobeyed God. If this applies to you in any way, do not allow parental pressures to hold you back from what God wants to do with you."

Ray couldn't believe it, as it described his situation so clearly. This was the first and only time this man had met Ray and he had no idea of Ray's background. Ray knew that God could be calling him, but he was so worried about what his parents would say if he were to leave the family business. However, Ray also knew that God was speaking and that if he didn't do what God had told him to do, he would be living in disobedience. He gave in to God that night and told him that no matter what storms would occur, he would obey him. Ray surrendered his future to God and gave him total control of the whole of his life. That night he received four opportunities to work for God in various countries in the world. Although we knew that none of these offers were right for Ray, it was a real encouragement to Ray to continue to seek God for the way ahead.

At 11.00pm that night Ray phoned me, totally forgetting the fact that it was 4.00am in Scotland. However, when he told me what had happened and how God had totally changed his life, I didn't mind at all being woken out of my sleep, in fact I was thrilled. When I came off the phone that night, I thanked God for answering my prayers and for all he had done in Ray. When I looked in my diary to see when I had started praying and praising God for Ray, I was amazed to discover that it was exactly a year to the day that God had spoken to me and told me he would change my husband's life. Wow! God is so faithful.

When I met Ray in Canada several days later, I honestly felt like God had given me a new husband! I was truly astounded at what God had done. As it says in Psalm 145:13, *The Lord is trustworthy in all his promises and faithful in everything he does (NIV).*

Can I encourage you to continue to pray and believe God for a miracle even if you are not at this time seeing God answer your prayers in the way you would like? God will indeed bring his promises into being, and even now will be working behind the scenes to make sure his will is accomplished. If God can do it for me, he can do it for you.

During that early morning phone call, Ray asked me to bring £50 when I joined him in Canada a few days later. He explained that his money was running out and in fact for most of the time that he had been in Toronto he had been living on a very small McDonald's hamburger and a small carton of milk for his main meal. It was only after I got off the phone that I started to think to myself, "How am I going to get £50?" Unknown to Ray, finances were in short supply at home too. We had received several bills at once and I really didn't have any cash to take with me. Before going back to sleep, I remembered that a retired minister had given me £10 to take to Ray while he was in Canada. So, I thought to myself, that means I have to find £40. I said a quick prayer, "Lord would you somehow provide £40 for me?"

The very next morning, when the post came, I noticed a hand-written envelope from London. As Ray and I didn't know anyone in London at the time, I was intrigued to find out who could possibly be writing to us. As I opened the envelope, out fell four £10 postal orders. No letter at all, just four £10 postal orders! I couldn't believe it. I fell to my knees and with tears running down my face I thanked God for his amazing love and grace to me. This was the first time I had seen God provide finance for us – little did I realise that it would be the first of many.

7

A LESSON IN FAITH

When I joined Ray in Canada, we learned a huge lesson about faith that we have never forgotten. When a family heard that Ray's wife was coming across to see him for two weeks, they invited us to stay with them in their beautiful home in Toronto. One day our hosts' grown-up children asked us if we would like to go out with them for a meal. We said we would love to, but because Ray and I did not have very much money we thought we had better check our finances and see if this was possible. We discovered that we had enough finance for us to pay for one meal and so we decided to share a meal. This is an accepted practice in Canada as the portions are so huge. So, when we arrived at the restaurant with our hosts' family, we told them we didn't want a starter and that we would share our meal and asked the waitress to bring two plates. We loved the meal and of course there was plenty for us to eat, however we knew that after paying for our main course, our money would be gone. So, when the waitress came to ask us what we would like for dessert, we immediately declined declaring that we were full and could not possibly eat a pudding! Our friends pressed us again and again, but we knew we did not have enough money so we declined many times. They went ahead and ordered amazing desserts and when they came, my mouth watered so much. A huge pint jug full of strawberries, ice cream and cream – it was my favourite dessert and all I could do was to sit there and watch them eat it all. I really would have loved that dessert, but I had to pretend that I couldn't possibly eat it. When it came time to get the bill, we took our carefully calculated finances out of our pockets, but our friends immediately said, "Oh did we not tell you that this meal is on us? This is our treat." We could not believe it! You see, we hadn't prayed and asked God about this meal. If we had, things could have been different. We missed out on a huge blessing, all because we didn't hear, obey and trust God. However, we learned our lesson that day and we have never done this again!

Many years later when Nick Cuthbert, a good friend of ours, was preaching at an event where we and the rest of our band, Heartbeat, were playing, he said, "Never say you cannot afford something, instead go to the Lord and ask him if he wants you to have it. If he wants you to have it, then you can afford it." I have never forgotten what Nick said or the lessons we learned from our meal in Canada. We can so often miss out on God's many blessings because we don't ask him what he wants us to do.

We have a Heavenly Father who loves to bless his children. I'm convinced that many of us do not receive what God has for us because we do not listen to God and then exercise our faith. Romans 10:17 tell us, *Faith comes from hearing the message, and the message is heard through the word about Christ (NIV).* It also says in John 16:24, *Until now you have not asked for anything in my name. Ask and you will receive and your joy will be complete (NIV).* We often have not because we ask not. Let's ask and find out what is on the heart of God for us.

Perhaps as you are reading this book you can identify with what happened to us in Canada. As we counted our pennies and restricted our budget, it seemed the correct thing to do. However, our decision was made without hearing from God and exercising our faith in him. Perhaps you are not receiving the blessing of God because in some way you are restricting him.

I often hear people say that they cannot afford to do this or that, but saying that means that their vision is not on the Lord, it is on the circumstances around them. Next time you hear yourself saying something like this, take time to pray and ask the Lord if he wants you to have whatever it is. Don't make the same mistake as we did and miss out on God's many blessings.

8

THE CALL CONTINUES

When we came home from Canada, Ray gently explained the whole call of God to his parents, but as you can imagine they could only see that Ray was leaving not only his job in their business but the family as well! It felt like a rejection of them. Ray wanted to honour his parents and so he gave them a year's notice to get someone else to take his place in the family business. His parents were devastated. They always wanted the family to live near one another. At one point, Ray's parents had talked about moving to Australia, but said they would only do it if the whole family moved there. So, to hear that Ray and I were moving to England was not what they wanted to hear. There were many times when Ray's mum travelled with Ray and his dad through to Saltcoats where the shop was located. She was so upset at us leaving that she would cry on the way there and on the way back. It was very difficult for Ray and also for Ray's parents and if God hadn't spoken so clearly, he would have found it so easy to stay and not go. But God confirmed our calling so clearly through many different ways over a period of six months.

Shortly after we arrived home from Canada, we received a phone call from Clive Calver, who as I said earlier, was the National Director of British Youth for Christ. He asked if he could come and speak to us about the possibility of us joining British Youth for Christ. Little did we know at the time that his visit was going to be very significant for us.

It was great to have Clive in our home and Ray spent most of the day quizzing Clive about the baptism of the Holy Spirit. Our church had been torn apart by different opinions of what this baptism meant. Ray's dad was one of the most vocal against it being an experience we needed to have. I listened to the discussion that Ray and Clive were having, but I thought it didn't really apply to me as I was already filled with the Holy Spirit. However, at one point I went to the bathroom and whist sitting there, God spoke clearly to me. He told me to ask Clive to pray for me. I argued back and forth with God saying, "If I ask him to pray for me, he is bound to ask me what I would like prayer for and I haven't a clue what to say. So, tell me what I should say? Why do I want him to pray for me? God totally ignored my questions, and continued to say, "Ask Clive to pray for you!" I sat there so long that I was sure that Ray and the others would think there was something wrong with me! I went back into the room unsure what to do, but just at that point my friend, Sheila Walsh, who had spent the day with us, asked me if I could drive her home. I was so relieved that I didn't need to ask Clive to pray for me, and immediately went to the car to take her home. However, what happened in the car was as much a surprise to me as it was to Sheila. I started to cry. Tears ran down my face. Sheila asked me why I was crying and I told her I didn't know! Why was I crying? I began to tell her what I had experienced whilst sitting on the toilet, and she encouraged me to ask Clive to pray for me.

On the drive back from Sheila's home, I made a deal with God. I asked him to make it easy for me to ask Clive to pray for me. As I arrived at my home, I looked in the mirror to see if anyone would know that I had been crying and thought there was no sign, however the minute I entered the room where Clive and Ray were, they took one look at me and asked me what was wrong! I blurted out that God had told me to ask Clive to pray for me, and Clive didn't ask "what for" as I had anticipated, instead he said, "That's great because God told me this afternoon that I was to pray for you!" Clive then laid his hands on me and prayed for me to be filled with the Holy Spirit. He then prophesied over me that God would give me spiritual children all across the world. At that time, I could not see that prophecy happening, but now after 40 years of loving and serving Jesus in the UK and beyond, God has fulfilled that prophetic word and continues to do so. I have seen so many give their lives to the Lord and be transformed by his love and power. It was also through that prayer that God opened me up to the gifts of the Holy Spirit – you can read the rest of the story in my book *Nancy Goudie's Spiritual Health Encounters*.

During the time Clive spent with us, we took some time to pray about our future, and it was during this prayer session that Clive gave us both a prophecy. What he did not realise at the time was that Ray and I had never heard a prophecy in our lives before. When Clive was speaking the prophecy over us, I thought to myself, "Wow! This is God." Ray, however, was much more sceptical. Afterwards I said to Ray, "Wasn't that amazing?" Ray retorted back, "Well, if that was God, I'd like him to confirm his word." One of the things God said through the prophecy was, "Do not worry about your loved ones, I will look after them; you follow after me." Psalm 37:4-6 was also quoted in the prophecy.

The very next morning, after Ray had gone to work, a letter arrived from a friend called Howard Drysdale who was in the Royal Navy. The letter had been written several weeks before, but in it he said, "Ray, I feel I need to stop what I am saying and tell you something I believe God wants you to hear; in fact I believe he may have told you this already." He went on to quote the prophecy almost word for word and even used the same scriptures. I picked up the phone and called Ray at his work. I read out what was written in the letter and asked him what he thought it was. He said, "That's the prophecy Clive gave us last night." I replied, "No, it's not. I am reading from a letter we have just received from Howard." Ray was astonished. We were so excited that God confirmed the prophecy in such a special way. The Lord knew that Ray needed him to continue to confirm over and over again that he wanted us to obey him and that he would look after our loved ones.

Ray and I then decided to take our call to our Baptist church leadership. When we got married Ray and I had joined a Brethren church in Ayr, but after two years we moved to New Prestwick Baptist church which had, in fact, been the church that Ray had attended in his youth. I was particularly nervous about taking our call to them as I wasn't sure how they would respond. However, as Ray and I shared our hearts and our call, we were astonished at the response from our pastor and the whole eldership. Some of them were in tears; others had huge smiles on their faces and all of them confirmed, including our pastor who didn't believe that prophetic words were for today, that this was indeed God and that we had to obey. They prayed with us and told us they would support us in any way they could. We didn't realise, at that time, that our partnership would last with the majority of these people for many, many years.

We continued to receive confirmation after confirmation as the weeks went by, but although Ray was 90% sure that God had called us, he was still waiting for that extra 10%. I couldn't understand it. We had been receiving confirmation through scripture, through others, through our church leadership and through the peace in our hearts. What more could Ray be looking for? Ray explained that he knew how much our decision was hurting his mum and dad and he just needed to be 100% sure.

We went to see a lovely old couple in our church, George and Peggy Kerr, and explained our whole call in great detail. After we finished, George turned to Ray and asked him what he was waiting for. Ray responded by explaining that he was 90% sure but he still wanted to have that extra 10% confirmation. George wisely said, "Maybe the extra 10% you need is you exercising your faith and jumping into God's plan for your life. There always has to be a certain amount of faith and obedience expressed on our part in every faith walk. You exercise your faith and the 10% will be there." We left with joy in our hearts, knowing that if we obeyed and put our faith into action, God would take care of us and our loved ones.

As I said earlier, Ray decided he wanted to give his parents a year's notice and so it was decided that we would not leave Ayr to join BYFC until June 1980. The pressure on us throughout that year to stay was enormous but despite it being one of the hardest things Ray has ever had to do, we knew that no matter what we could not stay. It would have been sheer disobedience to God's call on our lives. However, when we eventually did leave, Ray decided that we would come home every month during our first year in full time ministry and work in the shop for his parents for one week. I wasn't sure how this would work, but what we decided was that we would work for BYFC for three weeks doing missions etc., without having as many days off as we should have and keep all those days off for the week where we would travel to Scotland and he would work for his parents. It was intense, but he wanted to help as much as he could. My husband had a kind and generous heart.

My parents and my family were thrilled that we were following God's will for our lives and encouraged us as much as they could. Interestingly enough, when I was a young girl, I said that I would be a missionary one day. I thought it would be in the West Indies, but it turned out that we became missionaries in the UK. Who would ever have thought?

9

THE PREPARATION

During that year, we decided to start a simple Bible study on a Friday night in our home. We didn't advertise it, instead we just told a few friends that if they weren't doing anything on Friday night then come to our home and we could study the Bible together. The first time we did this we had five people there including Ray and myself – the second week, we had four, but we were not put off. We decided to pray and fast beforehand and commit our Friday nights to God. What God did was stunningly amazing. Our numbers grew and grew. All we did was to have a simple Bible study with a good Scottish supper afterwards, but suddenly people were getting saved and discovering God was real for themselves. By the time we left Ayr a year later, our simple Bible study was attracting over 40 people every Friday night. We taught people about faith, prayer, evangelism and fasting during the year but to be honest we were only learning about it ourselves.

During the year, we decided to do an evangelistic event in Ayr and invited Eric Delve to be the preacher. We put a worship band together and trusted God to bring an audience. We prayed, we fasted, we sought God together and we advertised the event as much as we could. We held it in a modern Church of Scotland building and on the evening of the event, the place was packed. We saw quite a number of people respond to give their lives to Jesus; it was just incredible. God had used the people in our small Bible study and we were so excited.

During 1979, I remember a specific time when I prayed and laid down all my gifts (I think I could count four gifts that I thought I might have!). One was singing and I told the Lord that I would not use this gift again unless he opened the doors for me. In 1973 Ray and his brother, Derek, had started a band which we called Unity. To be honest it was more like a modern-day choir with a band and orchestra. It was way before its time. All the Goudie boys and their wives were in Unity. I started out as a narrator in a Christmas show we did and then when the band started properly, I became one of the many singers along with my sister-in-law, Yvonne and my good friend, Sheila Walsh. We had great fun as we sang and performed at various places all over Scotland and England. It was where all of us gained experience in how to sing and speak using microphones! I remember one of my friends was asked to introduce herself from stage. All she had to do was to say her name and where she worked. She said, "My name is Christine and I'm a bank!"

We recorded two albums and also had our own show on Scottish television which was simply called Unity Sings. When the band stopped in 1978, the main opportunity I had to sing was gone. I was more of a backing singer rather than a lead vocalist, but just a couple of days after I had laid this gift down, I got a phone call from Dave Pope. He was calling to ask if I could get some time off work to come and join a national tour that was happening called Our God Reigns. Luis Palau, the Argentinian evangelist who had spoken at Spring Harvest when Ray was deeply convicted, was going to be the main speaker. Ray was already going to be the drummer and Dave was asking if I would sing with him, Graham Kendrick and Sheila Walsh. I saw this as God opening the door for me, and I immediately said, "Yes." I don't think I would have been brave enough to say "Yes" if I hadn't had that time alone with the Lord.

The tour started at the Royal Albert Hall in London for several nights and then toured the largest theatres of our land. I felt very grateful for this opportunity of serving Jesus in this way. I got to tour with my husband and also with my close friend, Sheila Walsh, and our two newer friends, Graham Kendrick and Dave Pope as well as listen to Luis Palau every night. Every venue was full – the only problem was that during the latter part of the tour, I got pharyngitis and had to sing with a croaky voice. People joked and said I sounded like Graham! I loved the tour and learned that as you give your talents and gifts over to the Lord, he is the one who can open the doors wide for you.

After our year at home was over, our church commissioned us and sent us out as their missionaries. They asked Clive Calver to come and speak at our valedictory service, which they arranged in May 1980. The day of the service just so happened to be the day when, two years previously, God had promised me that he would change my husband's life and had told me that if I could see what he was going to do, I would not believe it. That was two years running that the Lord did something significant on the day he told me to praise him for what he was about to do. We didn't pick the day, the church and Clive did, not knowing that it was a significant date for us. Again, we were amazed at God's faithfulness to us. Never did I imagine in a million years on that day when I was so distraught at Ray giving up his faith that God would do so much. As we knelt that day to be prayed for by the elders of our church, tears poured down my face as I remembered the goodness and faithfulness of God. If God had not intervened in our lives, our story could have been so different.

Our only cloud on that day was that Ray's family was not there to witness us being sent out by the church. Ray's mum and dad went on holiday and only our sister-in-law, Shiona, Ray's eldest brother's ex-wife, attended. However, it was a joy to have my mum and dad and my family there to witness and support our call. My family were so thrilled that God had done so much in our lives already and encouraged us to follow God's call even though it meant us living many hours away. It truly was hard for Ray to obey God, but as he trusted God, Ray's relationship with his mum and dad eventually improved and after a couple of years got much stronger.

10
PREGNANT WITH A VISION

On 1st June 1980 some good friends met with us at the train station to see us off on our new adventure. As we sat on the train waving goodbye to that small group of friends from our Friday night Bible study, tears came to our eyes. We were leaving the security of our lovely home, our families, our friends, our church, our jobs and even our dog to go somewhere we had never been before. We were trusting our God for our future. We had heard the call, we had obeyed and stepped on to the train taking us to Wolverhampton where BYFC was based and now we needed to trust that God would show us the way forward. We rented our three-bedroom bungalow in Ayr to two good friends, Howard Drysdale and Stephen Beckwith who said they would keep our bedroom for us so we could use it whenever we came back. We were so grateful for this arrangement when we came back to Scotland each month so that Ray could work in his parent's business. They also looked after our dog. We had to leave our fantastic sporty car because it belonged to Ray's parents' business and so, as we left by train that day, it felt as though we had left everything to follow God's call, but we can truthfully say that God has more than repaid us for all we left behind. In Mark 10:29-30, it says, *"Truly I tell you, Jesus replied, no one who has left home, or brothers or sisters or father or mother or children or fields for me and the gospel, will receive a hundred times as much in this present age; homes, brothers, sisters, mothers, children and fields - along with persecutions - and in the age to come, eternal life (NIV).* I can testify to this being true. We even got the persecutions!! The Lord has been amazing to Ray and me. People say we gave up so much, but it's nothing in comparison to what he has given us. He has been so incredible. He has provided everything we needed for life and godliness (2 Peter 1:3) and has been extremely faithful to us and to his word. As the train pulled out of the station, we were excited as well as a little apprehensive about what lay ahead.

We were so pleased that our friends, Rob and Liz Marshall who lived in Wolverhampton, had asked us to come and stay with them. Living with people we knew and loved was such a huge blessing. The house they were renting belonged to British Youth for Christ and they gladly opened their home to us. I have to say that although it was wonderful to stay with them, the whole move to Wolverhampton was such a culture shock to us. The house was situated in the red-light district and prostitutes gathered outside the front door as they looked for business. We had come from a middle-class town in Scotland and here we were in one of the poorest areas of Wolverhampton. The house had dampness running down some of its walls; in fact, Rob and Liz could not use the front room of the house because the damp was so bad. Whilst we had not been used to this, I have to say that we were loving life and we were extremely grateful to God for his call on our lives. We knew we were doing what God had called us to do and being with our good friends, Rob and Liz, gave us the extra security we needed during our initial months in BYFC. When they moved from that rented house to buy their own home, we moved with them. What great friends!

When we walked through the door of the British Youth for Christ offices on our first day, we received another surprise. There was a small group of office staff sitting in a circle. As they looked up to see who was coming through the door and before anyone even said 'hello', we were told in no uncertain terms by one of the administrators that we were late. We had been told by Clive Calver to be there for 9.00am but realised after we arrived that they had a prayer meeting at 8.45am but no one had told us. When we asked what desk we should work from, we were told we could have a small corner of someone's desk. The person who was in charge of the offices was ill at the time and if he had been there, I know our welcome to British Youth for Christ would have been very different. It was not the best start to full-time Christian work. However, the joy and fulfilment in our hearts at being at the centre of God's will overcame whatever problems and difficulties we encountered. We knew this was where God wanted us to be. It really doesn't matter where you are, as long as you know you are doing what God wants you to do. The best place to find fulfilment is in the centre of God's will for your life. Ray and I knew we had done what God had called us to do and we were at the beginning of a great adventure.

Our first nine months in BYFC were very difficult and I'm sure if God had not called us so clearly, we would have been tempted to give up and go home. We were pregnant with a vision of starting a team/band that would show young people who Jesus really was. Whilst we prayed and asked God to birth our dreams, we were asked to head up the creative arts section of BYFC, which meant working with musicians such as Graham Kendrick and Sheila Walsh. Although we had some fantastic times working with Graham, Sheila and others in BYFC, those nine months felt like the worst nine months of our lives. We really did not enjoy what we were doing in the office section of our job and yet God taught us and shaped us so much through that time. We learned loads about leadership through Clive Calver, Ken McGreavy and many other great leaders in BYFC. We are so grateful for the love they showed and the investment they made into our lives.

Right at the time when we were at our lowest, we were offered a job by another Christian organisation. It sounded so tempting when they explained that we would head up a team in their organisation and not only get a bigger salary but we would also be paid to take people abroad for a holiday each year. We were very flattered to be asked, but as we talked through the possibilities and prayed about it, deep down we knew we were to stay where we were at present. I remember on several occasions, when tensions were high, having to physically stop Ray from lifting the phone and telling the other organisation we would join them. Even though we were going through some difficult times, God knew what he was doing. It was hard but we learned so much through our first nine months that helped us enormously in our leadership skills at a later stage.

11

THE BIRTH OF THE VISION

It was during those nine months that we carried and birthed our dream of having a team who were musicians but who were sold-out to God. We wanted people who were great musicians but that music wasn't first in their lives, instead Jesus was. As we prayed throughout the year, without advertising, God brought us four people who were to join Ray and I in the band we called Heartbeat – Jackie Stoner, Colin Vallance, Chris Rolinson and Jonny Billingsley.

During our first year in BYFC, as we were praying about starting Heartbeat, we formed a band to play for Dave Pope and sometimes Graham Kendrick too. We played and sang worship on the main stage at Greenbelt with Graham in August 1980. We were there to just be a part of a prayer team with Graham, but then he was asked if he could lead worship with a band on the Sunday morning. He invited Ray, Sheila and myself to be a part of that band. What an experience to look out from stage on the thousands of people in the audience. There seemed to be a sea of faces as far as the eye could see.

Ray and I have been close friends with Sheila since our teenage years when we sang together in Unity, the band I mentioned earlier. Sheila is now a well-known speaker and author based in the States, but at the beginning of her ministry she was an unknown singer. She was classically trained, but through her experience in Unity and then in BYFC, she began to sing other styles of music. She has always had a beautiful voice and a deep and real passion for Jesus. During our first few months of being in BYFC, Dave asked Ray and I if the band we had formed in BYFC would back him at a large Christian convention at Filey. Of course, we said we would because we loved to work with Dave. We were then asked if Sheila and the band would do a concert on one of the youth evenings at the Filey convention. We called ourselves the BYFC band. I'm sure no honours will ever be given for that very trendy name! None of us will ever own up to who came up with that creative name and to be honest, I'm not surprised!

We had just finished recording Sheila's first single before we went to Filey and so we decided to release it there. Graham Kendrick had written some songs for Sheila and two of them were put on the single. I remember the excitement we all had as we gathered beforehand to pray about our first gig together. I also remember feeling so nervous as I stood on stage to sing backing vocals for Sheila, but when the music started, the nerves went. It was great fun. The whole production that evening was stunning and the place was buzzing! At times we could hardly see each other for the amount of dry ice on stage! At the end of the gig we completely sold out of Sheila's single! However, a few people were perturbed at the loud music, the flashing lights and the dry ice and went to report to the leadership of the Filey convention that "the devil's music was being played at the young people's event." Dave, who had invited us to play, was summoned by the leadership. We were relieved that he was able to put their minds at rest.

When we went back to Wolverhampton where we lived at the time, we began preparing and recording Sheila's first album, Future Eyes. Ray was the Executive Producer and also the drummer on the album. Colin Vallance played bass and Chris Rolinson played keys and wrote some of the songs alongside Graham Kendrick. Ray got his brother, Derek, to write one of the songs with Chris too. I remember at times sitting in the recording booth beside Sheila while she sang – she wanted a friend with her so she didn't feel so lonely. From those small beginnings, Sheila became a household name in the Christian world.

A few months before Heartbeat started, Ray and I shared our vision with a wise and godly couple, Alex and Peggy Buchanan. As we spoke with them and they prayed for us, they warned us not to think about starting a band/ team such as Heartbeat unless we were going to make prayer a priority. They stressed how important it was to seek God's face and hear his voice. As we left them, with their words ringing in our ears, we determined to make prayer a priority not only in our lives but also in the life of the team. As we travelled around the country with a vision to be a demonstration of God's power and love, we did not realise the enormity of what God would accomplish through us. We were right at the beginning of an amazing story of God's faithfulness and although we didn't realise it, we were in a 'school of learning', discovering what it meant to 'live by faith' in every area of our lives.

Our whole heart and vision was to see the youth culture in our nation transformed by the love and power of God. We wanted to see God transform lives in two ways - one in the mainstream and so we went into schools, colleges, universities and prisons sharing our music, but also sharing our faith in God and through this area of our work we literally saw thousands coming to know the Lord. The second way was in the church. We wanted to see the church fall headlong in love with Jesus and for revival to come to our nation. We wanted to encourage the church to go deeper into intimacy and discover a life filled with fun, adventure and deep encounters with a supernatural God. We saw some incredible things happen in both these areas during the 1980s in particular. The vision today as I write this book in 2020 is still the same even though it has grown and developed through the years. We live to see lives transformed.

As I mentioned earlier, during the first year of us being in full time work with BYFC, we used to work three weeks of every month without having a day off so that we could save up our days off and take the fourth week off. This enabled Ray and I to go back to Ayr so that Ray could work in his mum and dad's business. It was tough, but Ray really wanted to bless and honour his mum and dad as much as he could and so every fourth week of every month saw us driving back to Scotland. Clive Calver's dad had died around that time and so Clive kindly gave us a loan of his dad's car in order to make it easier for us to travel north as well as helping us with our work in BYFC.

It was around this time when our church in Scotland began to have some conversations with us about us returning home to work as youth leaders in our church. We did what we always do with every opportunity that comes our way, we began to pray about it.

At the same time, David Pawson (an International speaker, pastor and prophet) came to speak in Ayr Town Hall on a BYFC tour and Clive Calver asked if David could come to our home to rest during the day. We just happened to be in Ayr at that time and so after he had rested, we began to talk with David. During the conversation, we told him about the opportunity we had of coming home and working in our church and how this could perhaps be God's will for us. He didn't say much but what he did say greatly impacted us. He said, "Oh, do you think so?" He went on to say, "If they don't accept the root of your ministry, then they should not expect the fruit of your ministry." We didn't say anything but inside we were thinking this man is an incredible prophetic man of God and although we didn't really know what he meant at the time - his words deeply troubled us. Later we said to each other, "Does he not think this is something that is on God's heart for us?"

We took what he said to God in prayer and asked the Lord that if this was not his will for our lives that he would close the door, but asked that it would be the church that would do the closing rather than us. We felt we didn't want to say "No" and offend our church who at that time was supporting us financially. A few weeks later, our church contacted us and told us that even though they were feeling excited at the thought of us working for them, they felt it was not the right time for us to come home and be their youth workers. God had answered and we were so thankful we had not made a mistake. A couple of months later, David Pawson was speaking in Wolverhampton and so Ray and I decided to go along and hear him. Afterwards we went to speak with him and we wondered whether he would remember us. When he saw us, he immediately asked how it had worked out with our church. We told him what we had prayed and what had happened. He then said, "That's so good. I have been praying for you both every day since I saw you. I've been praying that you would not go back to Scotland. I didn't feel it was right for you." We couldn't believe it - David Pawson had personally prayed for Ray and me every day for months - wow! What a blessing!

12

THE HEARTBEAT YEARS IN BYFC

During the summer of 1981, we were invited to play at a new event called Royal week. It was to be one of the first things we did as our newly formed band Heartbeat. One of the speakers there was Doug Barnett. He was a fantastic speaker and during that week Ray and I got to know him. Ray went to him for some advice as to the way forward with his parents and what he said was very helpful. He told us that we needed to 'cut the apron strings' and that this would be a freeing thing for both Ray's parents and ourselves. After this, we spent quite a bit of time seeking God as to how we should do that. We got a word from God that we needed to 'remove the stone' (Isaiah 62:10) and as we prayed, we felt this meant that we should sell our home in Scotland. So, when we went back to Ayr, we put our home on the market and it sold the very next day!

Once the house was sold, we bought a house in Preston beside my brother, Jack and his wife Susan and made that house our base for the next while. When Ray's parents realised that we were not coming back to Scotland, strangely enough our relationship with them vastly improved. Selling our home was definitely the right thing to do. From that time, Ray's parents got behind us and supported us in the work that we were doing. The prophecy we had received from God regarding our call said that God would look after our loved ones and that certainly happened. God was faithful to Ray's parents because a number of years later the town in which they had their shoe shop went through a difficult time. One of the main factories closed and the town centre became like a ghost town. However, just before this happened and before they had any knowledge of this, they decided to retire and put their shop up for sale and it sold very quickly. God blessed them by selling the business at the right time. We noted with interest that if Ray had stayed and still been in the business, he would have been out of a job!

After Heartbeat started, we left the management side of the Creative Arts in BYFC as the missions for Heartbeat around the UK started to increase hugely. We were asked by BYFC to be the worship band on tours such as Mission England which was a preparation for Billy Graham coming back to the UK. We travelled all over the UK on this tour and also on many other national tours. Churches and YFC centres started to invite Heartbeat to do schools, colleges and university missions up and down our nation. We saw incredible things happening as we discovered that there was a hunger in the youth of our land for a God who loved them and cared for them. They were not interested in attending a church as they saw church as dull and boring, but when we told them about a God who was real and who could do miracles, their hunger for spiritual things began to increase hugely.

We regularly visited various schools to play in their assemblies, to take several lessons and also to do lunchtime concerts. At each event, whether it was two of us in a lesson or all of us in the assembly or lunchtime concert, we would give out leaflets which told them about an end of the week event that we were putting on in a neutral hall. We never charged the pupils for the event, but we told them they had to have a leaflet to get in. We never knew how many people would attend, but we spent a portion of every day in prayer, praying that many young people's lives would be completely transformed by the love and power of God. We also had prayer meetings with the local church or churches who had invited us into their area, and prayed that we would see God's power released in that town or city.

We told the school children not to just come to see a band playing, but to come on Friday night to see God's power in action. We told them that we were expecting God to be there and that he would be transforming lives and healing people physically.

Throughout the 80's, we saw thousands of young people respond to give their lives to Jesus and so many hundreds of people healed. We thought what we were seeing was very ordinary, but really it was extraordinary. We thought it was normal but actually it was anything but normal. Looking back over those years we can now see that what we were experiencing was really like a revival. As we prayed and believed God and as we laid our lives down for him, we saw outstanding things happen through the work of Heartbeat. Many years later, as I go to speak at various churches and events, many people will come and tell me that they gave their lives to God at a Heartbeat concert.

During our first year of Heartbeat, Chris Rolinson left the band to go and work with my friend, Sheila Walsh, and funnily enough her keyboard player, Dave Bankhead joined Heartbeat.

I remember one of our first Heartbeat schools' missions was held in Garforth near Leeds. The organiser was a young lad called Derek Tiffany and in the team organising the event was a girl called Gill Riley. Gill invited her friends, John and Rose Lancaster and their family from Clitheroe to come and hear the band. From this one mission many significant things happened – many young people heard about a God who loved them and because of this, lives were radically changed. Derek became a good friend who not only supported the work that we did financially, but eventually many years later after he was married and had a grown-up family, he and his wife came to work for ngm for five years. He became my personal assistant and Ruth was ngm's receptionist and cleaner. Also, John and Rose invited Heartbeat to do a mission in their home town of Clitheroe. We had no idea at that time that John and Rose Lancaster would become partners with us in the work that God had called us to do.

Through the work of Heartbeat, John and Rose's children, Julie and Steven, gave their lives to God and John was physically healed at one point too. When we arrived in Clitheroe in 1982 to begin the schools' mission, we were told that Ray and I were to stay with John and Rose. What we didn't know was that John and Rose were converting a barn into a new home for them and their family. They were staying in a caravan outside the front door! We were the first people to stay in their new home before it was properly finished. As they showed us into what was to become their bedroom, they told us, "You will notice that there are no curtains on the windows, but don't worry it's only the cows in the field outside who will see you undressing!" I prayed they were right!

John, Rose, Ray and myself became close friends and throughout the years have spent many wonderful times together. Their love and friendship have always meant so much to us. We knew them when they had didn't have much money but even with very little resources, they were very generous. Many years later, John and Rose became multi-millionaires; their incredible story is in a wonderful book Rose has written called *Give the Best Away*. Fortune hasn't changed our friends; they are still the same John and Rose and they are still mega generous!

I remember at the end of our last concert of the Clitheroe mission as we sang an encore, Jackie and I hugged each other and then we both broke down crying on stage. Jackie had told us that she was leaving Heartbeat and our sadness overflowed in tears. Jackie went on to do incredible things in her life. She became an author, has got a doctorate and now advises the Government as well as the European Parliament on issues to do with children, but we have remained strong, close friends throughout the years. I remember meeting her in London after many years of not seeing each other and walking to a coffee shop with our arms around each other so thankful for our friendship. She is now married to Colin who was also in Heartbeat, but I will share this remarkable story later in the book.

Trish Maguire became our next lead singer and when she got married some time later, her husband, Malcolm Morgan joined us as our youth worker. Trish is the only person in Heartbeat to leave, get prayed for, receive leaving gift and then within a few weeks come back again. We often teased her that she had only left to get the gift, but really she left because she was getting married but then God called her and her husband to work with us. Malcolm was one of the best youth workers we've ever known. He has a such a warm and friendly attitude and a real heart for getting beside people. Our friendship with Trish and Malcolm has also lasted throughout the years. They were strong warriors who stood with us for years. They have always been faith filled carriers of the presence of Jesus and when they eventually left Heartbeat many years later, they went on to be key leaders in various places in the world and are now planting a church in Greece. They have never been afraid to live by faith and depend on God for their finances.

13

THE HEARTBEAT YEARS IN MALMESBURY

After we had been in British Youth for Christ for just under three years, Ray and I felt that God was asking us to leave BYFC and live by faith, depending on God for all our finances both individually and corporately. We felt we should set up Heartbeat as a separate ministry. This was indeed a very scary thought!

In BYFC, we each had a salary of £2,500 per year and although it was very small at least it was regular. As we prayed about leaving BYFC and depending on God for our finance, we decided to share our thoughts with the rest of Heartbeat. I remember vividly sitting with the team whilst Ray and I explained what we felt God had been saying to us. We were careful to say that God *might* only be saying to the two of us that we should live by faith for our finances. However, we asked them to pray and see if they felt this was something from God for all of us. As we finished sharing what God had laid on our hearts, our keyboard player, Dave Bankhead exclaimed, "Well, I think I need a stiff drink!" He may have only been joking, but his comments did bring home to us the reality of what God might be asking us to do.

After a week of each of us praying on our own, the six of us sat down together to discuss what each individual felt God had said. We had an amazing team of people; each one of them was very special and we knew they would really seek God's heart for the way forward. We were amazed and thrilled when every one of them told us that they were in this move with us. Each one felt that they should move out of BYFC and begin to live by faith and depend on God for our finances. As we sat and discussed the future, we knew we were on the edge of an exciting journey of faith yet I am sure if we had been honest, each one of us would have said that we were little apprehensive about the way ahead. We had no idea what we would encounter, but we did know that God was walking with us and that gave us confidence to take the first step.

Ray and I went to share our thoughts and the scriptures God had given us with the leadership of BYFC. Clive Calver had just moved on from BYFC and Rob White had taken over the reins. We had valued our time in that organisation and we were so thankful for all they had done to help us in our early years as Heartbeat. Rob and the rest of the leadership understood totally what we were saying and released us in August 1983 from being salaried staff of BYFC. We left not having any PA equipment, no lights, van, offices or money! All we had was our personal gear: our drums, keyboard, guitars etc., and the promise that God would supply *all* our needs.

As you can imagine we spent quite a lot of time together during our last few months in BYFC praying and seeking God as to where we should set up our base. We came into contact with a man and two girls who used to be the administration team for another ministry called Living Sound. They all lived in and around Malmesbury, Wiltshire. A few months earlier they felt that God had told them to leave Living Sound and that he would show them a team that they could serve in administration. As we prayed and talked together for some weeks, it became apparent that as well as them providing the secretarial and administrative support we needed, we should all move to Malmesbury, Wiltshire and set up our base there.

The Shaftsbury Society has a school there for children with special needs and they had kindly offered us a wing of their building where we could set up our offices for a peppercorn rent. We were so excited. God provided not only administration help for us (up until that point, I had been doing all the administration on the road) but had also given us four small offices and a lounge with kitchen combined. In August 1983, we all began to move our homes to a very beautiful part of the country that we did not know even existed. We were to live and have our offices in Malmesbury for the next ten years. However, about a year later, we were to go through one of the biggest lessons of faith that we could learn.

The man who had become one of our administrators decided he wanted to leave Heartbeat, and as he had found the offices in the first place, he wanted Ray and me and the rest of the team to leave so he could use them for his new ministry. As you can imagine we were shocked as we felt the offices were not his, but had been given to Heartbeat. However, as usual we all went to God in prayer over the issue and also, we phoned our faithful and wise pastor and friend, Ken McGreavy.

When Ray and I started Heartbeat in 1981, we had approached Ken McGreavy, the pastor of British Youth for Christ at the time, and asked him if he would mentor us and stand with us as we pursued God's vision for our lives. Ken said he would and he and Hazel, his wife, have been so faithful to us over the years. Ken became a very good friend of ours and Hazel and their family became very close to us and were, in fact, like family. Ken and Hazel prayed for us both every day, in fact Ken often told Ray and me that he would not pray anything for himself that he had not first of all prayed for us. He was an amazing mentor and friend. He wrote us a letter that said if we ever needed help, just to call him and he would come from wherever he was to see us. His love and commitment to us both was so wonderful.

Over the years, Ken gave Ray and I mountains of wisdom and advice as well as regular spiritual teaching for all of us in Heartbeat. In the early years of Heartbeat, he would come and stay with us for a few days almost every month and teach the truths of the Bible to us all. These days were so special and he taught us so much about how to live a life totally sold out to God. When we set up Heartbeat as a registered charity in 1985, Ken and Hazel became two of our Trustees. Our relationship with Ken until his death in 2010 was one of the most precious things in our lives. Hazel remains such a dear friend and continues on our Trustee board to this day.

Ray and I arranged to meet Ken at a service station on the M4 about halfway between our homes. When we discussed with Ken what was happening with our offices, we were shocked to hear that he felt that we needed to do what God asked Abraham to do with Isaac and put our offices on the altar. We could not believe that Ken was telling us that we should sacrifice our offices and give them to our administrator. Ray and I looked at each other, surely that could not be what God was asking us to do? The more we talked and prayed with Ken, the more it became obvious that this was indeed the right course of action.

As we drove back to Malmesbury, we began to wonder how the team would receive the news that we needed to give the offices to our administrator. We needn't have worried though because after the initial shock, they began to see that no matter what, God would provide for us. We called Brian, our administrator, and told him that he could have the offices and began to make plans to set up our administration base in our rented home. We also informed the school that we would be moving out of the building. It just so happened that the head of the Shaftesbury Society at the time, Gordon Holloway, was coming to visit the school in Malmesbury and while there he asked if he could see Ray.

When Ray met him in the Headmaster's office, the first thing Gordon said was, "I only need to know the answer to one question. Do you want to leave the offices?" When Ray said, "No" he immediately responded and said, "That's great. The offices are yours. We never gave the offices in the first place to your administrator; we gave them to Heartbeat and we still believe God wants you to have them. I will chat to Brian and will let him know that the offices belong to you." We could not believe what God had done. We thought our offices were dead but here was God raising them back to life again. As we had been obedient to what God had said, God performed a miracle.

Thousands of years previously, when Abraham went up the mountain to sacrifice his son, he knew he had heard from God and that he must obey. He knew that this meant that he may even have to plunge a knife into his precious son's body. He knew he had to trust that even if he had to sacrifice his son on the altar, that somehow God would raise Isaac back to life. God wanted to find out whether Abraham would be obedient to him. When God saw Abraham's obedience and his heart to do whatever the Lord asked of him, he stopped him from harming his son and provided a ram as a sacrifice instead (Genesis 22). When situations and decisions seem incredibly tough, it is good to listen and read about how God has dealt with others in a similar situation. Ken had indeed heard the word of the Lord for us. Never in our wildest dreams did we think that God would give us our offices back. We knew God would somehow provide for us, but we were prepared to set up an office in our home and work from there. As we 'killed off' our offices, God raised them back to life for us. As you can imagine, we were ecstatic and so grateful to God and to the Shaftesbury Society for the outcome of this difficult situation.

Many years later, I was speaking at an event near Malmesbury when I saw someone I knew in the audience. It was Brian's wife. I was delighted to see her and we spoke in the interval. She explained that her husband had specifically sent her to the event so she could speak to me. He wasn't very well and in fact he knew he was dying. He had asked her to come and see me that morning despite the fact that he needed her with him at all times as his carer. He wanted to say he was sorry and to ask us to forgive him. I didn't have much time to speak, but I said to tell him that Ray and I really appreciated his message and that we didn't hold anything against him whatsoever. We had forgiven him a long time ago. I asked her to convey our love to him and told her that we would be praying for him. I wanted to chat more, but she wanted to leave as she understandably needed to be at her husband's side. What happened that morning meant so much to Ray and myself.

14

GOD'S PROVISION

A few months after we had come off salary with British Youth for Christ and whilst we were still in transit to Malmesbury, Ray's father phoned us to say that he had just attended a church meeting where it had been decided that our home church would no longer financially support Ray and myself in the work we were doing. It was a huge shock to us both. You see, when the church sent us out as their missionaries to the UK, they had committed themselves to give £400 a month to BYFC to go towards our salary. When we left BYFC, they then said they would redirect this money to Ray and myself as part of our support. We were incredibly thankful to our church for being so supportive, but what was going to happen now?

Ray and I could tell that Ray's parents were very upset at the church's decision and felt that they should warn us that the cheque we were expecting in the next couple of weeks would not arrive. What Ray's parents did not know, however, was that a week or so earlier, Ray and I had felt challenged from God to give away everything we received as our regular income for that month. We regularly received three gifts, one large gift of £400 from our church and two smaller ones of £30 from two friends. This was not enough for us to live on so we always had to reach out to God each month to receive the extra finance we needed for our mortgage, bills, food etc. A great need for money to support evangelism had arisen and as we prayed, we had felt challenged by God to give away everything we received regularly and depend on him for all our needs for that month. Although we regularly gave to God's work, this was the first time that God had ever asked us to give away a full month's income. As we gave it, I can remember thinking to myself that we only needed to get through the next few weeks and then the church money would come in again. Now here was Ray's dad telling us that the church money would not be arriving ever again!

To say that we were shocked was an understatement. We could not believe it. Perhaps Ray's dad had got it wrong? However, when no letter or cheque arrived over the next three months, we realised that he had heard correctly. On the night we heard the news, fear crept into our hearts. Fear is a horrible visitor; no wonder it tells us 365 times in the Bible that we should not fear! Fear crushes our faith and stops us in our tracks.

We talked long into the night discussing what God was doing. Did he want us to give up our work in evangelism with Heartbeat? Did he want us to go and get jobs? We talked, prayed and cried together and resolved that in the morning we needed to call our wise friend, Ken McGreavy. We knew he would pray for us and together we would discover what God was saying. After hours of talking, Ray went into the kitchen to get a drink and discovered the old dishwasher we had was on fire. This seemed like the last straw – what else could go wrong?

The next morning, we phoned Ken and told him our sorry tale. Ken immediately invited us to travel down to his home in London to see himself and Hazel. As we got into the car at Preston, we put a teaching cassette by Floyd McClung on in the car. As we listened to Floyd as we travelled down the M6, we realised that God was speaking to us. Floyd said, "At times you may feel you are out on a limb for God and when you look back it's as if you see the devil sawing off the branch." This was exactly what Ray and I had felt. We had given everything we had to live on. We had no savings at all to fall back on. We needed God to do something miraculous in order for us to survive. We had a mortgage to pay and we needed food to eat, but as we looked for God to provide, it was as if we saw the enemy sawing off our branch. Were we going to fall big time?

Floyd went on to say, "I tell you even though you see the devil sawing off the branch, God will enable the branch to stay in the air and the tree will fall down." Right at that moment, God spoke to us and said, "Ray, Nancy, what have you been praying for?" We suddenly remembered that we had been praying for God to increase our faith. We heard the Lord say, "I'm just answering your prayers."

What a relief to know that God was still with us and that all he wanted us to do was to trust him.

As I mentioned earlier, there are three steps to discovering real faith pumping through our veins. The first is hearing from God; the second is obedience to what God is saying and the third is trusting God and his word. Hearing, Obeying and Trusting. We had *heard* God tell us to give away our regular income; we had been *obedient* and had released the finance. Now we needed to take the third step of *trusting* God despite the difficult circumstances. As we travelled in the car, we prayed and thanked God for what he was doing and asked him to help us trust him and to grow in our faith. As we finished praying, we realised that the fear had gone and our joy had returned. Our heavy hearts had disappeared. God was with us and if God was with us then he would somehow provide. It may have looked as though we had nothing but in actual fact, we had everything because we had God! When we arrived at Ken and Hazel's home in London, we were delighted to tell them that God had already spoken to us. Before we left Ken and Hazel prayed with us and gave us a gift of money to help us with our petrol and food. They were great friends!

During the next few months, God did some pretty amazing things. The branch certainly did stay in the air. We had been trying to sell our home in Preston for months with no success, but that month our house sold, which freed us to move from Preston in Lancashire to Malmesbury in Wiltshire to the base that God had given us. When we arrived in Malmesbury, Ray and I put our bed in one of the offices and shared the lounge and kitchen with the rest of Heartbeat during the day. A few weeks later God provided a huge home rent-free for three months. The local vicarage was empty as the local Church of England was waiting for a new vicar to arrive. They very kindly told us that we and Malcom and Trish, who were also looking for a home, could stay in the vicarage for the summer until the vicar arrived. Our income was greatly reduced however God reduced our outgoings even more for a period of time.

Our church in Scotland had been going through some really tough issues at the time and all the elders and some of the deacons who had commissioned us and sent us out as missionaries had left to start up another church nearby called Kyle Community Church. When they heard that the church they had left had stopped supporting us, they immediately decided to take up an offering for us each month. That offering together with small gifts we received was such an amazing answer to our prayers. Kyle Community Church supported us for almost 30 years as their missionaries. Their constant financial and prayerful support was an amazing blessing to us both as a couple and eventually as a family. They were extremely loving, caring and generous. They never put demands on us and certainly never tried to control us, but continued to faithfully pray for us. After we had been in full time work for thirty years our support from Kyle Community Church stopped as all of the original elders and deacons who had commissioned us and sent us out were no longer alive or no longer attending that church. We will always be so grateful for the many years we had this partnership with them. We will always be grateful for their love and support at a time when we needed it the most.

This experience taught us how to grow in faith. We honestly never thought that when we asked God to increase our faith we would go through such pressure, but we learned so much about God's faithfulness when we had absolutely nothing in our bank to pay our bills. We could only rely on our God who is never in need. I love what God says in Psalm 50 v 9 & 12, "*I have no need….If I were hungry I would not tell you, for the world is mine and all that is in it*" (NIV). Then in verse 15 he says, "*Call on me in the day of trouble; I will deliver you and you will honour me*" (NIV). He has everything we need, and to access it we only need to look to him. There have been many similar journeys we have had during our lives and each one has helped us to grow more in love with our Lord Jesus. I have often said throughout the forty years I have lived this way that every Christian should live by faith for their finances for at least a year of their lives. It certainly is the quickest way of getting to know the Lord and discovering that he is real and alive today.

One of the lessons we have learned along our journey of faith is that it is extremely important to honour God with our money. Tithing was never taught in my church in Scotland. I mentioned earlier that I attended a Christian Brethren church for twenty-two years of my life where I was taught that giving ten per cent of your money was part of the 'old covenant' and that really all your finances belonged to God which is true. However, in reality, many people in our church only ever gave the small change in their pockets and even ten per cent was never reached.

Many years before God led us into full-time Christian work, he taught Ray and I an important lesson about tithing. One Sunday evening, not long after we were married, we attended a church in Glasgow where a Scottish evangelist called Ian Leitch was speaking. During the service, I strongly felt that God had told me to give Ian some money. This kind of thing had never happened to me before and so I thought I would chat it through with Ray whenever I got a chance to do so. After the meeting we were invited to someone's home for supper and discovered that the preacher, Ian, had been invited too. We had never met Ian before, but that night we really clicked with him and spent most of the night chatting with him. As we were leaving, he delighted us by inviting us to spend a weekend with him and his wife, Morag, at his home in a couple of months. We didn't realise it, but this friendship was to last many years. We were to learn so much through Ian and Morag Leitch.

On our way home, Ray surprised me by telling me that during the service he had felt God say to him that we should be giving Ian a gift of money. We spent the rest of that car journey discussing what we should do. How much should we send? Would Ian think it weird if we sent him money through the post? We didn't know if Ian was on a salary or how he got his money. As there were so many unanswered questions, we decided to think and pray about it individually and discuss it again in a couple of days.

When we brought the subject back up again in a couple of days, neither of us was any clearer about what we should do. It did seem strange to us at that point to send some money through the post to someone we didn't really know. Maybe he didn't need it; maybe we didn't hear from God? So many doubts filled our minds that we delayed doing anything for another few days. When we talked about it again at a later stage, we convinced ourselves that it was now too late to send any money and that we probably got it wrong anyhow. We had both heard God speak to us so clearly and yet we allowed our doubts and fears to distract us from what God had said. We ended up not doing what God had asked us to do. In the coming weeks we forgot all about it.

After a few months, it was time for us to drive to the east coast of Scotland to where Ian and Morag lived. During that weekend, we asked Ian about his financial base and discovered that he lived by faith and depended on God to send him enough money to live on. Ray asked him if there had been any time that God had let him down. Ian replied, "It's funny you should ask that, because there was a time just recently, in fact it was just around the time that I met you, where I was praying for God to send me some money to cover a bill. My time limit came and went and I couldn't understand why God had not sent the money on time. Eventually, however, God did send the money from a contact in the States." Ray and I looked at each other and then confessed to Ian that we knew why God had not sent the money at the correct time! We had disobeyed God and had not done what God had asked us to do. Ian then asked us a question that was to lay a huge foundation in our lives for our future. He asked us if we tithed our finances. We admitted we didn't and told him all our excuses as to why we didn't. Ian went through the Bible with us and showed us why it was essential that a least ten per cent of our income should go to God. We remember quite clearly telling Ian that if we gave ten per cent of our salary to God, we would be even more in the red each month. We explained that we had very small salaries and at the end of each month our bank account went into the red for a few days before salaries arrived. We told Ian in no uncertain terms that we could not afford to tithe. Ian's reply stuck in our hearts and minds as he said to us, "You can't afford not to tithe. If you trust God in this and do what he is telling you to do, instead of being in the red each month you will be in the black."

We arrived home knowing that we needed to take the step of trusting God for our money. The very next month we tithed our finances and immediately gave ten per cent away. It felt good to be doing what God had instructed us to do and at the end of that month, for the first time ever in our married life, we were in the black. We had received an unexpected tax refund which put our account in the black. Every month since, we have continued to be in the black. God is amazing! Trust him and you will see what he can do. It is so important to put God first and honour him with our finances. This is something that we as a couple have done every month and also when we set up Heartbeat/ngm as a ministry we tithed the ministry's money too. We continue to do this individually and corporately every month. In ngm we decided to give to ministries that are similar to ourselves as well as those who are working among the poor or disadvantaged.

God says in Malachi 3:8-9 that if we do not tithe and give offerings then it amounts to *robbing* God. But when we tithe, God says he will *throw open the floodgates of heaven and pour out so much blessing that there will not be room enough to store it* - Malachi 3:10 (NIV). In Matthew 23:23 Jesus also makes it clear that we should not forget to tithe. Why is it that we struggle so much to give back to God just a little of what he has given us? Jesus quite clearly says in Matthew 6:24, *You cannot serve both God and money (NIV)*. Money can have such a hold on our lives as I discovered a few months later.

My husband, Ray, was one of the most generous people I have ever met. He would give away his last penny to someone who needed it more than he did. However, when he came to me a few months after we had begun to tithe and told me that he wanted to give away the only savings we had, I was indignant. It is one thing to give God ten per cent, but surely God would not ask me to part with our savings. At that point we had £200 in an account put aside for something special like a holiday and here was Ray saying he wanted to pray and ask God if we should give it away to someone else. That night in bed I could not sleep; instead I argued with God. I was determined that God was not going to get his hands on that money. That money was mine and I wanted to spend it on something that would be special for Ray and me. I argued back and forth with God for what seemed like hours and then in the middle of the night I hit the bed with a clenched fist and shouted out loud, "No!" The act of shouting at God suddenly brought me to my senses. I could not believe what I had done. I loved the Lord so much and yet here I was shouting "No" at him. I very quickly repented and told God I was sorry. I told him that if he wanted my savings, he could have them, in fact he could have every penny I had. As I poured out my heart to God, a huge relief flooded my being and to be honest I couldn't believe it had taken me so long to say "Yes" and give in to God.

One of the biggest hindrances to our faith is not honouring God with our finances. Without necessarily realising it, we can get very precious about *our* money. God broke something in me that night that changed my attitude to finances and helped me to realise that there is much joy in giving; in fact, there can be more joy in giving than in receiving. Nowadays, I love being able to give to others much more than receiving. I love to see the joy in people's faces as they see their need met. Try it and see and you will discover what I mean. Give with a cheerful heart, for God loves a cheerful giver (2 Corinthians 9:7).

Throughout the years, God showed me that if I obeyed him and gave out of the little I had, he would provide abundantly for me. I know from experience that it is true that you can never out-give God. No matter how big our shovel is, God's shovel is always bigger. As we shovel our tithes and offerings out with our little shovel, God will use his massive shovel to pour out his blessings into our lives.

God knew all those years ago that if we didn't get these principles right in our lives, then it would be impossible for us to live by faith and depend on him for the finances that we needed, not only to survive but also to succeed. Can I encourage you to put your finances under the Lordship of Christ? All our money and possessions belong to him anyhow, we are just caretakers of it. Let's make sure that we look after his money the way he would want to us to do. We must not hold it to ourselves, but surrender our will to his and do what he tells us to do with the wealth he has given us.

We tell the folks who join us in the work that God has given us to do that they cannot expect God to answer their prayers for finance if they are not honouring him in the first place with their personal finances. It's not a matter of how much money we have; it is a matter of allowing God to have full access to all that we have and being open to when, how and to whom he may want us to give. As we were told many years ago, you cannot afford not to tithe.

15

THE HEARTBEAT YEARS – OUR MIRACLE VAN

Just after we left British Youth for Christ and had set up our own ministry under the name of Heartbeat the need for a van became evident. In BYFC we had used a van which we called the Bread Bin, as it seemed to want to cook you red hot. We hadn't liked the van very much, but in comparison to the van we had just borrowed, our van in BYFC began to look like the best thing since sliced bread! Ray took one look at the van we had borrowed which was supposed to take us on a five-hour journey to Lowestoft at the end of the week and said, "This is ridiculous! This van will not get to us to the end of the street, never mind the other end of the country." Ray immediately encouraged us to go to God in prayer, as he felt God had a better and more suitable van for us.

We called the whole of Heartbeat together, and as we prayed and asked God for a van we heard him speak clearly to us. God simply asked us, "What kind of van do you want? Be specific!" We discussed the kind of van we would need and came up with a complete profile of a van. We felt that a Mercedes would be the best make, possibly a 307D. It had to be a certain height; depth and length because of our equipment, but it didn't need to be brand new. It could be around two or three years old and we reckoned it would possibly cost us between £5,000 and £6,000. We wrote all the information on a piece of paper and we even had a photograph of the type of van we wanted. We put the information and the photo in the middle of the floor and again prayed to God.

As we prayed and told God this was the kind of van we wanted, we felt we should contact a friend of a friend who dealt in Mercedes vans. During the phone call, the guy informed us that these vans were really scarce as most people held on to them for a long time, however he needed to know our time scale, when did we need the van? He almost collapsed when we told him that we needed the van by Saturday, as this was when we were going off on our mission to Lowestoft. He told us he would phone us back as soon as he had made some enquiries, but as we put the phone down his last words were ringing in our ears: "It will take a miracle to get this type of van by Saturday!" We laughed and said, "He doesn't realise it, but that is exactly what we are needing – a miracle!"

During band rehearsals the next day, which was Thursday, we received a phone call from our garage friend who told us excitedly, "You will never believe this! I have found the exact van you wanted. It's a 307D with the exact dimensions you asked for. It is two years old and will cost you £5,400." You can imagine the excitement we had in our hearts as we sent our engineer to go and look at the van, but there was one little problem! We didn't have the money; in fact, we didn't have a penny towards this van. We prayed again asking God to complete the miracle by giving us enough finance so that we could purchase this vehicle. We then went back to our rehearsals. Ten minutes later we had a phone call from someone Ray and I did not know but who lived in our local town of Malmesbury. During his prayer time that morning with his wife, this man had heard God clearly speak to him and say, "I want you to phone the offices of Heartbeat and offer them an amount of money they need to purchase a van." We had our van and we went off to our mission in Lowestoft with our miracle and a new story of God's amazing faithfulness.

One of the important lessons we learned through that journey of faith was the need to be specific in our prayers. Often our prayers can be vague. We ask God to bless us but we are not specific about exactly what we would like God to do. This is one of the hindrances to seeing faith grow. God was teaching us that it was important to be specific in our prayers. We read in Mark 10 that when Jesus asked Bartimaeus what he wanted, Bartimaeus didn't say, "Oh I'm not really sure what I want you to do!" No, he was specific and immediately replied to Jesus with the words, *"Rabbi, I want to see"* -Mark 10:51 (NIV). It was obvious to everyone that Bartimaeus was blind but to unlock the miracle of receiving his eyesight required him to be specific.

If God were to ask you today, "What do you want me to do for you?" I wonder how many of us would be specific with God. Would we have to stop and think what we would like to receive from God or would your response be immediate? Bartimaeus' need was such that he knew immediately what he wanted. We learned that day to be specific in our prayers and not to be afraid to ask God for a miracle. In the months and years ahead, we were to see many incredible miracles.

16

THE HEARTBEAT YEARS – THE INCREASE BEGINS

We met Ian and Dorry Townend in March 1983 when we were looking for a guitarist to join us. When we first met them, we had no idea that these two people were to become two of our closest friends and that our friendship would last a lifetime. Ian is Scottish by birth but through joining a band called Living Sound, he met and married Dorry who is American. A year after they were married, they felt the call of God to come to the UK. They did not know where in the UK God was calling them to, but they knew that like Abraham they had to obey God and that meant leaving their home, friends and country and relocating to England. Just as they were praying about this, a friend from England called them and asked if they were feeling a call to come and serve God in England. When they explained that they had indeed been praying about this, he explained that he felt God was asking them not only to hear the call but to obey by packing their bags and travelling to England. He explained that if they did that and trusted God, then God would open doors before them. This was the encouragement they needed and so with their church's blessing, they left; putting themselves fully into the hands of God.

When they arrived on British soil, they were told about a couple called Ray and Nancy Goudie, who were in a full-time Christian band and who were looking for a guitarist. Ian was a guitarist/singer and Dorry was a singer. Within a week, Ian was in Heartbeat and was playing at Spring Harvest with us. Within a month or so, Dorry became one of our singers. They did not realise it at the time, but they were to be in Heartbeat for the next seven years and as they would say now, "We were at the beginning of one of the greatest adventures in God that we have ever known."

When they arrived in Malmesbury, they had hardly any financial support and no home to live in. Similar to us, they lived in our offices for some time before exploring how they could get a home of their own. In the natural realm it seemed crazy to be thinking of renting or buying because they were living on $75 per month support from their church. The Lord spoke to Ian and Dorry through the parable of the talents in the Bible and from that parable they knew the Lord was telling them to buy a home rather than rent one, even though there seemed no reasonable way of doing this. Some months previously God had given Ray a verse of scripture, which we believed was a promise from God to all of us in Heartbeat. The verse came from Hosea 11:11, *"I will settle them in their homes" declares the Lord (NIV)*. We knew that God would somehow give each of us a home as we put our faith in him.

As a team we went to spend some time at Colin Urquhart's base called The Hyde. Colin's book *Faith for the Future* had been a huge encouragement to Ray and myself as we had been going through similar experiences of living by faith. We felt it would be good to spend some time together as a team in a faith-filled atmosphere, so we went on a retreat there. At the same retreat was a man who was a building society manager and out of the blue he told us that if we ever needed a mortgage, we should get in touch with him. When we explained that we didn't have a regular salary as such, he told us this was not a problem, as he believed in our employer more than he believed in some of his regular clients' employers.

When Ian and Dorry found a house they wanted to buy, they knew it was going to take a miracle to enable them to purchase it as they had no money to put down as a deposit. As Ian, Dorry, Ray and I prayed we felt it was right to approach our friend, the building society manager, for a mortgage. When we did, he gave them a 100% mortgage on the house. Ian and Dorry did not need a deposit and by the time their mortgage came through, God not only increased their regular monthly support but each month gave them enough money to cover the mortgage payments and their other bills. When Ian and Dorry left us many years later they sold their home for more than twice the amount they had paid for it. God blessed their step of faith in a huge way.

Shortly after we arrived in Malmesbury, we were introduced to a wonderful guy who lived there called Dave Strange. Dave became our engineer in Heartbeat and thus another great friendship was formed. Another guy who joined our technical team a little later on was Mick Nobbs. Mick, like Dave, had a real loving and compassionate heart. They made a great team and we made some incredible memories with them throughout the years.

When we arrived in Malmesbury, there were six of us in the band, and together with our administration team, we became nine. Throughout our ten years in Malmesbury, our numbers grew as more people came to join us; people like Sarah Shepherd who was a brilliant dancer. She is another one whose friendship down the years has meant so much. In fact, many years later, Sarah's 18-year-old daughter, Charis, came to work with us in ngm. Sarah would not only dance during some of our songs, but we also gave her a spot in our concert for her to dance and send a message through her creative performance.

My own brother, Jack, had a call of God through our mission in Preston in 1984 to come and join us as our administrator. What a joy it was to have him and his wife, Susan and their family come to live in Malmesbury with us from 1985 to the end of 1989. We never would have thought that many years later Jack and Susan's daughter, our niece, Natalie would come and join us in ngm as a dancer and find her husband, Jon who was also going through our training programme. It was wonderful having family live with us in Malmesbury and so good to have Jack as our administrator. I mentioned earlier that Jack and I have always been close, but what I didn't say was that when I married Ray, he and Jack became close friends too. It was wonderful for us both to work so closely with Jack, especially during the time when we released singles into the mainstream charts in the UK. However, that story is still to come!

Our numbers grew during our ten years based in that area. The Lord added many amazing people to our team. We were often complimented about the team that we had with us on mission; they were certainly a great bunch of people who truly loved God and wanted to do what he wanted them to do and go where he wanted them to go. Serving God was always at the top of our agenda!

Ray and I managed to buy a lovely brand new three bedroomed townhouse on the banks of the River Avon. Each time we had a new person join the team and they didn't have somewhere to stay we would invite them to stay with Ray and myself until they found a more permanent place to live. It was a great way of getting to know each new team member. Malmesbury is a beautiful small town that has an incredible 12th century Abbey. It is steeped in history and we absolutely loved staying there.

17

THE HEARTBEAT YEARS - SIGNS OF REVIVAL

During the 80's we saw so many thousands of people come to know the Lord. We did missions all across the UK working with local churches. Many of the missions remain in my memory because of the spectacular things that God did. We saw things that evangelists all over the world pray to see. We saw thousands of young lives changed forever as they accepted God into their lives and many were also healed emotionally and physically. It was incredible. As I said earlier, we thought it was normal, that everyone saw the things we saw. It was only many years later that we realised that it was extraordinary! It was all because of God's grace! Before every mission, we would always spend time fasting and praying. Even before we left our base, we would ask God who and what we were going to encounter in our next mission and get any words of knowledge or words of wisdom he wanted to share with us. I believe the preparation we put in beforehand was essential to the success of the mission.

I remember being invited to Birmingham by a local church, to work as we usually did within the schools of the area. We handed out leaflets which gave them information about an event we would be holding in the town hall. It held 600 people. As usual we put time aside in our busy schedule for prayer and it was in those prayer times that God spoke about many of these young people going to a lost eternity if we didn't tell them about Jesus. There was an urgency in our prayers to see many lives transformed. We were on our faces before the Lord with tears in our eyes praying for these precious young lives. On the Friday night, after visiting many schools and taking classes, assemblies and lunchtime concerts, the town hall was packed. The place was so packed that the Christians were asked to leave so that we could get everyone in from the schools. The audience was young and noisy, but very receptive as we played our music and told our stories. At the end of the night, Ray got up to preach the gospel message. The rest of us were praying silently and expecting God to move. When he did, we were astounded. Ray gave the appeal and asked those who wanted to give their lives to Jesus to stand. Everyone stood! We have a video of this, and you can see me in the video going up to Ray and whispering in his ear, "They must have misunderstood you. I think you should do the appeal again."

Ray got them all to sit down and explained clearly that only if you wanted to give your life to Jesus were you to stand up. He told them what it meant to become a Christian and that it was making God boss of your life. It was turning away from those things in your life that were wrong. He told them only to stand up if they seriously wanted to go God's way and not their own way. They all stood again. I noticed that in the balcony an older couple had stood too, and so I thought the audience had again misunderstood. Surely this older couple were Christians? I again approached Ray saying, "You have to do it all again, they definitely don't understand." He told them all to sit down once more and told them in no uncertain terms that God is not mocked. He went on to say, "only if you want to give your life to Jesus Christ then please stand." Again, everyone stood including this older couple in the balcony who had only heard the music as they passed the hall and decided to come in. They were not Christians but when they heard the message of the cross, they wanted to give their lives to Jesus. We had never had such a response before.

The pastor asked the organizer, who was a member of his church, "How many booklets of Journey into Christ do you have? The organizer told him 100 and he immediately responded, "That is never going to be enough." It was a good problem to have as we worked our way through 600 young people all wanting to give their lives to Jesus.

Another place that sticks in my mind was Northampton. We had visited several schools and on the Friday night around 100 people gave their lives to Jesus. I want to tell you about 10 of them. These 10 all came from the same school. They got so on fire for God that they wanted to start a Christian Union in their school and tell all their friends about what God had done for them. A Christian teacher helped them set up the Christian Union, and then they began to pray. They prayed before school started, but then discovered that this was not long enough. They then started to pray at lunch time as well but again eventually discovered that this was not long enough and so they started to pray after school too. They were praying three times a day that all their friends would come to know the Lord Jesus. What happened was wonderful. A year later, they had 200 people attending the Christian Union. I remember retelling this story many years later at an event held in the NEC, Birmingham, and afterwards a young couple approached us and told us that one of them was one of the ten I had talked about and the other had come to know the Lord through the Christian Union. They had got married years later.

Before one of our missions in Worcester God spoke clearly to us about prayer. With the backing of several churches and after a year-long foundation of prayer, we spent a week in Worcester presenting the message of Jesus. The aim for the mission was to make a real impact on the whole community. Richard Wood, the local co-ordinator at the time, had worked extremely hard and there was a real air of expectancy as the week arrived. We organised a two-hour prayer meeting every day for the mission but were disappointed when only a few people from the local area turned up. However, all that was about to change.

On our opening night we discovered that the local electricity board had wired the 1300-seat hall incorrectly which meant we had to hire a generator. This arrived late and we were soon faced with a massive PA and lighting rig, an audience queuing up outside and experienced engineers frantically trying to get power. No matter what was tried, the generator would not work. Our first reaction was to blame the enemy for disrupting the mission, but there was an inexplicable sense in our hearts that somehow God was in this with us. When we realised that we were not going to get power that evening, we asked all Christians in the audience to stay and gave out tickets to the rest to guarantee them seats for another night. What happened next was quite incredible.

As Ray led the remaining audience in a time of prayer, a local Christian man shared that he felt people needed to be praying and not just relying on Heartbeat to do their part. As he spoke, Christians all over the hall started to repent. People, including leaders and pastors, were on their knees crying out to God to forgive them and to bring revival. The prayer meeting went on for some time as God broke through. Earlier in the day, when only a few people had turned up for the prayer meeting, Ray and I had wondered what it would take to get the Christians praying. We never imagined for a moment that God would turn off the electricity! The very next morning we heard from our engineers that everything was working and that during the night the system appeared to have fixed itself! The daily prayer meetings were amazing with over 100 people praying together. As we prayed, many who had come to pray saw God move in their lives in incredible ways, including one person getting out of a wheelchair and walking as God healed them.

During our time in Worcester we saw the 1300-seat hall packed each night, with over 400 people giving their lives to Jesus and God touching many Christians in a deep way. I will never forget one night when Ray asked people to come to the front if they wanted to give their lives to Jesus. Before he had even finished the appeal, a teenage girl got up and ran to the front falling to her knees at the front with tears running down her face. When I asked her why she responded so quickly, she said that she'd heard Jesus calling her name and could not wait to give her life to him.

We also visited a town called Thornbury, never imagining that years later we would be living in that town and that's where we would have our base. At the invitation of the local churches, we visited three schools in the area and then hired the Armstrong Hall for the last night. Our newsletter reported what happened:

Friday night saw the Armstrong Hall in Thornbury overflowing. Every available seat had been taken and sadly, over 100 teenagers had to be turned away. It still amazes us that although everyone is told that they are coming to more than a concert where they will hear us share our faith, explain what it is to be a Christian and give people an opportunity to respond, they still flock in to hear the good news. Over 70 responded. On the Sunday morning at the local church, one fourteen-year-old girl said that when she became Christian at our concert, she felt as though she'd had a bath on the inside.

This type of thing happened to us again and again. We literally saw thousands come to know the Lord throughout the time that Heartbeat existed.

We also worked with other speakers and mission organisers at times in the early 80's. Canon Michael Green was one of the people we worked with and it was such a joy to do so. He was a lovely man with a great heart. However, our clientele was a little different to the crowds he normally saw. We went into a number of schools to invite the young people to the events at the end of the week. I remember one school would not let us play in their assembly hall as it was exam time but they did say they would allow us to play in the school's grounds at the end of the day. We didn't think this was a good idea and so we explained to Michael and his team that we didn't think it would work. They, however, did think it would work and therefore because we were their invited guests, we said we would do it. During the last hour of school, we could see the teenagers looking out of the window obviously wondering why a band was setting up on their school grounds. We set up on a grassy part of the school grounds and when the last bell of the day sounded, we started playing our music. All of a sudden, teenagers came from every direction towards us. We thought, "Oh Michael and his team were right, it is working!" We then quickly changed our minds, as the teenagers ran right past us and on to the many buses that were waiting to take them home. We didn't have one person who stayed to listen to our music. It was the shortest concert we had ever played. After one song, we packed our gear away and went back to the mission headquarters!

We did, however, manage to get to play in other schools and on the Friday night the young people we had seen came in their droves. On all the missions we did with Michael Green, the young people packed the halls so much that many of them were hanging over the balconies as they listened to the message of the cross. Michael was thrilled as so many responded and gave their lives to the Lord Jesus.

One really funny and embarrassing thing happened when working with Michael Green. We have never forgotten it, and I'm sure Michael never forgot it either! We had been asked to do a gig in a large old Church of England building. In the afternoon we were sound checking and rehearsing for the evening event when Ray had severe pains in his stomach and he knew he needed to get to a toilet immediately. He asked one of the young vergers where the toilet was and he was told that there were no toilets in the building. I think he saw the look of horror on Ray's face and told Ray that the only toilet was in the Vicar's vestry, but that he was sure the Vicar wouldn't mind him using it if it was an emergency. Ray assured him it was an emergency and followed his instructions down some small winding stairs. This led him into a small room, but it was full of vicars, local church leaders and of course Canon Michael Green. These were all special guests who had been invited to attend the event in the evening.

Ray then discovered that the toilet was a very small space only separated from the small vestry they were all meeting in by a sliding door that didn't fully shut! He somehow managed to squeeze himself onto the toilet and quickly realised this was going to be very embarrassing! There was no soundproofing and of course the door did not shut properly. Ray felt as though he was sitting on the toilet in the middle of all these vicars! He told me later that he had this picture in his mind of a cartoon where a smell is shown as a cloud in the shape of a pair of hands wafting across the room, slapping all these vicars across the face. After the obvious explosion and then all the wonderful sound effects and the release of the smell, Ray then discovered that the toilet paper was not the silent, nice, soft, kind but was instead the hard, noisy, crinkly type! Ray didn't know how he was going to face all these dignitaries when he left the toilet. With a red face, he quickly opened the door and ran! We all howled with laughter when we learned about his predicament!

Throughout the 80's we were absolutely loving what God was doing and the results we were seeing. Not only did hundreds of young people come to know the Lord, but many were going home to tell their parents what they had done, and they too wanted to find out more. After another mission, we heard of one young person who became a Christian at our event then went home and led her whole family to know the Lord including her aunt, her uncle and cousins. It was wonderful. After visiting Northern Ireland, one of the young girls who had given her life to the Lord contacted us to tell us that her mum and dad had also become Christians. To us this was normal as it happened every week.

Just recently in 2019 whilst I was writing this book, I met with Malcolm and Trish and they told me what had happened to them when they were leading a church in South Africa. A man approached them and asked if they were Malc and Trish from Heartbeat. When they said they were he told them that he had become a Christian as a young lad at one of our missions and afterwards he went home and led his mum, dad and family to the Lord. We might never have heard about this had he not been in the same place at the same time as Malcolm and Trish.

18

THE HEARTBEAT YEARS - MORE MIRACULOUS MISSIONS

When we were invited to Preston to head up a large city-wide mission, we asked our friend Gary Gibbs and the drama team Back to Back to join us. The Charter Theatre, which seats 800 people, was booked for five nights. This was a huge step for us as we normally only filled a hall for one night in various places in the UK. We spent 3 weeks visiting the local schools and trusted that God would bring an audience to the Charter Theatre so that we could communicate our faith. We had a big banner outside the Charter Theatre which said, God's Power in Action. We told the many schools that we visited not to come just to see a band, but to come and see God's power in action in the Charter Theatre. We handed out so many free tickets and prayed like crazy. Prayer always was and still is central to all we do.

We gathered to pray one last time before the first event at the Charter Theatre. We never knew how many people would come and so we prayed that God would provide an audience. This theatre is built in a shopping centre and so after that prayer meeting, I decided to quickly nip to the shops for something I needed to buy. As I went out of the theatre, I could not believe the sight I saw. There was a huge queue of people waiting to get in two hours before the show was due to start. The queue went all the way down the stairs and into the level where the shops were. I ran back inside to let the rest of the team know that God was answering our prayers. It was incredible. That evening, we had to again ask the Christians in the audience to leave their seats and go to another hall in the venue where Malcom would lead through a prayer meeting whilst the event was going on. The 800-seater theatre was packed every night and hundreds came to know the Lord both in the main venue and in the prayer meeting!

I remember talking to a young girl on one of the nights. She desperately wanted to come to the event and so she asked her mum and dad, who were divorced, if they would both come with her. They often did things together for the sake of their daughter. On that evening, not only did the girl respond but so did her parents. They all came to know the Lord and when we left Preston, the parents were going through counselling to try and put their marriage back together again. I just love seeing lives being transformed by the love and power of God.

Our newsletters from that era were filled with miraculous stories of people being transformed. In Hastings we worked with our friend, Nick Cuthbert, who had been asked to be the main speaker at this mission. We held our final event in the Pier Ballroom which holds just over 1000 people. By 7.20pm it was so full that the gallery had to be opened up so that an extra 100 people could attend. During this mission we saw not only teenagers respond but two teachers separately responded and gave their lives to the Lord. At one of the local schools, the staff had been particularly interested in our faith. One teacher was booked to go to the theatre on the Friday night, but after chatting to us decided to change her plans and come to our event. She prayed with Trish at the end of the concert and gave her life to God. During that same week, a young teenage girl gave her life to the Lord and the next day at school she was surrounded by her friends who all wanted to know what had happened to her. Her friends had been playing with the Ouija board during the day and having called up an evil spirit they asked some questions about her. The evil spirit told them, "We lost her last night." It sent shivers through that young girl as she realised the reality of what God had done.

It sounds here on paper that it was easy to see what we saw, but there was a lot of hard work, a lot of prayer, a lot of sacrifice and a lot of enemy attack. I remember being on mission in Portsmouth when I woke up in the middle of the night feeling that there was an evil presence in our bedroom. As fear tugged at my heart, I heard a sound from Ray as if he was choking. Before I could say anything, Ray shouted "Jesus" and suddenly the demonic presence was gone. Ray was then able to tell me that he had woken up with what felt like hands around his neck. He felt as though he was being strangled, but when he shouted the name of Jesus the pressure around his neck lifted. That day we had visited one particular school where the RE teacher had strongly objected to us coming into the school. We discovered that the teacher was into the occult. The Head Teacher however was very keen and invited us to sing and speak to all the pupils in the school. He brought each year group into the assembly hall so that they would have a chance to hear our music and our message. When Ray experienced this in the night, we knew we had a battle on our hands.

At the end of our time in the school, we held our usual event and prayed that many pupils would come and hear how to give their lives to Jesus. We normally always held our end of the week concert in a separate venue but the organisers of this mission decided to hire this particular school for the evening event. That night the hall was packed and many responded to say they wanted to give their lives to Jesus. We went back to our hosts' houses rejoicing at all that God had done.

However, the next morning it was as if all hell had been let loose. Ray had a phone call from Graham Cooke, who was one of the organisers of our mission. Graham was a leader of a local church at the time, and is now well known across the globe as an international speaker. He called us to say that the headmaster had asked if Ray and Graham could attend a meeting in the headmaster's study. We had no idea what it was all about. When Ray walked into the room, he said it was like walking into the lions' den. Seemingly, the headmaster had received so many complaints about the previous night that he wanted to investigate what really happened. In the headmaster's room, there was a school governor, the RE teacher, a pupil and a parent and for the next hour or so accusations were shouted at Ray and Graham.

The headmaster was told that we had bouncers who controlled the audience. In reality, we had no bouncers, only a few older Christians who were helping to make sure the event went well. They said that Ray had preached a message that if people did not give their lives to Jesus that night, then they would go to hell and would endure a long, slow, painful death. In reality, Ray did not mention hell once and obviously did not say they would experience a long, slow, painful death. They then said we had locked those who responded in a room where we would not let them out unless they gave us their names and addresses. In reality, all we had done was to ask those who responded to go into an unlocked room where the counsellors could pray for them and after they had become Christians we asked if we could have their names and address so that we could give them to the local church. This meant that the local church could invite them to further activities that would be organised for them. They also gave an example of two sisters who attended the event. One of them gave her life to Jesus and went home thrilled at what God had done in her life, the other did not respond to God and went home in tears with the conviction of God on her. They could not understand why both sisters who had attended the same event could come away with completely different experiences. Although we explained all these situations, they didn't accept what we said and continued to shout their accusations at Ray and Graham. The headmaster eventually said he would look into the matter but that from now on all schools in Hampshire would be closed to Heartbeat.

We went back to God in prayer and asked that God would reverse the decision to block Heartbeat from all the schools in Hampshire and that people would see the truth. We knew we weren't fighting against flesh and blood and we needed to pray that the Lord would move in this situation.

During the next few weeks, the press got a hold of what had happened and so folks from Graham's church responded letting people know that the accusations were completely untrue. People said, "Actually, I was there and this is what really happened; this is what Ray said." They then took the opportunity of sharing the story of how they themselves had become Christians. The newspaper was filled with incredible stories of salvations for weeks on end. It was incredible.

Eventually, months later, Ray and Graham were again asked to go to the headmaster's study. Ray travelled back down to Portsmouth to go with Graham to the meeting. This time only the headmaster was present. He said, "I have asked you to come here today so that I can apologise to you both. I have looked into this matter thoroughly and cannot back up any of the accusations that were thrust at you. I have discovered that there is no truth in any of the accusations and all I can say is that there must have been a certain ethos around that evening." He then asked Ray and Graham what we would like him to do. They asked him to clear Heartbeat's name and open the doors to the schools in Hampshire again. The headmaster agreed. Then they asked that Graham would be put in charge of who came into the school to teach Religious Education. He agreed to this too. God completely turned this situation around. What the enemy meant for evil, the Lord turned around for good.

Another place we went to was Tower Hamlets in the east end of London. We were told when we arrived that Tower Hamlets was the Evangelists' graveyard! We were there for two weeks and before we even started in the schools, we were told that one major school had pulled out due to industrial action. It meant our schools work was limited. One of the schools we did visit had a 60% Muslim presence and this meant that we only saw approximately 300 teenagers that week. We began to wonder whether the graveyard would claim us too but thankfully the second week was much better. In this week, again only one main school was visited. We spent a lot of our time in prayer as we prayed for a breakthrough for this mission. In the final concert, we saw 450 people attend and around 50 people gave their lives to the Lord including some adults.

I spoke to one lady who came only because she had gone to her doctor with mental and emotional problems. Her doctor, who was obviously a Christian, gave her a prescription and on it he wrote – Go to the Heartbeat concert. She did and gave her life to the Lord and was changed completely by the love and power of God. It was so exciting. Another man that evening saw his withered veins completely restored. He had been injecting himself with drugs for years and that night God healed him and transformed his life. Afterwards we were told that this mission was the biggest breakthrough that the church had seen in that area. What a joy to work for Jesus.

In Stroud over 100 churched people had to give up their seats at our end of the week concert to make room for the crowds who were still waiting outside. We were in the biggest public hall in the area, but even though it was a 500-seater, it was still not big enough to accommodate everyone who wanted to come. After asking the Christians in the building if they would leave and go to a prayer meeting instead, we still could not get everyone in and had to turn about 100 people away. Many were saved and quite a number healed that night. A man told us how he had come to the evening in real pain as he had a disc complaint in his back. He explained joyfully how he felt the Holy Spirit go through him and was showing everyone how he could touch his toes! However, it was at this event that we discovered that even though some people see God's power in action and are actually healed themselves that doesn't automatically mean that they will want to choose to give their lives to God. We prayed for a young lad who had a problem with his knees. He loved skateboarding and wanted God to heal him. When we prayed for him, he was completely healed. He was overjoyed so we asked him if he wanted to give his life to the one who had healed him and he clearly told us "No". Even when people see that God is real and that he is a compassionate, loving, healing God, it doesn't mean that they will choose to give him their lives. It saddened our hearts and I have never forgotten that young lad and often wondered if he changed his mind in the days, weeks, months or even years ahead.

Just recently one of my contacts on Facebook told me I had led her to the Lord when she was 15 at the same Stroud concert. She saw us when we came into her school and decided to come to the concert on the Friday night. She came from a family who didn't know Jesus but that night I prayed with her to become a Christian. Now 35 years later she is still following Jesus. She told me that she and her husband now have five children and all of them are continuing to grow in their faith and her home is filled with worship songs. She had been a worship leader for 20 years. God had deeply impacted her life through what we did in her school all those years ago. I love how it didn't just impact her but has affected her family too. It's wonderful how when one person gets to know the Lord there is a ripple effect and many, many more are also affected. I guess we will never know just how many people were transformed through the work of Heartbeat until we get to Heaven. So, no matter who you are, keep sowing seeds and you too will see many coming to know the Lord.

I remember going to Torbay where we were working beside our friends Eric Delve and Ian Coffey. There were several events happening at the one time as part of Mission England. On the day of our last event we were preparing to do our concert in a 1000-seat leisure centre when we heard that Ian, who was due to speak that night, had to go home urgently. Ray was asked if he would speak instead. The hall was packed and we saw many respond to the invitation to give their lives to God. One mother, whose daughter became a Christian that night, talked with us afterwards and decided that she too would give her life to the Lord. Many were also physically healed as God's Spirit moved. We heard later that a local minister had received a phone call from a woman whose two daughters had become Christians through our concert. She asked him if she could have what her daughters had got!! He led her to the Lord there and then. It was just wonderful to see many lives transformed by the love and power of God.

About a week or so later we were just about to start our final concert in another area of the UK where we had done a week's mission, when someone from our office arrived with a letter that was addressed to Ray. He had a few moments before we were due on stage and so he opened the letter. He shouldn't have done that! It was from one of the ministers in Torbay who had been at our final event where many young people had given their lives to Christ and several had been healed. In his letter he expressed his concern about Ray releasing healing. He didn't think healing should have been mentioned at all. Ray was always very pastoral when he prayed for God to move in healing power, however this minister was anticipating that there must have been people at the event who were not healed and that he would be left to answer their questions. Ray was always clear to say that God loves everyone, but that as a sign and a wonder God was going to release healing and that *some* in the audience would experience healing. He also always expressed how God loved all of us and wanted all of us well. In his letter the minister criticized Ray for mentioning that God was a healing God. He said he would rather not have seen the healings because it just left him with pastoral problems and questions he could not answer. Our hearts were sad that instead of being thrilled at the many lives won for Jesus and the many who were instantaneously healed, we received a letter of criticism and complaint.

We learned a lesson that night. Ray should not have opened the letter until our mission was over. It was clearly a tactic of the enemy to discourage Ray and put a stop to what God wanted to do that night. Ray found it difficult to read the comments in this letter, especially just before going on stage to preach. However, we need to know that when we see people saved and healed there will always be people who don't agree with the way God does it.

It's at those times when we need to do what Jesus did, keep your eyes on our Heavenly Father and do what we see him doing.

I remember one time we went to Kidlington to do a mission there in the schools. We visited schools in the area and as usual we met to pray during the week and also just before the final event. It was at the prayer meeting before the event that I received a word of knowledge that there would be someone at the event from one of the schools who was a habitual stealer and that God wanted to free that person from that habit. During the concert that evening, I gave out the word of knowledge and something incredible happened. When I mentioned that someone had a habit of stealing, quite a number of people in the venue turned around and pointed at this little chap in the middle of the hall. They all came from the same school and when I described this chap in my word of knowledge, they recognised who it was. He had stolen from them all. I never expected that to happen and felt a little sorry for the guy at the time, however, during the appeal that same lad gave his life to the Lord Jesus.

During the early 80's we were asked by Colin Urquhart to lead the young people's event at Faith Camp. When we started, very few people came to the young people's event, but even from the first year, we could see the potential. We were in charge of this event for many years and the numbers grew hugely until we had over 1,000 young people attending. It was as if we had a camp within a camp. The leadership were so supportive of all we were doing and gave us their full backing. It was incredible what we saw happen as we came under the covering of Colin and his team. Our newsletter report in 1985 was this:

Words cannot express what we saw God do during the week. People who were not Christians became Christians. People were set free from bondage. Many were filled with the Holy Spirit. The gifts of the Spirit were released in many people, gifts of tongues, prophecy, words of knowledge, numerous healings and miracles. There was repentance and recommitment to Christ. The power of God fell so heavily at times that the events inside the tent became like scenes from some of the past revivals: people weeping and getting right with God; many lost in worship and adoration, singing and speaking out in tongues; some kneeling and lying prostrate while others fell to the floor as the power of the

Holy Spirit came upon them.

We had some very significant healings at Faith Camp. I remember one young lad aged 15 who had very bad eczema. As he responded and stood at the front, God healed him. You could see dry, flaky skin falling off and new, soft skin appearing. When the miracle was complete, he had piles of dry skin around his feet! He said it was the first time he had felt soft skin on his body. What a wonderful miracle! Another time a young lad on the front row shouted out "Brilliant!" Ian went to find out what had happened and discovered him reading his Bible with one eye shut! Evidently, he had a weak right eye and couldn't see close up. During the worship, God touched him and his eye was instantly healed. He was reading the Bible with the eye that had been healed. I remember people being touched by the Spirit of God at the very back of the meeting as well as the front. Often people are touched at the front more than the back, but people were going out in the Spirit at the back with no one touching them at all. Even after the evening event was finished, people were having supernatural encounters with God in their tents. We loved working at Faith Camp every year – it was such a joy and we always saw so much of the supernatural!

One of the things we initiated and organised for many years was to invite all the young people and many of the adults at Faith Camp to come into the centre of Peterborough and put on an event where we could declare to the whole town that God was very much alive. Heartbeat sang, led worship and spoke whilst some of our youth workers mingled with the crowd and talked to those who responded. Every year we made a huge impact and saw people turn to God.

During the '80s we saw many signs of revival as we travelled throughout the UK. As I said at the beginning of this chapter, we thought this was normal, but this was certainly not normal, this was supernatural. As we became laid down lovers of Jesus, God poured out his grace on many. When we were in Northern Ireland we saw God move in many incredible ways. One of the supernatural stories that sticks in my mind is when we had just performed at a school in Lurgan. After the short performance, a girl approached me. I could see she was shaking. She said, "I've never seen you before in my life and yet last night I had a dream and you were in it. You were telling me in my dream that I had to get right with God. I came into school today and there you are telling me that I need to get right with God. What is going on?" I explained to her that God sometimes speaks to us through dreams and that to me it was obvious that God was speaking to her. I asked her if she wanted to get right with God and she immediately replied saying "Yes." There and then we prayed together and she gave her life to God. We absolutely love seeing lives transformed and seeing salvation and forgiveness poured out in our land. Our hearts longed for more and even today we still cry out for the Lord to bring revival to our land.

19

THE HEARTBEAT YEARS – HEALING POWER

The first time we ever saw someone being healed was in the early 80's when we were finishing one of our missions. We had been singing and speaking in the schools in the area and at the end of the week, as usual, we invited the school pupils to come and see us play in a local hall. After we had spoken, sung our songs and Ray had preached, Ray invited people to stand up if they wanted to know the Lord. Many responded, but as one young teenager stood, he suddenly shouted out, "My arm! My arm!" We discovered after Malcolm, one of our team, had spoken to him that he had come into the event with his arm in a sling. His wrist had been broken and after six weeks he had gone to the hospital to get the plaster removed, but instead of it being healed, they had discovered that the bone had set incorrectly and therefore he would have to go back into hospital and get his bone set correctly. As the guy stood to say he wanted to ask God into his life, he felt a heat go through his arm and he was instantaneously healed.

None of us were expecting God to heal that night, we hadn't prayed for healing but God did it anyhow. We were astonished and so were the boy's friends, who all came to know the Lord too because they had seen God's power in action.

Sometime after that, Ray and I attended a conference for leaders on the subject of healing, which was hosted and organised by Ken McGreavy. The evangelist who had been asked to speak at this event was Ian Andrews. Ian, who has since that time become a close friend, has seen God use him in incredible ways as he speaks throughout the world. He talked about how the Lord had commissioned us to preach the Gospel *and* heal the sick (Luke 9:2) and how as evangelists we needed to take up the challenge of not only preaching the gospel but healing the sick too.

We left the conference feeling that God had placed a seed of faith in our hearts that when we preached the gospel at any of our Heartbeat missions, some people would get healed as a sign that God was real.

Our first mission after this conference was in Bristol. I remember us all praying like crazy before the event that God would move in salvation *and* healing. We were very nervous as Ray got up to speak that night, but we were thrilled to see that at the appeal many gave their lives to Christ. Ray then took a deep breath and in fear and trembling said, "Now I believe that some of you are going to be healed." As Ray prayed and released the Holy Spirit to bring healing, the rest of us were all praying, "God, just one! Just heal one person, Lord!" Our faith was so small, but despite our weak and trembling knees, with faith in our hearts, we trusted that as we did what he had asked us to do, he would deliver. That night we were amazed, relieved and excited to discover that 11 people were healed of various diseases. God is incredible! Ray and I cannot heal anyone, but from that trembling beginning, we have literally seen God heal hundreds of people over the years.

I remember a girl in Northern Ireland being healed of a back complaint. She was listening to Ray preaching during a Heartbeat concert and as she did, she saw a vision of Jesus standing behind Ray. Jesus looked at her and pointed to her and in that instant, she was healed of a back complaint she had had for years.

Another young teenage boy told us that he felt he had been healed of a hole in the heart. We encouraged him to go to his doctor and get checked out medically before coming off any medication the doctor had given him. When we visited Northern Ireland a year later, he came to see us to tell us that he had been back to his doctor and after an examination and X-rays, the doctor said he did not understand it but there was no hole in his heart now.

At one of our missions in England, we prayed for a teenage girl who had a cartilage problem in her knee. We knew medically she could not be healed

Ray's parents' timeshare apartment which we had been able to transfer to Florida. Ian and Dorry, who by then were back living in the States, had arranged to meet us there. We knew it cost a huge amount of money to visit many of the attractions so we prayed about what we should do. We knew that Ian and Dorry would understand if we could only go to a few of the theme parks, but we did not want to be party poopers and spoil their holiday either. We prayed but didn't feel it was right to order our tickets on our credit card before we left the UK.

During one of Ray's seminars at Nashville, he happened to mention that he was going on from Nashville to Florida for a holiday. He didn't mention our need of finance at all. After the seminar was over, a lady approached him and asked if he was planning on going on any of the Disney attractions while in Florida and if we had bought our tickets yet. When Ray replied saying we were planning to go to Disney but had not yet bought our tickets, she gave him her name and address and told us to phone her when we reached Florida. She explained that her husband worked for Disney and was allowed to give free passes to up to five of his friends. When we arrived in Florida, we were able to get into as many of the Disney attractions as we wanted for absolutely nothing and even got to see behind the scenes too as he was a graphic designer for Disney. This time God didn't give us money, but gave us free tickets instead.

Sometimes people who don't know God have suggested to us that these things could be coincidences. All I can tell them is that these coincidences seem to happen to us again and again and again. If they had only happened to us a few times, then perhaps you could put it down to coincidence. But when these things happen thousands of times not only to us, but also to many people working with ngm and also to thousands of other people across the world, you can no longer put it down to coincidence. We have to put it down to a God who is not only real, but who also cares about the smallest of details in our lives.

The most unusual thing happened to us around 2010. We had been praying for a holiday for our family and also our friends' family. We decided where we would like to go which was a hotel that had lovely lodges for rent. We knew it would be big enough to accommodate us all. When I looked on the of this, so needed God to do a miracle by providing her with a new cartilage. She felt the heat of the Holy Spirit go through her knee as we prayed and immediately knew that she had been healed. She went back into school on the following Monday and asked her head teacher if she could now take PE lessons as God had healed her knee. Her head teacher wisely told her she needed to go to the doctor and get a letter from him confirming that she could now restart PE lessons. She went to the doctor and told him that God had healed her. He was not convinced until he examined her knee and proclaimed that he did not know what had happened and that although it was medically impossible, she was indeed healed. He gave her the letter she wanted and she was able to start PE lessons again. Isn't our God incredible? This happened again and again as we prayed for people with problems with their knees.

After one of our events in Redhill, a man wrote to us and told us that in January of that year he had heart problems and that after tests his doctor had told him that he had had a mild heart attack and he was promptly put on medication. During our worship event, he had felt the power of God go through him and he knew he had been healed. The pain went instantly and his heart started to beat properly. When he went back to the doctor, he was put through an ECG which showed no signs of him ever having had a heart attack. What a fantastic God we serve!

At one of our events in Preston a man with a massive hernia suddenly shouted, "It's gone!" His massive hernia had disappeared. In Northern Ireland after one of our packed concerts, we not only saw people come to know the Lord but God also moved greatly in healing. People suffering from cartilage problems, psoriasis, asthma, eczema, toothache and blurred vision were all healed in that one concert.

A story that definitely needs to be told happened at our mission in Blackburn. As we prepared for our event at the end of our mission in Blackburn, Ray told me he had a word of knowledge that there was someone coming to the King George's Hall that night who had leprosy. I thought he was joking at first because who on earth has leprosy in the UK? I said, "Are you serious Ray? This isn't Africa. No one has leprosy in the UK." I looked into his eyes and saw that he was not joking so I said, "OK, let's go and share this with the team and then let's give it out tonight." I remember Ray explaining it to the rest of Heartbeat and Dave Bankhead said, "Well, maybe we should just say skin disorders rather than leprosy!" Ray said, "No, God has definitely said leprosy!" So that night, my brave husband stood in the King George's Hall in front of a packed audience and told the gospel message. He asked people to respond and again over a hundred people stood to say they wanted to give their lives to God. Then Ray told the audience that as a sign and a wonder God was going to heal a number of people. He went on to say, "There's at least one person in the audience tonight who has leprosy and if that's you, then right now God is going to heal you." We heard later that two people were healed from leprosy that night and about 6 or 7 were healed from skin disorders.

A number of years later, I was preaching at Clitheroe and for the first time ever I told that story of how Ray got a word of knowledge and dared to trust God and how two people were healed from leprosy. What I didn't know was the organisers of the Blackburn mission were in the audience and at the end they spoke with Ray whilst I was praying for people who had responded in the meeting. They told Ray that on the way to the event in Clitheroe they had said to each other, "I wonder if Nancy might tell the story of the word of knowledge about leprosy." They were thrilled when I told the story, but then they said to Ray, "But she got the story wrong." Ray said, "What do you mean?" They said, "Ray it wasn't just two people healed from leprosy there were 6 people healed from leprosy and about 6 or 7 from skin disorders." Just amazing! If Ray hadn't stepped out and believed God, a number of miracles would have been missed.

I am praying that these stories will inspire you not only to believe for healing in your own life, but also to take up the challenge to pray for healing for your friends. When people who don't know God see him move in healing power, it makes them realise that God is indeed alive; they then have a choice as to whether they want to know him personally.

Often people think that it is only special people who have a healing ministry who can pray for someone and see them healed, but that is not the case. God will use anyone who has a small grain of faith. A number of years ago, when my son Aidan was only three or four years of age, I discovered that he had prayed for someone and had seen her healed. Aidan knew that when we are ill, we as a family always pray and ask God to make us better. One day whilst having his lunch in the ngm offices, he overheard his cousin, Natalie, who was part of ngm at the time, mention that she had a huge headache that she could not shift. Without prompting from anyone, Aidan got up from his seat and went over to Natalie, laid his hand on her head and said, "Lord Jesus, please make Natalie better, Amen." A simple prayer combined with a simple faith. Instantaneously, Natalie was amazed to discover that she was healed. God will use the simplest of prayers and the smallest amount of faith to perform a miracle.

Jesus tells us in Matthew 17:20, *"If you have faith as small as a mustard seed, you can say to this mountain, 'Move from here to there' and it will move. Nothing will be impossible for you"* (NIV).

It is important to remember, however, that faith has its origins in God. There is nothing we can do to work faith up. We cannot manufacture it, but we can ask God to increase our faith.

As I have said many times, neither Ray nor I could heal anyone, only God can heal. There have been times when we have prayed for individuals and they haven't been healed. I remember the time when Ray read a story about a man called Smith Wigglesworth who hit a lump on someone's hand with his Bible and it completely disappeared. Shortly after this, someone came forward at one of our Christian camps with a lump on his wrist and Ray remembered what Smith had done. Ray told the boy to hold out his wrist. The boy said nervously, "What are you going to do?" Ray replied, "I'm going to hit it with my Bible but don't worry it will be fine." Ray then hit it with his big Bible. The boy cried out in pain, "Ouch – that was sore!" Ray told him to hold out his hand again, and to be honest, I am so surprised he did! Ray repeated the action, but still the lad was not healed. You see you cannot ride on someone else's anointing. You have to hear what the Lord is saying to you.

I remember Ray and I going to a church event to hear the amazing evangelist, Reinhard Bonnke speak. We were travelling by car to a large church not too far from London and we realised that we were going to be late and so we prayed. We asked God to keep two good seats for us near the front. When we arrived, we noticed the place was packed and people were being shown to seats in the balcony. As we were passing the entrance to the ground floor of the church, someone came out and pointed to Ray and me and said, "You two, follow me!" We did and he led us into a packed arena. He took us down to the front near the platform and pointed to two seats in the middle of the third or fourth row. It was as though those two seats had our name on them. We could hardly believe it. It wasn't as though someone recognised us, we were just picked randomly out of the crowd. We knew it was God answering our prayers. That evening we were inspired as we listened to Reinhard Bonnke and we saw many people being healed. Reinhard then released a healing anointing on those in the audience and Ray and I were both impacted. When we went back to Malmesbury, Ray asked if there were any healing needs in the team. There were some and so he prayed for them and as he did, they were instantly healed. It was so easy! This lasted about two or three weeks and then stopped. Ray asked Ken why the anointing had stopped and Ken told him that you can only ride on someone else's anointing for a short while, then you have to push into God and make that anointing your own.

It is interesting to note that during the 1980's and 90's we found that when we prayed in evangelistic situations for people to get healed, God healed many. However, when we prayed at Christian celebrations, church meetings or worship events there were not so many healed. I believe it must be lack of faith that is the reason for this. There seems to be a huge problem with unbelief in the church. We say we believe in a miraculous and incredible God, but do we really mean this? Often unbelief is lurking in our hearts and what we forget is that unbelief is a sin and in order to get rid of it, we need to repent. This sin that we so easily accept can be our downfall. Let's start to believe what the Lord says and what the Bible says and ask God to forgive us for our unbelief. Let's start to trust in our amazing God. Is anything impossible for him? No, nothing is impossible for him.

Sometimes there is a clear answer as to why healing hasn't happened, but at other times there is no answer. Healing can be a difficult subject; one person is healed and another is not and we don't understand why. It's in those circumstances that we hold on to the fact that our God is a kind and loving God who cares immensely for us all and wants us all to be well.

A number of years ago a good friend, who had been one of the organisers of one of our missions, was chatting with me. We were reminiscing about what God had done in the 80's when he said, "Of course you heard about the blind boy who came to one of your concerts and was healed?" I said, "No, tell me the story," and so he did. A man brought his blind son to our concert and told him to enjoy the music and said he would come back and pick him up afterwards. When he came back, he discovered his son was totally healed. God had healed him during the concert. His eyesight had been completely restored and we didn't get to hear about this story until years later.

Earlier in this chapter I mentioned a man called Smith Wigglesworth. If you know me, you would know that apart from the Lord, the man who has inspired me so much is Smith Wigglesworth. He was a simple plumber from Bradford who dared to believe God for salvation and for healing and as he did, he saw miracles of salvation and healing all over the world. He even saw a handful of people raised from the dead. He used to sing a song and repeat its message everywhere. It was called, "Only believe!" Someone once asked him how he came to have such great faith. He replied, "First the blade, then the ear, then the full corn in the ear." In other words, it grows. Exercise your faith and you will see it increase. I wonder what would happen in our world if we all began to believe God?

20

THE HEARTBEAT YEARS – LEARNING TO LIVE BY FAITH

When the Lord told us to leave British Youth for Christ and begin to depend on him for our finances, we knew it was important to continue to keep close to him. Whatever need we had, we would always go to him first and ask for his instructions. This is something we still do today! If the Lord tells us to write and mention our needs to our prayer partners then that is what we do. If he tells us not to tell anyone, again, this is what we do. If he tells us to go and directly ask someone if they can help us in our faith walk, then again that is what we do, although I have to say I find this one quite difficult to do. Ray and I have never found it easy to ask someone to help us. However, listening closely to God and hearing, obeying and trusting him has always been of utmost importance in our life of faith.

I remember a time in Malmesbury when we were praying for a car (we have so many stories over the years of believing God for cars). Ray and I heard from God that we should give away the car we needed to replace and so we heard, we obeyed and we trusted. We gave the car to my brother, Jack, who was in Heartbeat and who as our administrator needed a car for more local journeys. When we had done this, we went back to God and asked, "What now Lord?" We couldn't hear anything! Do you ever get these times when you ask the Lord what to do, and you hear nothing? It's happened a few times to us throughout the years. A number of people give up at this point, but we have always pressed in to God and continued to listen.

Ray suggested that instead of praying together we should go pray separately for a bit. After some time, I had still heard nothing, but Ray felt he had got a word from God. I was so pleased. I asked him eagerly, "What did he say then?" He answered, "Do you remember that bit in the Bible where the disciples are told by Jesus to go and get a donkey? I said a hesitant, "Yes", wondering where this was going. He went on to say, "Jesus then told them to tell anyone who asked them what they were doing with the donkey to say, 'The Lord has need of it.'" I answered with an even more hesitant, "Yes", while he went on to say, "Well I feel the Lord has told us to go to your brother, Jim, and say to him, 'The Lord has need of your car, Jim.'" My reaction was immediate. "No way," I cried. "There is no way I can go to my brother and ask him for his car!" My eldest brother and his wife were emigrating to the States. Jim was a pastor in Parkstone, nr Poole in the south of England and was soon to be moving to be a Senior Pastor in the States. There was no way I could ask him for his car; I felt it would start a family row!

Ray then said, "Well look I may have got this wrong, so why don't you go away and ask God if this is right and if he says it is right we will do it, if you don't get a positive answer, then we will just forget it." I thought this was a great idea and so I went away to pray with confidence in my heart that there was no way God would ask us to ask my brother for his car. However, the moment I began to pray, I realised that Ray had heard correctly; we had to go and ask my brother for his car.

So, after prayer, I lifted the phone to call my brother. When he answered he told me he had been just about to call me. He asked me what I wanted and I said, "Jim…."and there was a big long pause, then I said, "Ray wants to speak to you!" As I handed the phone to a very surprised Ray, I mouthed to him, "I can't ask him!" Ray bravely took the phone and said, "Jim we were just wondering what you are doing with your car since you are moving to the States." Jim replied, "Are you interested in buying it? I could give you it at a great price if you wish?" As Ray stuttered and stumbled over his words, Jim went on to say, "Pray about it and let me know if you and Nancy want the car."

We put the phone down with great sadness in our hearts, we knew we hadn't done what the Lord had told us to do. We hadn't told Jim the words our God had told us to say, "The Lord has need of your car, Jim." The next day we were off to Weston-Super-Mare where someone had loaned us their lovely cottage so that we could have a week's holiday in it. Now I must say that there is nothing wrong with Weston-Super-Mare, but it was the worst holiday of my life. Every day, as we spent time with the Lord, he would remind us, "You haven't done what I asked you to do!" At the end of an agonising week, we arrived home determined to call my brother to say what the Lord had told us to say despite the possibility of being misunderstood. On the way home, I told Ray, "Ray, you call Jim and I will be your prayer warrior while you ask my brother for the car!" I just couldn't bring myself to lift the phone and ask my brother. As I went upstairs, I closed our bedroom door and got on my knees and I prayed loudly. I could not even bear to hear Ray make the phone call.

Ray bravely lifted the phone and when Jim answered, he told him, "Jim, when Nancy and I called you last week, we both bottled out of telling you what God had asked us to say. Jim, the Lord told us to call you and tell you, 'The Lord has need of your car, Jim.'" Jim immediately responded by saying, "That's great Ray, you can have it!"

Jim then began to explain what had been happening with him and his wife, Anne. Before we called the previous week, they both felt that they should give their car to us. They were just about to phone us when I called. When Jim came off the phone, Anne asked, "Why didn't you give them the car?" He explained that something had held him back and he then had doubts as to whether it was right to give us the car. After the phone call and throughout the following week, Jim tried everything to sell the car. He had advertised it in his church, in the newspapers and on the radio and although this was a time when second-hand cars were selling very quickly, he didn't even have one enquiry about it. At the end of the week, he said to Anne that he just needed one more confirmation that it was right to give the car to us. It was at that point that Ray called to say, "The Lord has need of your car, Jim." You can imagine our excitement when Ray came off the phone. We had our car but we just wished we had been obedient the week before, because it would have saved us from an agonising week. I believe God stopped my brother giving us the car until we had not only heard, but we obeyed and then trusted – we were learning more about H.O.T. faith.

It was only after Ray came off the phone that we realised we didn't even know what kind of car my brother had. It could have been an old wreck of a car for all we knew, but it turned out to be a beautiful Saab with only a few thousand miles on the clock and a heated driver front seat! We always fought each other as to who drove the car – especially on cold days! God is so amazing; he gives great gifts to his children. Trust him and see what he will do for you. But do remember what the Bible says in James 1:22, *Do not merely listen to the word......do what it says (NIV)*. We need to not only hear, but also obey and trust if you want to see a miracle happen.

Throughout our lives we discovered that fear can stop us from doing what the Lord wants us to do. My fear of the reaction from my brother and my family stopped us enjoying a holiday in Weston-Super-Mare that we badly needed, and almost stopped us from doing what God had told us to do. When Ray first stepped out in faith and believed God for healing, he had to first overcome his fear of failure and of God not turning up. When God called us into full time work, Ray struggled with the fear of telling his parents that he was leaving their family business and moving to live in England. Fear, if not dealt with, can leave us paralysed and devoid of faith. In every adventure of faith that we have had throughout the 40 years we have been in full time ministry we have always had to overcome fear. Don't allow fear to stop you from doing what God wants you to do. Your adventure awaits you, but first you need to conquer your fear.

Throughout our 40 years of living by faith in God, we have many stories of how God has provided for us. Every month we had to pray for God to give us enough money to pay for our mortgage, bills, food and petrol. I remember my brother telling me when he gave us his car to make sure the car always had a lot of petrol in the tank as it ran better that way. However, we often didn't have enough money to pay for petrol so that we could have a full tank.

I remember travelling home from a mission by car one day with others from Heartbeat. The petrol tank was almost empty and we couldn't find a petrol station anywhere. So, we prayed for God to put enough petrol in our tank to allow us to get back to Malmesbury. What happened was miraculous. As we prayed and continued to pray, we watched the petrol indicator going up instead of down. Our only explanation was that God had indeed put petrol in our tank! We got home because God had filled our empty tank with enough petrol to get us home and when we got there, we still had petrol in our car. It was miraculous.

Over the years we learned so much through living by faith for our finances. Some people told our team that this way of living was not right and that we should not expect others to give us money. However, the truth is that not only has God told us to live depending on him for our finances, but also that 2000 years ago Jesus himself lived by faith. In the Bible it talks about Jesus being supported by wealthy women (see Luke 8:2-3). We get our example and huge encouragement from him. Not only that but as he sent out his disciples to minister, he taught them principles of living by faith. He told them not to take a staff, no bag, no bread, no money and no extra clothes (see Luke 9:3). In other words, he wanted them to depend on God to provide for them. There have been many people in the past who have lived by faith - one of whom I love to read about is Hudson Taylor who became a missionary to China. Get hold of one of the books about his life and you will be so encouraged in your faith. Smith Wigglesworth too lived by faith and told the Lord that the day God didn't provide for him, he would go back to being a plumber, which was his trade. He never returned to plumbing because God always provided, in fact he provided more than enough because out of what God gave, Smith gave thousands of pounds to overseas missions. George Muller, the great evangelist who founded orphanages, lived by faith and prayed for God to provide food for hundreds of orphans. Get a hold of a book about his life and discover the miracles he saw happen as he and the children waited for their breakfasts.

Someone once said to one of our workers when she told them she was now living by faith, "Don't you mean dying by faith?" That cynical comment told me a lot about the person who said it. He expected that we and our ministry would die and not have the means to live. Another man who came to visit our ministry to ask if he could have a job with us went away telling people that ngm was on the brink of bankruptcy! He couldn't understand how people could live by faith in God for finances. When he realised that the job he was being interviewed for was one where he would have to depend on God for his finances, he couldn't understand it and therefore expected that the ministry would end soon. I can tell you from over 40 years of experience of living this way and seeing God provide, not only for us but also for the whole ministry, that we are certainly not dying by faith. That doesn't mean that we don't have days where we don't know where we are going to get our next penny from, it just means that when we do have a need, we know where to go to find the answer. As I said earlier many people have lived this way before us. Read their stories and be encouraged in your walk with God. Our God is the same yesterday, today and forever.

Over the years Ray and I have been so encouraged by those who have given to us regularly to enable us to do the work God has called us to do. People have sacrificially given us finance and gifts just at the right time. Their generosity does not go unnoticed by us or by our Heavenly Father. Money, at times, has been pushed into our hands; holidays given to us and clothes paid for without us mentioning finance. At one point we even had a lady give me a credit card in my name; a second card from her account so that we could put petrol or food on it up to a certain amount each month and she paid the bill. What an incredible thing to do and such a blessing and an answer to prayer for us for the time she did this.

I also remember when Ray and I were on a plane in South Africa, a lady who I had started to speak to during the journey to Cape Town pushed some Rand notes into my hand just before she got off the plane. I don't remember mentioning finance to her at all, we just talked about what we did. There have been many times when we haven't had money to buy what we would have wanted but we always had enough money for what we needed. There have been times when we were on holiday in Santa Ponsa in Majorca (due to the generosity of George and Jean Sinclair, two friends and leaders from our church in Scotland who owned a small apartment there), and we only had enough money to share a pizza, side salad and a coke between us each day for our main meal – but it was all we needed at the time. We've experienced many lean times as well as times of enormous blessing. Like Paul we have known what it is to have plenty and known was it is like to be in want (Philippians 4:12).

I remember once sitting in a friend's car when he told us he had so much money he didn't know what to do with it. Both Ray and I had to keep our mouths shut and not mention the great need we had at that time in our own lives as well as the ministry of ngm. We didn't feel released to say anything to him at all.

I remember one time I was in Scotland preaching at a church. Afterwards I had arranged to see my mum and dad at a hotel for a carvery lunch. I desperately wanted to pay for my parent's meals, but I didn't have enough money. So, I prayed that somehow God would give me the extra money I needed to pay for their meals as well as mine. My mum introduced me to an older man in the hotel and she told him that I was involved in Christian ministry. He chatted for a little while and then went back to his seat. We didn't talk about money at all. A little later, on his way out of the hotel, he came across and shook my hand to say goodbye. Without my parents noticing, as he shook my hand, he transferred some notes into the palm of my hand. It was enough to pay for my parent's meals. God hears our every prayer.

Ray and I individually have had so many answers to our prayers for finance. I remember when we knew a bill was going to arrive through the post for £5,000, but we didn't know how we were going to pay it. We went to God and asked him what to do. God took both Ray and myself to the story of the feeding of the 5,000 and told us that we would have enough finance when the bill came in. We praise God for his word and kept on praying and thanking God that we would have enough to pay every penny of this bill. When the bill needed to be paid, we had just enough to pay the bill. We praised God, but then I said to Ray, "You have to know Ray that the greater miracle is still to happen." You see, we had put everything we had to pay this bill, which meant that throughout the following month of December, we didn't have any money for food, or bills, or my Dad's birthday (he was going to be 90 that month) or for Christmas presents for our boys. We didn't mind not having presents, but we didn't feel that it was right for our boys not to have presents at Christmas and so we went back to God in prayer. We thanked him for paying the bill, but asked him about the month of December. How were we going to get our food and everything else that we needed for that month? The Lord spoke so clearly and said, "You've forgotten something!" I said "What have we forgotten Lord?" He said "You have forgotten in the story of the feeding of the 5000 that there were 12 full baskets left over. I'm going to send baskets of money to you during this month." That is exactly what God did. Throughout the month little baskets of finance arrived just at the right time. We had money for our food, our bills, for my Dad's birthday and also for our Christmas. In fact, at the end of the month, we had money left over. I really love how God looks after each of us when we turn to him.

We have been in restaurants and when we asked for the bill, we were told that someone else had paid the bill. We didn't know who it was, only that the bill was paid. I remember one time in Malmesbury when we didn't have enough money to pay our babysitter. When we got back to the house, we showed him two Heartbeat albums that we had just been given. Each member of the band got a free album, so Ray had one and I had one. I got out my cheque book to write a cheque for our babysitter knowing that we had no money in the account, but trusting God that somehow the money would be there when the cheque was cashed. As I did this, our babysitter said, "I hope you don't mind, but would it be possible for you to give me one of your Heartbeat albums instead of money?" I put my cheque book away and thanked God for his answer to our prayers. We didn't need two albums. Another prayer answered.

The Lord taught us so much about leaning on him for our finances both for the ministry and for us as individuals. Each project is a new challenge. How are we going to get the finance for this? What does God want us to do? Whatever he tells us, we obey! It's not always easy and sometimes the faith journey starts when we think it should be finished. I remember finishing a wonderful mission in the UK. We had seen so many young people saved, healed and set free. The church we were working for had said they would cover our expenses and give us a gift. As we left, they put an envelope into my hands and so on the way home I opened the envelope to discover that they had not given us a gift and the money they had put in the envelope would not even cover our petrol. I have to say I cried. We were all so tired and worn out from the mission. We had all been individually and corporately depending on this gift, not just to get us back to Malmesbury but also to help us all with food etc. All the way home I cried, prayed and forgave them for not honouring what they had said. It was an important reminder for us all that God is our provider and not our mission organisers. I have to say that many of our mission organisers were very generous but there were a number who could have done with some teaching on honouring those who serve in the gospel. I remember going to a church in the south coast. There were three of us travelling to a Baptist church where I had been invited to speak to their women for a full day. During the day, we saw a woman stealing from my bookshop. She took one of my CD's without paying for it. It cost £10. On the way home, I opened the envelope that the church gave us for taking the day's sessions. Again, they had promised to give us a gift. Their gift was £5. This time we laughed and said that by going to the church and serving the Lord there, we were out of pocket by £5 as the woman had stolen a CD. These were important lessons for us to learn. Our dependence is not on others, but instead is on the Lord. He is our provider.

At one point we were praying and asking God for the money to go on a holiday. Ray and I were preaching in Belgium in the summer and so we asked the Lord if we could go on from there and have a week's holiday in Holland at Centre Parcs. The event was paying for us and our son, Daniel, plus a nanny to fly to Belgium, so we knew we needed not only the money for the accommodation, food etc., whilst we were there, but also transport to the camp itself.

Money started to come in and very soon the whole accommodation was paid. The organiser heard that we were going to Centre Parcs in Holland and offered to drive us there and come back for us when the holiday was over and take us to Brussels airport. We were so thrilled. All we needed now was money for food for the four of us and perhaps some money for ice creams and postcards. However, when the time came for us to leave to go to Belgium, we only had a small amount of cash, certainly not enough for all our food. We prayed and God gave us an assurance in our hearts that it was going to be okay. We had a brilliant time in Belgium, and if I am honest God was doing so much there that our need was forgotten. However, God had not forgotten. At the end of the last meeting, a man came up to us and told us that he believed that God had told him to give us an envelope. Inside the envelope was the equivalent of £170. No one knew of our need. We had not mentioned it to anyone. We took the money to the leader of the mission and told him what had happened and he said, "You must take this money as a gift from God as God often speaks so clearly to this man." We were blown away. We had a great holiday!

Many years later, Ray and I had been invited to speak in Nashville at a Worship Together conference. After the conference we were going to stay at

internet, I noticed there was only one lodge left and also because it was half term, the price was hugely inflated. We prayed about what to do, and the Lord told us not to call about the lodge until the day before we were due to go. It was hard to discipline ourselves not to call, especially when we knew there was only one lodge left, yet we knew we didn't have the money to pay the inflated price. The enemy would tell us many times that the lodge would be gone, but we had heard and so we obeyed. On the Friday, I lifted the phone and with my heart beating wildly I called the company responsible for the lodges. I not only asked if they had a lodge free, but also asked them for a discount since it was so close to the holiday dates. They replied that there had been a lot of interest about this lodge and they were convinced that it would be rented before the end of the day, however they did offer to take a small deduction from the cost. I knew this was still far too expensive for us and so I mentioned that on a previous visit I had paid much less. They asked how much I had previously paid and when I told them they laughed and said that even if they did reduce the price, they would never reduce it by that much. They continued to insist that the lodge would be rented before the day was concluded. At the end of the telephone call, they asked me to call at 7pm that evening to check if it was still available for rent. At around 4pm, my phone rang. It was the same woman. She had called to ask how much I would be willing to pay for the lodge. I told her a price that I thought was reasonable and she told me she didn't think I would get it for that price, but she would go and check with her superior. We continued to pray. They called back a short while later to agree our price. I gave her my credit card details and paid the holiday in full. We were so thankful to God for his instructions and rang our friends to tell them to pack their bags.

We spent an amazing holiday together, all eight of us thoroughly enjoyed our time away. At the end of the holiday we paid the electricity costs and left thanking God for a great holiday.

However, God hadn't finished being generous towards us. When I received my credit card statement, our holiday wasn't listed. I called the holiday rental line and told them that we had stayed in the lodge for a week, but there was no charge showing on my statement. She told me that it was far too soon to see it on my credit card statement and to wait for another month and by then it would definitely be showing. However, the holiday was still not listed on the next statement. I called again and they assured me that it would go through soon and that it could take up to three months before showing on my bill. However, when the charge wasn't showing for the third month, I called again. After about six or seven phone calls, they eventually said they would look into it again for me. They eventually called back and said, "Mrs Goudie, there is no notification on our system of you ever staying in our lodge." I told them we were definitely there and that we had paid an electricity bill at the end of the holiday. It was then that they politely but firmly asked me not to call again. I was stunned. I didn't know quite what to do. When I told a good friend of mine what had happened and asked for her advice as to what to do, she said, "Nancy, this is wonderful. Take it as a gift from the Lord." It was only then that I could let it go and thank God for his generosity. To be honest there was nothing else I could do as I had called them so many times.

But that's not the end of the story. The amazing thing is that the following year the whole thing happened again. We went to the same lodge, and my credit card payment never appeared on my statement. We had stayed at the same place two years running for nothing. As an old hymn says, God moves in mysterious ways, his wonders to perform! Who would ever have thought that this would have happened not just once but twice!

During the years we have taught so many people to depend on God for their finances. If one person in our team struggles financially, we pray together asking God why. Throughout our journey we knew that God only needed to stop the finances coming in and he had our fullest attention. Whatever God said through our prayer time we would then put into practice through obedience. We would also usually take up an offering from within the team to help the person in their walk of faith. We always felt that unless God specifically said not to give because he wanted to release finance in another way, then we would always do what we could to help. We still do this to this day!

As I have said earlier, we make sure we tithe individually and also corporately. One of the things we have done in ngm throughout the years is to support local and national organisations who work with the homeless or stand up for justice issues, like Care (Christian Action, Research and Education), Care for the Family etc. We also give to other Christian workers and ministries.

When we first set up our Heartbeat bank account in 1983, we felt God tell us to give a tithe of our money to others who were doing similar work to us. Not only would we be sowing into their work, but we also knew it would help to destroy any unbiblical competition that might arise in us.

Even now, 40 years later, we are still discovering the joys of living by faith. Seeing God provide supernaturally is always amazing. It's worth all the struggles to see God provide all that we need as we trust in him. I hope all these stories will encourage you to trust in God for all your needs too. Whether you are in a well-paid job or not, live by faith and put your trust in God for all the finances you receive. It's such a blessing to live this way! Who would ever have thought?

21

THE HEARTBEAT YEARS – THE VISION EXPANDS

One day whilst Ray was out walking with the Lord, he heard the Lord tell us to pray for our nation. We had prayed for our nation many times but usually it was city by city or town by town as we prepared to visit them and do a mission. Prayer was always central to what we did, but Ray felt this was different and that we were to pray for the nation as a whole. And so, in our spare time, the whole of Heartbeat began to meet together to pray for our nation. We thought it was separate to our normal ministry, but what happened was that those prayer meetings soon became central to our vison.

As God began to show us pictures of our nation, our hearts and our vision began to change. He showed us a rubbish tip and the smell from this rubbish tip was rising up to God. Our nation had turned its back on God. As we had travelled extensively throughout the whole of the UK, we were well aware of the state of the nation. Crime was on the increase; abuse, both physical and sexual, was common. We had met children as young as nine who had been thrown out of their homes because their parents didn't want them any longer. Old ladies at the age of 90 were being mugged, raped and sometimes left for dead. The number of people having abortions had increased and a large percentage of teenagers had slept with someone by the time they had reached sixteen. In fact, in one city we met teenagers who told us they were having sex with animals. More and more people were becoming homeless and there was much racial tension. We only had to look in our newspapers to discover that our society was in a dreadful mess. However, it was only when we asked God the following questions: "How do you see our nation?" and "What do you feel about our nation?" that we broke down and wept. God began to show us how heavy his heart was at the sin and sorrow he saw every day, but also, he showed us his heart of deep love for the people of our nation.

We began to pour out our tears to God and repent on behalf of the nation, telling God how sorry we were that we had turned our backs on him. We prayed for revival for our land. However, as we prayed what surprised us was that God began to take the spotlight off the nation and turn it on us. We were a team of sold out, fired up people who loved God passionately and had given up everything for God and yet in his spotlight we saw things in us that contributed to the rubbish tip – things like pride and selfishness or even just saying an unkind word to someone and thinking it didn't matter. God spoke to us and said, "No longer am I prepared to put up with the things that you think don't count." When we heard God speak, we all began to repent of our own sins and ask God to forgive us. We prayed revival prayers as we publicly confessed our own sins. We were all on the floor in tears at each prayer meeting as God highlighted even small stuff in us that we needed to put right. It was a very special time where God was cleansing us. Revival always starts with the church.

During one of these half nights of prayer, when there was a real sense of expectancy, God began to speak powerfully through visions and prophetic words. In a vision, I saw an incredibly huge tidal wave coming in towards the shores of our land. As the wave broke, it crashed on to England and spread out to encompass the whole of Britain and went into Europe and other nations too. God spoke to me and said, "I am bringing a new move of my Spirit to this land. It's not old-time revival or religion, but it's something new and fresh by my Spirit. I want my people to pray and prepare for what I am about to do, but even if some of my people don't pray or prepare, I am coming anyway."

What a great God we've got! It is not as though we deserve revival, but God in his grace and mercy extends his love towards us. The vision God gave us that evening became central to everything we did in ngm. Everything in our ministry now comes out of the conviction that God is going to pour out his Spirit in these last days in a huge and mighty way. We don't know how he is going to do it nor when it will happen but we do know that God is calling us, his church, to be prepared and ready for all he is going to do.

There was a sense in my heart that preparation needed to be inward as well as outward. God wanted his people to purge anything that was within them that was not of him. He also wanted us to have a *big* vision of what he wanted to do. I was reminded that evening of a scene I saw in Spain a few years earlier, while Ray and I were there on holiday.

We had been walking along a street in a small village when we noticed a huge crowd of people trying to get into a large church building. As we drew closer, we noticed that the church was absolutely full and that many people couldn't get in. We wondered what was going on, as you don't usually see churches packed to capacity like that. We got as near as we could and peered into the building to discover that it was just a man at the front preaching. We don't know what he was saying as he was speaking in Spanish however, God spoke to us very clearly at that moment. We felt God saying that the time would come when the churches in Britain would be too small for what he was going to do. There would come a time when churches would be so packed that some people wouldn't be able to get in. With conviction in our hearts, we said, "Yes Lord, do it!" We didn't realise at the time that this would happen even in some of our own concerts because the numbers of people wanting to attend were so huge!

We had no idea that our half night of prayer would be significant, but it was out of the prophecy of the tidal wave that the Heartbeat song Heal our Nation and the tour of that same name were born. In the first recording of this song, the prophecy I received was put in the middle of the song. Heal Our Nation was written by the songwriters in the band, Dave Bankhead, Trish Morgan, Ian Townend and of course, Ray, and we recorded it in our own studios in Malmesbury.

Sometime after we arrived in Malmesbury, The Shaftesbury Society asked us if we could do anything with a dilapidated building which was almost next to our offices on their grounds. Ray took one look at it with eyes of vision and said, "This could be our recording studio!" We took it to the Lord in prayer and felt we should ask our prayer partners to help us with the finance we needed to transform this building. At the same time a church in Stroud asked us to share the vision with their church members one Sunday morning. We told them that downstairs we wanted it to be a studio, but upstairs we wanted it to be a place where we could hold our prayer/worship meetings. A builder spoke with us afterwards and told us that he felt he should do the upstairs of the building for us for nothing. What a blessing! God provided the money for the studio downstairs by providing one gift after another. Within a short amount of time the transformation had begun. The studio was used for many years not only to produce the Heartbeat albums and singles, but also other worship albums and other recordings even after Heartbeat had finished.

We sang the song Heal Our Nation as a cry from our hearts for God to come and move in power in the UK, but once the song was recorded, many people across the world took it up as a song to sing before the Lord for their nation. I have met many people in other nations who have told me how this song has been used in their nation as a heartfelt prayer for God to come and move in power. As I am writing this book in 2020, again God has raised this song as a cry from our hearts to Heal our Nation and change our coronavirus world. Who would ever have thought?

We toured all around the UK with the message of revival and we saw many respond to the message we brought. We wanted to see this new move of God's Spirit move across the land. In the 90's God did release a mighty move of his Spirit on our land. This was called The Toronto Blessing. A number of people wrote to us at that time asking if this was the tidal wave? I don't know, certainly God did move in extraordinary power, but oh we want to see so much more. We want to see not only the church transformed, but we want to see salvation released so that thousands of people are swept into the Kingdom. During the years to come, we wrote a song called The Great Awakening which said in faith, "There's gonna be a great awakening. There's gonna be a great revival in our land." We are now living in 2020 in unprecedented times when God is moving in many fearful and panicking hearts all around the world. Our cries are still the same; Lord we long for you to move in power, come and heal our nation and heal our world.

Heal our Nation

Lord we long for you to move in power
There's a hunger deep within our hearts
To see healing in our nation
Send your Spirit to revive us.

Heal our Nation
Heal our Nation
Heal our Nation
Pour out your Spirit on this land.

Lord, we hear your Spirit coming closer
A mighty wave to break upon our land
Bringing justice and forgiveness
God we cry to you, 'Revive us.'

'I looked and I saw a mighty tidal wave heading towards the shores of our land. As the wave broke, it quickly spread throughout the whole nation, and as I watched, God spoke. "I am sending a new wave of my Spirit, bringing healing, justice and forgiveness. The time is near and I want my people to get ready, pray and prepare themselves for what I am about to do."'

Heal our Nation
Heal our Nation
Heal our Nation
Pour out your Spirit on this land.

(Trish Morgan; Ray Goudie; Ian Townend; Dave Bankhead. Copyright
Thank You Music)
(Prophesy written by Nancy Goudie)

22

THE HEARTBEAT YEARS - SOUTH AFRICA

During 1984, Ray and I both felt that we had heard God speak to us and say that one day he would take us to Johannesburg. When God first told us that he would take us to that city, we didn't even realise it was in South Africa. However, from that time on we prayed that when the time was right to go, we would know it. I remember we responded to a call one day in a church in Stroud when the preacher asked people who felt they had been called to Africa to stand. Ray and I knew we had to stand and publicly tell people that we believed one day God would take us to South Africa.

About six months later it became obvious through our readings in the Bible and through God's whisper to our hearts that the time was right to prepare to go. In our travels, we had met a national Christian leader who, when he heard that we were thinking of going to South Africa in 1985, invited us to travel with him. It so happened that he was going there on a speaking tour in April of that year. It was such a relief to be travelling with someone we knew, as we felt so alone in our adventure of faith. We had never been to South Africa before and to travel into the unknown seemed so daunting. The Christian leader gave us the name and number of his co-ordinator and asked us to contact him to find out what flights he was on and see if we could co-ordinate our flights. We phoned his contact and discovered the cost of the flights and asked the rest of Heartbeat to pray for us. We did not know why God wanted us to go; just that we needed to be obedient and that he would show us why when we got there. We felt it was not a personal thing, but that God would show us something about the ministry of Heartbeat over there. However, before we were even to get our feet on the plane, we had to overcome many obstacles.

When God speaks to you and tells you to do something, it's at that point that the enemy will try everything to turn you away from your calling. You know that God has called you, and yet it seems as though it would be easier to ignore that calling and bury your head in the sand. So often we need to fight our way through difficulties and show God that no matter what, we will respond to what he is saying. You see, we had heard and we had started to obey, but we had to learn to trust. As I have said many times throughout the years, trust is one of the things that is so important in our everyday lives.

First of all, some in Heartbeat began to question our calling. Ray and I felt it was right to write a letter to Heartbeat's prayer partners and ask them to pray for us while we were in South Africa and also to give them the opportunity of helping us financially with the tickets. We had no money to go on this trip and we needed around £1,500 for the flights. However, some of the people in Heartbeat weren't sure if this was right, as they perceived our trip to be a personal vision and not a Heartbeat one. No matter how many times we said that we believed this trip would affect Heartbeat as a whole, it was not seen in this light. Although we were the leaders, we didn't feel it was right to push this decision through. We worked as a team and we wanted everyone on board as much as possible. Ray and I felt disappointed, but we allowed the questions to push us back into God and continued to trust him for the way ahead. We learned an important lesson at that point. It is important that when questions or obstacles to your faith arise, rather than backing off and running away from God, we should run into God and ask him to continue to confirm his calling and show us the way ahead.

At the same time, the leader who had invited us to come on his trip seemed to change his mind. He phoned and left a long message on our voicemail saying that people in his team had been accusing us of muscling in on his trip. We phoned back and explained that the only reason we had booked our flights to coincide with his was because he had encouraged us to do so. We explained that we were setting up our own itinerary in South Africa, and that his co-ordinator had only helped us book our flights to and from South Africa.

Unfortunately, we could not change the tickets by then as the travel agency had confirmed them, otherwise we would have done. The leader was receiving criticism from within his team because he had invited us when others within his church network had wanted to go. All these hassles added to our insecurity. Questions like, 'Are we sure God has told us to go?' kept coming into our minds, but the more we prayed about it, the more God kept confirming that we were doing the right thing.

Because of the questions from the Heartbeat team, we decided to only ask our personal prayer partners to stand with us, rather than ask our corporate Heartbeat supporters. We shared the vision with them in a letter and money started to arrive in the post. Our personal prayer partners were responding to the urgent need that we had, and soon we had received all the money we needed for the journey.

At the same time, we were asking God where we should go when we got to South Africa. Our friends at Kingsway Music told us that if we were going to South Africa, we had to make sure that we met a man called Malcolm du Plessis, a leader of a church in Durban, who was well-known for his pioneering and creative ministry in the realm of praise and worship. We were also given the name of an English couple in Durban who, when we contacted them, said we could stay with them for a few days. It turned out that they knew us from a mission we had done previously in Oxfordshire. We were also given contacts in East London, Cape Town and Johannesburg. As we prayed, we felt God tell us to book a 'rover ticket', which would take us to Durban first, then East London, Cape Town and then end up in Jo'burg.

We attended a New Year party at Sheila Walsh's home. At the time she and her husband, Norman, shared a home with church leaders, Gerald and Anona Coates. It was at this party that we met Cliff Richard for the third time (we, in our band, Unity, had played and sang at a concert with him in Glasgow many years before and Ray had also played drums for him at Filey camp) and when he heard that we were going to South Africa, he told us that we must visit Cape Town as it was very beautiful. So, when the opportunity came to spend some time in Cape Town, we jumped at the chance. Funnily enough, without us realising it, we discovered once we'd arrived in South Africa that the national Christian leader was following almost the same itinerary as us. We had no idea of his itinerary in advance, but we discovered that he was going to almost every city that we were going to and that apart from Durban, where we arrived on the same flight, we arrived at every city just before he arrived there to speak. In Jo'burg we were staying with people from the same church where he was speaking and so both in Durban and Jo'burg we got to hear him speak.

However, because of the nature of our visit and the problems we had, it was a very nervous Ray and Nancy who boarded the plane in London. We did not see the people we were supposed to be travelling with until well into our journey. All the tension we felt just added to our insecurity.

When we arrived in Jo'burg, after the long flight from London, I remember a very funny incident happening to me. When we went to check in for our internal flight to Durban, the guy at the check-in desk asked me to smile. I thought it was a strange thing to say, but I thought I'd better co-operate with his request, so I looked at him and smiled. The guy then asked again, and so again I beamed an even bigger smile back at him. It was only when Ray looked at me as if to say, "What is wrong with you?" that I realised the guy behind the counter had not asked me to smile but asked if I wanted a smoking or non-smoking seat? I felt such an idiot! I had totally misunderstood his accent. He must have wondered why this woman was just standing there grinning at him!

When we arrived in Durban we were taken to the home of Richard and Jill Lawton, the couple who had kindly said we could stay with them. They were fantastic and made us feel so welcome and showered us with love and acceptance. They even gave us their own bedroom to sleep in. However, despite their warm welcome, we still felt very insecure about being in South Africa. We kept asking ourselves, "Why has God brought us here?" To make things worse, when we attended their church service in Durban, people kept asking us why we had come to South Africa. When we answered, "Well, we know this sounds really strange, but we came because we felt God tell us to come, and that he would show us why when we got here." The look of disbelief in their eyes was more than evident and again that added to our insecurity.

On the fourth day of being in Durban, just before we were due to fly out to our next port of call, we met Malcolm du Plessis. He had just returned from a trip out of town, but from the moment we set eyes on Malcolm, we knew we would just love him. He was the most unusual, flamboyant person we had ever met and we quickly became good friends. However, we did not realise just how significant this meeting would be. He began to tell us about a band called Friends First, which he had founded. To our utter amazement we found that our Heartbeat vision and the vision that God had given him were almost identical. He had been responsible for getting together a group of multi-racial Christian singers and musicians to record an album as a prophetic challenge to the church *and* to their nation. He told us that many churches had prayed for them and helped them financially with the project. They believed that God wanted to use them and their music to be a voice to their nation against the evil of apartheid. Their exciting music was reaching high in the South African mainstream charts at the time.

We began to tell him about the work of Heartbeat and how we had just completed a tour called Heal our Nation. We told him about our half night of prayer when God had met with us in such a clear way and told us about a tidal wave of his Spirit coming to our land. We told him about the song we had written called Heal our Nation and the message we carried to the church through our tour. He excitedly told us that we must meet a friend of his called Joe Arthur, who was in the Friends First band and who had produced all their singles and albums. We were thrilled to discover that Joe lived in Cape Town as we were going there in a few days. Malcolm arranged to fly to Cape Town and meet us there and introduce us to Joe.

Before we had left England, one of the most pressing needs in Heartbeat at the time was the need to find a producer who could produce our next album. We had tried to hire quite a number of people, but no one had been able to do it in our time scale. After meeting Malcolm, Ray and I wondered if God had not only brought us to South Africa to sharpen our vision but also to meet the guy who would produce our next album.

When we arrived in Cape Town, we immediately really liked Joe and his wife, Dee. We loved the vision and music of Friends First, and were very impressed with what we heard Joe had produced. That night we prayed that somehow, we would be able to meet Joe again and be able to chat with him some more about Heartbeat and our need for a producer. When we discovered that we were all booked onto the same flight to Jo'burg the very next day and that we were all going to the same concert in Rhema church, we just knew God was working behind the scenes and that this was a God- appointment. The four of us were seated next to each other on the plane and we chatted at great length all the way to Johannesburg. We decided to ask Joe if he would come and produce our next album and he immediately responded positively. It was a miracle that he had the space in his diary and was willing to fly to England over the exact dates that we had put aside for our recording.

That night we saw Joe perform at Rhema church and we could not believe how talented this man was – his voice was stunning! We felt rather embarrassed in the light of his amazing talent that we had given him our Heartbeat cassette and hoped that when he listened to it he would still want to come. Praise God he did!

On our way home on the plane we reflected on all that God had said and done and as we prayed, we thanked him for his amazing grace to us. We came home knowing that God was telling us that we must be a voice to the nation and not just a voice to the church. From that one trip to South Africa, God had sharpened and expanded our vision and we also now had our producer. Joe Arthur turned out to be the perfect producer for the next part of our journey. We could not wait to tell the team what God had done.

We could not believe how much had come out of one adventure of faith and how easy it would have been to miss it and stay at home. If we had submitted to our insecurities and given in to our problems and difficulties, we would not have been in the right place at the right time. It was a learning time for all of us in Heartbeat, and although we all had to push through some reservations, the team were fantastic at getting behind us and praying for us before and during our trip. On the plane on the way home, the Christian leader who had invited us to travel with him apologised for the problems we had encountered before we left and thanked us for the encouragement we had given to him while he had been in South Africa. He told us he could not believe how everywhere he went, he heard about this Ray and Nancy Goudie who had been there before him and how we had said positive and encouraging comments about him.

If God has told you to do something, no matter how strong the opposition is against you, do make sure you obey God first and he will bring huge amounts of blessing from it. However, first of all you need to be sure that it is God who has spoken to you and not just your own thoughts or inclinations. There are many ways that God speaks to us; I have listed some in chapter 4. However, one of the most common ways in which God communicates with us is through the Bible. As I have previously said, if we are not regularly reading his written word, the Bible, then it will be more difficult for us to hear his voice. I cannot emphasise enough how important it is to read the Bible. God has given us a wonderful book full of his instructions and promises and it is essential that we not only read it, but that we hide it in our hearts by memorising it. If God wanted to speak to Ray and myself, he would often do so by showing us something from his written word. However, in our walks of faith, as we have heard from God through the Bible, through peace in our hearts, through hearing his still small voice, and through other people, we have found that it was also important to share what we feel we have heard to others who are wiser and more mature in their faith. If we are truly hearing from God then it will stand up to scrutiny, and submitting it to others will keep us from going in a wrong direction.

23

THE HEARTBEAT YEARS - BEING A VOICE TO THE NATION

On our return home Ray began to write with others from Heartbeat the song called Voice to the Nation. Some of you reading this book will remember that we released a single into the charts called Tears from Heaven from an album called Voice to the Nation. We produced a booklet which was also called Voice of the Nation. Also, on our return from South Africa, Ray and I (mostly) or Ray and Jack (sometimes) visited many if not all of the national Christian leaders of our country to ask if they would pray for us as we released what we believed was a prophetic single telling the nation that God cared for our land. As we submitted our vision to them, each leader was so encouraging and supportive. We did laugh with Bob Gordon (a preacher/leader working with Colin Urquhart at the time) about his first response to our vision. He said in his broad Scot's accent, "If God's not spoken to you, you're dead!" We knew we were taking a huge faith step, but we had to trust God that he had given us the vision in the first place.

When Joe came across to the UK, he produced both the album Voice to the Nation and the single Tears from Heaven in our studios in Malmesbury. Many nights we would hear him in his bedroom in our house getting prepared for the next day of recording. He was inspirational and he became a great friend. Not only did he do a great job of being our producer, but he also passed on so many production skills to our band members that they went on to use later in life.

Our single, Tears from Heaven reached number thirty-two in the pop charts in Britain and Heartbeat appeared on Top of the Pops, The Roxy and many other TV and radio programmes too. Ray and I were so thankful that we had my brother there as our administrator to deal with the many phone calls we got from the press etc., during that period of time. Jack was the perfect man to deal with the press. He was also a great salesman. I remember he and Dorry used to have friendly competitions to see how many albums each of them could sell. Sometimes Dorry won and at other times Jack took the title of the best sales person. I remember him telling us that after much persuasion, he eventually sold a Heartbeat album to a lady he knew. She didn't really want to buy it, but Jack was very persuasive. However, the next week she returned to ask for a refund saying that she didn't have a record player to play it on. Jack had managed to sell a Heartbeat album to a woman who had no way of playing it. How we laughed – only Jack could have done that!

We also had amazing opportunities to share our faith with many of the national leaders of our country as well. We wrote to our Prime Minister, to the opposition party leader, to members of the Royal Family, to the head of the BBC and heads of other TV channels, to the Trade Unions and many businessmen, sending them a single and telling them that God loved our land and that the lyrics of the single portrayed God's heart for our nation. We received great responses from many of them.

We found the response to the single was very interesting. Many news items were reported that did not actually happen and many untruths were said as though they were true. Ray had many opportunities to speak about the single on the radio and one of his interviews was reported in the national press. One report said, Ray Gale says, "I hate the church." First of all, they didn't even get his name correct and secondly why would Ray ever say that he hated the church? Those words were never uttered by Ray. Ray loved the church. However, because people saw this report in a national newspaper, many believed it was true and without asking, began to condemn Ray. We received so many letters and phone calls from Christians slamming Ray. They didn't ask *if* Ray had said this, instead, they judged him as guilty because they felt the newspaper report must be correct. We learned the hard way that what we often read in the newspapers is not always accurate.

We also were criticised by many from the Christian press of trying to get the single into the charts in the wrong way, yet when it was investigated by the mainstream authorities, they announced that there was nothing wrong with the way that we had asked our fans to buy the single. However, I must say that some churches and people were so blessed and encouraged by the single that they kept bombarding the radio stations with requests to play the single, but some of their ways of doing this were not so wise. However, the opportunities to share Jesus with many people we met was so brilliant and so encouraging. Our reputation went ahead of us as we went into many TV shows. They told us that they didn't know what to expect after all they had heard about us from the newspapers, and that they had suggested to each other that we would be Jesus freaks wearing Jesus sandals. They were so relieved to see that we were normal trendy human beings and that there were no Jesus sandals in sight! We were a band who had a passion in life to share the one person who had changed us forever.

A number of months later we released another song into the charts, this time the song was called The Winner. This song was pushed by Radio 1 and the feeling from them was that this song would be a top ten hit. Joe had produced it and it was remixed by Pete Waterman of Stock, Aitken and Waterman in London.

Unfortunately, the timing of the single was not great. A national Christian event was happening at the time and therefore because of this, people's attention was elsewhere and so the single was not purchased in the same quantities as the previous single. It surprised the DJ's at Radio One that it only reached number 70 in the charts. Ray felt let down by the Christian leaders who had promised to make the single known at the Christian event and within their own churches.

We discovered something through this experience; we discovered that both Ray and I didn't respond to failure very well. We let it affect us and Ray, in particular, was very discouraged. We learnt through this experience to hang on to God through disappointments and discouragements and to rejoice even when things didn't turn out the way we had expected them to turn out. We discovered that Ray and I dealt with success well, in other words we didn't get filled with pride or self-importance but we remembered why it was that we were doing it and we continued to know that it was God and not us; it was his vision and we were only fulfilling what he wanted us to do.

But when it came to failure, we let circumstances and disappointments pull us down. Ray and I got on our knees and prayed to God to use what were seen as our successes and also what were seen as our failures. It is true to say that the others in the band generally dealt with the failure much better than Ray and I did, and we dealt with success much better than some of them did.

24

THE HEARTBEAT YEARS – THE BIRTH OF OUR FIRSTBORN SON

About nine months before the first single was released, Ray and I began to try to have a family. Family had always been on our minds from the beginning of our marriage, but we decided to wait five years or so before having our first child. However, when those years had passed, it was the time when God was calling us into full time Christian work and so the timing didn't seem right, so we delayed trying for many more years. I remember when I was 29 asking God when we would have children and he told me clearly, "If and when I want you to have children, I will put you in a place where this is possible." At that time, we didn't have a home of our own, so we relaxed and trusted that when it was the right time we would know. Several years later, whilst on holiday with two of our friends and their family, we both began to feel that the time could be right. We looked at our friends' children and thought it would be lovely to have some of our own. When we discovered in 1987 that I was pregnant, we were absolutely overjoyed. By then we had moved into our new home in the Inner Silk Mill grounds in Malmesbury; we were at last in a place where having a family was possible.

My pregnancy was really easy and so I continued to sing in the band until I was eight months pregnant. My last mission/concert was in August 1987 and so I then had a month before our son, Daniel was born on 25th September. I felt so huge in the last month and so it was great when the contractions started, or so I thought until the pain increased hugely. I remember being in the hospital in Malmesbury with Ray and telling him after a few hours of intense pain that I had suffered enough and he needed to take me home! I wish it could have been that easy! I also remember Ray being worried that I would damage my face as I pressed the gas and air mask deeply onto my face to try and get some relief from the pain. We discovered later that the canister was empty, but the nursing staff didn't realise. After 24 and a half hours of contractions and two and a half hours of pushing, the doctor asked if I wanted to see the baby's head. I told him, "No, please just get it out." I also cried out to the Lord saying, "Lord help me!" The doctor told me, "You don't need anyone to help you, you are doing really well". I said, "No I'm not, I need the Lord to help me!" When he told me the baby was out, I said, "Praise the Lord" and the doctor turned to his staff and said, "What did she say?" They told him, "She said, 'Praise the Lord'". They told me afterwards that they had heard so many women swear and scream during labour, but had never heard anyone pray or say "Praise the Lord!" I don't think they had ever encountered someone like me before!

When Daniel was laid in my arms, both Ray and I cried tears of joy. God had given us a perfect baby boy who would bring such huge joy into our lives. What a gift from God; we were overwhelmed by the grace of God. We named him Daniel as we knew Daniel in the Bible was someone who co-operated with the society he lived in, yet never compromised his faith. We prayed for this to be the calling on our firstborn son.

It was around this time that Ray went with Heartbeat to the BBC to record Top of the Pops. Our single had reached number 32 in the charts for two weeks running and so they invited us to sing on the highly popular show. I had taken six weeks off from Heartbeat and therefore missed this show and indeed all the TV shows we were in during this time. I missed it all because I was busy with my gorgeous son, but to be honest although I would have loved to have been there, I didn't mind at all because I had an incredible, wonderful and very precious gift from God in my arms.

When Ray and the band went to record Top of the Pops, they discovered that there were cameramen and others working for the BBC who were Christians. They told the band that they were praying for us. It astounded us how God had strategically placed people in the right place at the right time to encourage us with their comments and their prayers.

When I went back into Heartbeat after the birth of Daniel, I took him with us on a number of our concerts, it was so great to have our precious little son with us. However eventually there came a day that I had to leave him at home. I have to say it wasn't easy and there were times that I really struggled to leave, but it was made a lot easier by the fact that by then we had someone join Heartbeat who became Daniel's nanny and who was primarily there to help me in any way she could. This was a great help throughout the years. Some girls who worked as our nanny stayed for a year or so, but mostly they stayed for many years and this was so helpful. Whatever nanny we had to help stayed in our home and became part of our family. She was like a big sister to Daniel.

Daniel was dedicated upstairs in The Barn in our prayer/church meeting place one Sunday morning by Ken McGreavy. He prayed for Daniel and blessed our son and many of the team prayed and brought prophecies about how this child would bring so much joy into our lives. Already Daniel had brought so much joy to our lives. We absolutely loved being the parents of this gorgeous little baby. Some people told us, "Oh just wait until he is in the terrible twos, it gets worse," but every stage of his life was such a joy. To us, he was a wonderful, special and incredible gift from the Lord.

Sometime after Daniel's birth, I began to experience pain in my joints and went to the doctor to find out what was going on. He took some tests and told me he thought it was rheumatoid arthritis, however when the test results came back negative for this, he told me that they didn't know what it was. Ray and I prayed a lot about this with the team and asked the Lord to heal me, but the illness remained. It didn't bother me during the day, it was only when I was sitting or sleeping in one position, my joints would then become very painful until I got moving again. One day, I was praying about it and asking the Lord to heal me, when the Lord spoke and said, "Ask Heartbeat to pray for you once more and I will heal you." I was embarrassed to ask the team to pray for me because they had prayed so many times already, but because the Lord asked me to do so, I did what he said. They prayed and whilst they prayed Dave, our keyboard player, had a word of knowledge that someone close to me had spoken against me and this had been like a curse and caused this illness. They prayed against any negative words spoken about me and when they did, I just knew I had been healed. The next morning after sleeping, there was no stiffness whatsoever. The pain was gone. I was healed. A few days afterwards Ray and I went in the car to Bath and when I got out of the car at the other end, the pain started again. I asked Ray to stand with me. I was not having this illness back again. We prayed and commanded the pain to go and it has never returned. Sometimes when you are healed of something, the enemy tries to put the same illness back on you a few days later and I knew that if I accepted it, then it would have meant the illness would have returned. However, as Ray and I stood against it that day in prayer, it could not find a resting place in my body. I was determined that God had healed me, and indeed he had.

Ray as a cute baby!

My first photoshoot!

Me as a 3 year old with my baby brother, Jack

Jack and I ready for church

The Goudie brothers

Mum, Dad and I dressed for church but would have been more appropriate for Ascot

The McVicar family

Daniel enjoying a swing in a park in Malmesbury

Daniel and Aidan — Daniel was so pleased to have a baby brother

My best birthday present – Aidan born on my birthday!

Daniel trying out diving in our amazing holiday in Mauritius

Aidan enjoying our holiday in Mauritius

Me outside our home in Ayr with our dog called
Dylan (named after the singer)

Ray & I in 1981

Out celebrating Ray's birthday

Singing in the Dave Pope band

Speaking at the first Spiritual Health Weekend – 8 months pregnant

Singing on the Heal our Nation Tour

Wearing my tartan trousers to speak at one of my Spiritual Health Weekends

500 people gather at Bristol for my Spiritual Health Weekend

Ray playing the drums

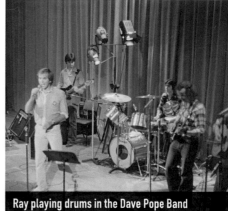

Ray playing drums in the Dave Pope Band

Ray preaching

Ray producing

Unity (1973–1978) – Not sure who picked the pink gingham dresses!!

Unity in concert

The first Heartbeat line-up at our Clitheroe mission with John and Rose

Singing in Heartbeat with my Andy Pandy trousers

A Heartbeat concert

Leading worship in Heartbeat

Queue outside the Charter Theatre, Preston two hours before the doors opened!

Myself and Trish in Heartbeat

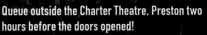

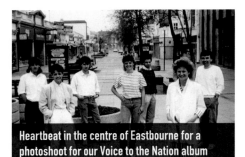

Heartbeat in the centre of Eastbourne for a photoshoot for our Voice to the Nation album

Heartbeat leading a celebration in the centre of Peterborough

Jack joins us as our administrator – 1985

Sarah Shepherd – Heartbeat Dancer

1981 – Heartbeat with Nancy on vocals and Ray on drums on television programme on STV

Heartbeat – outside our offices in Malmesbury

65dba

Rhythmworks

dba

Re:fresh

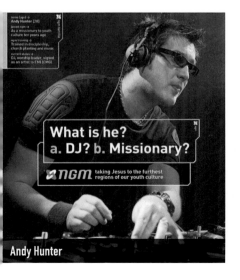

What is he?
a. DJ? b. Missionary?

ngm taking Jesus to the furthest regions of our youth culture

Andy Hunter

Tomorrow's Girl – Zoe (second one in from left) was in the band as a dancer

Doug Ross 'Kubiks'

Jimmy Ragstaff

Steve

Esther Howgill

OnOff Switch – Daniel was the drummer in this band (the one on the right)

Luv Esther

The Prodigals – The cast beside a bus advertising the show in Coventry

Our first floor Heartbeat offices in Malmesbury

The Barn before we turned it into our studios – many of our albums were recorded here

Before Caedmon was built – these garages are now incorporated into Caedmon building

Caedmon as it is today

John & Rose Lancaster opening Caedmon

Our beautiful Manor House – Lancaster House named after John and Rose

Our wedding – Ayr – 1973

Aidan & Leanne's wedding – The Goudie family – 2016

Leanne showing her sense of humour

Daniel and Veronica's wedding – Nancy reading the scripture at the ceremony

Daniel and Veronica's wedding – The Goudie family – 2018

25

THE DEATH OF HEARTBEAT AND THE BIRTH OF NGM

It was 1987/8 when we felt we should change our name from Heartbeat to ngm (new generation ministries) due to the large number of people who were now working with us. Heartbeat became one of the bands that we had within the ministry. In the late 80's we started another band called 65dba and then a band called Rhythmworks. We formed friendships with the leaders of a church in Belgium and sent Rhythmworks to work with them and plant a youth church there. We had many wonderful years seeing this work grow and develop. Throughout the following years several other bands and artists such as Andy Hunter, Steve, T-Girl, Underdown, Refresh, Bleach, Jimmy Ragstaff, Thundershock, together with many others were birthed through the work of ngm.

At various points throughout our lives, God has asked us to put something to death so that he could raise it back to life perhaps in a different form. Death is never easy but as we trust God to take us through the darkness, we will discover that what we move into is an even more fruitful place.

Ray and I had always said that if God told us to put Heartbeat or ngm to death then we would do it. We knew that God had put the vision of a music and mission team into our hearts, so if God said that the time for this ministry was over, then we would not want to continue. There is a huge difference, though, in saying a statement like that and actually obeying God and putting it into practice. By 1990, Heartbeat had been working in ministry for almost ten years. The personnel in the band had changed many times, by now we had Sue Rinaldi as lead singer, Su and Steve Bassett as backing vocalist and bassist. Ray no longer played the drums, instead Clive Urquhart (Colin Ur-quhart's son) had become our drummer and his wife, Jane, became part of the team working as a youth worker and intercessor. Dave Bankhead was still our keyboard player and Ian Townend our guitarist, although he was about to go back to the States with Dorry and Carl was due to be taking his place. I was back in the band singing and we had a vocalist from the States join us called Bobby. I cannot stress how much Ray and I valued everyone who was a part of Heartbeat during the 10 years that the band was in existence. The Lord gave us wonderful people to work with and Ray and I loved each of them enormously.

In those 10 years, we had literally seen thousands of people come to know the Lord and hundreds of people healed from various illnesses. We also saw thousands of Christians re-dedicate their lives to Christ. Our sphere of influence had moved from a national one to an international one. We had many missions and events in mainland Europe and many invitations to travel in the States. Our albums were being sold all over the world. One of the tracks from The Winner album had reached number 3 in the American Christian Music charts. We were receiving letters from people as far away as Australia and South Africa telling us they loved our music and the message we brought. Just when we seemed to be at our most successful, we felt God speak to us and tell us that it was time for Heartbeat to die.

We asked Ken McGreavy if he would pray with us that if God was asking us to put Heartbeat to death, he would make that very clear. Just after that, Ray went to a meeting where Gerald Coates was speaking. Afterwards Gerald took Ray aside and told him that a number of weeks previously he had felt a burden to pray for Ray, myself and Heartbeat. He mentioned this to Trish Richards, whom Gerald knew often heard prophetically from God for others, and he asked her if she had received anything from God for Heartbeat. She said she hadn't but the very next morning she woke up from a dream which she felt was for us. As Gerald explained the dream to Ray, it was not hard to see that God was talking about Heartbeat dying and that we would be moving from our base in Malmesbury.

A few weeks later, we met Lynn Green from Youth with a Mission at a mission we were doing in Swindon. At that event, Lynn gave Ray and myself a word from God about Heartbeat. He told us he felt God has said that unless the seed falls to the ground and dies, it would remain only one seed, but if it dies, it would produce many seeds. He told us to look at John 12:24. I can still remember Lynn telling us that day, "Ray, Nancy, I feel God is telling you that Heartbeat should die, and if you obey God in this, you will be much more effective in the future." His words shook us – was God really asking us to put Heartbeat to death? We took his words back to God and continued to ask him for wisdom. When we next saw Ken, he too told us he felt the time was right for Heartbeat to finish. It seemed so opposite to what the world would do, especially when we were seeing so much happen through our ministry worldwide, yet it would have been disobedient to ignore the promptings of God.

At that point, just before our Christmas holidays, we shared with the others in Heartbeat the words we had received from God and said that there was a strong possibility that Heartbeat would finish soon. We asked them to pray and see if they could sense what God was saying. As you can imagine, this was a huge shock to everyone, but we stressed that even if Heartbeat ended, that did not mean that they needed to leave ngm. We assured all of them that there would always be a place for them if they wanted to walk into the future with us because ngm would be continuing. However, we realised from the dream that Trish Richards gave us that some arrows would fly in other directions and therefore it was right for some to move on to other ministries. We continued to pray that God would show us all the way ahead. We asked them to pray and then let us know what they all felt.

As we gathered together at the beginning of 1991, it was with great sadness in our hearts that we all knew that this would be our last year. We and the team could not deny that God had spoken and so we decided that the band would finish in September 1991. Those last number of months were so difficult as we walked through a minefield of emotions within the team. However, because God had spoken so clearly, we knew it would have been wrong to keep the ministry going and so despite the problems we encountered, we planned our last event.

One of our amazing organisers, Heather Crate, took up the challenge of putting on our last farewell event in the De Montfort Hall in Leicester. As I looked out on the audience that night before going on stage, tears came to my eyes. The 2,200-seater hall was packed with people, many of whom had come to know the Lord through the work of Heartbeat. I was remembering that when Ray and I started Heartbeat in 1981 we could hardly get an audience of one to come and listen to us, yet, here we were ten years later in a huge, packed venue celebrating the many lives that had been transformed through our work. God had indeed been faithful and I couldn't hold back my grateful emotions.

Our trustees, Ken and Hazel McGreavy and Richard and Karen Collier-Keywood were in the audience that night. At the end of the event, Ray and I thanked everyone in Heartbeat for all they had done. Ray mentioned each one of the band publicly by name, making sure we conveyed our heartfelt thanks to them for the many wonderful years we had shared together. Within the team we had Clive Urquhart (our drummer) and his wife, Jane Urquhart (our intercessor in the team), Sue Rinaldi (our lead vocalist), Su Bassett and myself were the backing vocalists. We were joined on backing vocals by Bobby from the States and occasionally he sang lead too. Steve Bassett was our bassist and Carl, our guitarist, had only joined us in January 91 so his time in the band was rather short. Dave Bankhead, who was on keys, had been with us almost from the beginning. Our dancer Sarah Shepherd was also with us and of course Dave Strange was on sound. We loved them all and so it was with real sadness that we realised we would no longer be sharing every day with them.

Each of them chose to leave ngm and as the prophecy from Trish Richards had indicated, many of them went on to other wonderful ministries. Some of them would make a huge mark for our Lord as the years went on and Ray and I were so proud of everything they've accomplished.

Once those who had been in Heartbeat left in September 1991, ngm seemed so small. We were left with 65dba, who were based in Swindon at one of our church plants for a year, and two office staff besides ourselves in Malmesbury. However, we knew we had heard from God and no matter how small or how big we became we needed to follow him. It's never to do with the size of your ministry, it's to do with the size of your heart and your passion to follow the Lord wherever he leads.

We felt our time in Malmesbury was over and so we prayed about moving to Bristol where some of our friends were based. We had been invited by the leadership of Bristol Christian Fellowship to consider moving closer to them. We always had a brilliant relationship with this church and in particular with the leaders, Dave and Rhi Day, Neil and Zoe Edbrooke and Nic and Jenny Harding. We had done many missions and events with these guys over the years and it seemed right for us to move closer to them. Also, the prophetic word from Trish Richards had said that the main arrow would move a short distance away so this seemed to fit what the Lord had said. When we arrived in Bristol, their friendship and support, especially in the early days of us moving, was so helpful and encouraging.

26

THE NGM YEARS – MOVING TO BRISTOL

When we were considering what part of Bristol we would move to, we automatically thought we should be based in the centre of Bristol, but no matter how hard we tried to relocate ourselves there, there was always something that suggested the centre of Bristol was not the place to go. Eventually, we decided to settle in Thornbury where our friends, Neil and Zoe Edbrooke, were living and where there was a satellite church from Bristol Christian Fellowship.

Ray and I were offered temporary accommodation in Graham and Isabelle Roberts' family home in Thornbury. They were so very kind to us and we became good friends. We ended up staying with them for a month before we rented a home for six months. Those six months allowed us to get a feel for the area before we bought our own home very close to where Neil and Zoe Edbrooke and Jonathan and Gail Brooks lived. Jonathan and Gail were the leaders of Thornbury Christian Fellowship.

The church was so kind and welcoming especially the people who lived in Thornbury. Many of them became good friends. About a month after we arrived in Thornbury, Daniel was due to start school. Someone dropped off a parcel for us at Graham and Isabelle's home and in it was a brand new school uniform for Daniel. What a kind thing to do.

Even though we lived in Thornbury we still had to travel back to Malmesbury every day as our offices and studio were still there. We knew this could not continue and so we began to ask God where our offices and base should be. Each day on our journey to Malmesbury we passed a manor house called The Ridge, which was partly owned by Bristol Christian Fellowship. We knew the church only used the house occasionally for church meetings and so we began to pray whether this could be the right place for us to have our base. The more we prayed the more convinced we became that this was indeed the right place for us. It wasn't in Thornbury itself but it was only six miles away, very near the M4/M5 junction.

We approached the elders to ask if it was possible for us to have a couple of the bedrooms as offices and jointly use the large lounge for meetings and have shared use of the kitchen. They invited us to attend one of their elders' meetings so that we could discuss with them if this was possible. The meeting was held in the building in question. After Ray outlined exactly what we were asking and what it would mean, the elders then began to discuss the possibility. We knew the elders wanted to help us if they could but as the conversation progressed it was obvious, due to concerns over planning permission, that the answer was going to be no. I remember inwardly talking to the Lord saying, "Lord, I am convinced you want us to have this place as our offices, so it is going to be interesting to find out how you will change their minds."

As the discussion came to a close and the elders said, "Sorry, Ray and Nancy, I really don't think it is going to be possible." Suddenly one elder, who had remained silent throughout the whole discussion, made a comment that totally changed the situation. With that one comment, the answer now was that if we could get planning permission for the change of use, then the elders would allow us to have our offices there.

We went back to our team with renewed vigour to pray and fast, as it seemed unlikely that the planning permission for change of use would be granted. As you can imagine, it takes some time for planning permission to be given and during that time we had several people from the church say to us, "It is so sad that you will not be able to use The Ridge as your base." When we replied that we were praying and believing that we would be able to use it, they were totally surprised as they didn't think there was any way we would get the permission we needed.

We kept going back and asking God if we had indeed heard from him and that he would bring us a positive word from the planning department. There was great rejoicing when we received a phone call from one of the elders who told us that the planning permission had been granted. God had made the impossible possible once again! The church allowed us to rent two of the bedrooms and the landing and we shared the kitchen and lounge with them. They also allowed us to house our studios in one of their buildings in the centre of Bristol at no cost. As I said, they were such a great bunch of people.

27

THE NGM YEARS - MY BEST BIRTHDAY PRESENT EVER!

Ray and I were loving being parents to Daniel. He was a very easy child and real fun too, so when he was about two years old we decided we'd like to try for another baby, but it never happened. Whereas with Daniel I conceived the very first time we tried, with Aidan it was a very different story. It was so difficult, month after month to discover that I still was not pregnant. We couldn't understand it and so, as usual, we went to God in prayer, but no matter how much Ray and I prayed we could not hear from Heaven. That was until 1st April 1990.

On this day Ray, Daniel and myself were visiting our good friends, Bill and Jacqui Hilary in London and we attended church with them. Daniel was a little unsettled in the church and so I picked him up and took him outside. It was a beautiful, sunny day. I played with him for a while outside the church and whilst I did that I prayed. "Lord, please tell me. Am I going to have another child? I really want to know." Immediately, God spoke. I heard him so clearly. He said, "Hosea chapter 1 verse 6." I thought to myself, "What on earth does Hosea 1:6 say?" I picked Daniel up and went inside the church. I gave Daniel to Ray and immediately opened my Bible and read these words, *Gomer conceived again and gave birth to a daughter (NIV)*. God spoke again and said, "Nancy, I'm not promising you a daughter, but I am promising you that you will conceive again and you will give birth to a child." I quickly whispered what had happened to Ray and showed him the scripture God had given me. He too was overjoyed. God had spoken and so it would happen, but it didn't!

We tried for months and months, but every time the same result -disappointment! We went back to God, but he told us to trust him. The months and years went by and still no baby. We went to the doctor and asked if there was any reason why we were not conceiving and was told there was no reason whatsoever why we couldn't have another child. But month after month we were filled with disappointment!

Eventually when I reached the age of 40, I went and spoke to Ken about it. I told him the story and asked him if we did something wrong. He said "No you haven't." I said, "Did we not hear God right." He said "You did hear right." I laughed and said, "Was God joking with me because it was April Fool's day?" He replied, "No that didn't happen." I said, "Was it the enemy's voice and he was trying to deceive us?" He said, "No it's not that." I said, "Well, what is it then?" Ken replied, "Well, the only thing I can think of is maybe it's still to happen!" I was shocked and said, "What? At the age of 40?" I felt a bit like Sarah who when she heard she was going to conceive at the age of 90 said, *"Now that I am worn out and my husband is old, will I really know such happiness?"* (CEV). I thought to myself, "Could it happen after all this time?"

Ray and I didn't understand. This had been one of the clearest words I had ever received and yet it had not come to pass. We knew we couldn't do anything about it ourselves and so we left it in the Lord's hands. I said to Ray, "Well, if it happens, it happens, but if it doesn't then I will have a conversation with the Lord about it when I get to Heaven."

There were many times throughout the coming years, when I was asked by my doctor if I wanted to go on the pill or take some other precautions to avoid getting pregnant over the age of 40. I was told all the horror stories and advised to do something to make sure it didn't happen to us, but I couldn't do that. I wanted to give God every opportunity to keep his promise to me. If I had done what the doctors suggested, it would have felt to me like I was throwing God's promise away. About three years passed before the thought crossed my mind that I could be pregnant. I remember using a home pregnancy kit to find out and did it twice because I could not believe the result; at the age of 43 I was pregnant!

We were overjoyed although if truth be told a little apprehensive! Were we too old to be parents? Would this child be okay health wise? I was asked about six or seven times by different doctors during the term of my pregnancy if I wanted an abortion as there was a higher risk that the child could have Down's syndrome. I told them that even if he was a Down's syndrome baby, I would not abort this child. We wanted this baby; he was our promise from God.

I remember when we sat down with Daniel and told him that we were going to have a baby! His whole face lit up. He then told us that it had to be a boy! He had been praying for years for a brother who would play football with him. I also remember when we told everyone at ngm that I was pregnant! The look on the young people's faces as they realised that Ray and I weren't too old to still have sex! It was hilarious!

A few days after we discovered I was pregnant I had a show of blood and I went to see my doctor. It was too early to have a scan, but she booked me in for one when I was 8 weeks pregnant. She told me I could have lost the baby and therefore I could be carrying a dead foetus inside of me. You can imagine how that made me feel. Everything she told me was filled with gloom and doom, until I was walking out of the door and she called after me, "Congratulations by the way." I was totally confused, how could she congratulate me if my baby could be dead? Ray and I prayed and asked God that this baby would be good and healthy and that everything would be fine when I went for the scan.

I remember the day of the scan so clearly. Ray and I had to go to the hospital and after the scan we nervously sat waiting for the results. We were told we had to see the consultant rather than the normal doctor and this, as you can imagine, caused a bit of anxiety. We were praying all the time. He explained that he had seen some blood which would at some point just come away, but there was nothing to worry about and that the baby itself was absolutely fine. We were relieved. We didn't know when this blood would show itself or how much blood there would be. Believe it or not, I was preaching at a Cultural Shift event, when the blood decided to show itself. It completely threw me. I don't quite know how I got through the rest of my message. I could feel it happening and so finished the preach quickly and got to a toilet. I couldn't believe it happened whilst I was preaching! The rest of my pregnancy was great with no problems at all, although I did get a little tired of the various doctors and consultants who continually offered me an abortion because of my age!

On my 44th birthday, 27th February 1997, our second son, Aidan Jon Goudie was born. He is the best birthday present I have ever received. Despite all that the doctors told me that could go wrong, he was a perfect and beautiful baby boy. My perfect birthday gift! I remember counting his fingers and toes to make sure he had all ten before I called my dad and told him through my tears that he and my mum were grandparents again! We called him Aidan after the Celtic saint who was an evangelist to the English and Jon after John, the beloved disciple and of course my dad, whose proper name was John. We prayed that both our boys would be significant like the people they were named after.

Ray went to Daniel's school and took him out of his class early so that he could come to the hospital to see his baby brother. He was overjoyed that God had given him a brother. He could not stop smiling! This was the perfect answer to his prayers! However, as the months went by, he realised that it was going to be a lot longer before his baby brother would be able to play football with him. There were 9 and a half years between our first and second sons, not through our own choice, but we knew that this timing was from the Lord. I was allowed out of hospital that evening so I could enjoy the rest of my birthday and my precious present at home!

We discovered as the years went by that although Daniel and Aidan were so similar in looks, they were so different in personality. How could two children born to the same parents be so different? We would tell Daniel the boundaries and he always kept to them. Aidan, however, never kept one of the boundaries, he always crossed them in his early years. Daniel, as he was growing up, was like a little adult. When we had friends in our home for dinner, Daniel would sit at the table and listen in on the conversation. Aidan, however, couldn't sit still at all; he was so full of energy and excitement. Of course, by the time Aidan was born, we were older parents and we just didn't have the energy that parents would have had in their 20's. As the years went by Aidan certainly kept us fit. He loved sport and whether it was football, cricket or golf, our days normally involved at least one of these sports.

When I went through the menopause very soon after giving birth, the doctor told me, "You do realise that your son's birth is a miracle?" She was saying this because I conceived at a time when it would have been almost impossible to get pregnant just before the menopause. I replied, "Yes I do, in more ways than one!"

One story of what happened with Aidan when he was very young has always stuck in our minds. When Aidan was about 18 months old, we left him and his 11-year-old brother in the care of two friends, who were leaders in ngm, for a few days as we were celebrating our wedding anniversary. Our friends were married but they didn't have children of their own as yet. When we called home to check on Aidan and Daniel and asked how they were all getting along, we were told they were getting on well, but that they had had an interesting time with Aidan.

He had gone for an afternoon nap and sometime later they decided to go and see if he was awake. They said that as soon as they opened the bedroom door, the smell that hit them was overpowering, however the scene they saw shocked them completely. Aidan had decided to take off his dirty nappy and then thought he would be creative with the contents. He proceeded to paint the cot (which had many small delicately decorated wooden bars) with the contents of his nappy! Not satisfied with this, he decided to plaster it on his head, his body and even put it in his mouth. What a nightmare for our childless friends; we thought it might put them off having a family forever, but they eventually had kids of their own. Somehow it is much easier to deal with these sorts of things when it is your own child.

We loved having a family and we are so thankful to God for our two boys. During their teen years it was strange to see that it was Daniel who pushed the boundaries rather than Aidan. However, both have grown into amazing men who have wonderful and very deep hearts of faith.

I remember when Daniel was 14 years of age, he told me that he was going to read the Bible using my Bible reading planner. I was thrilled. It was amazing that a 14-year-old boy wanted to read the Bible daily! I have to admit I did wonder if he would really do it, but he did. At the end of a year, he told me, "Mum I did it! I've read the whole Bible!" I was so excited and encouraged, however the next morning I noticed that he was no longer reading his Bible. When I asked him why, he told me, "I've done it Mum – I've read it all. I don't need to read it anymore!"

I had to explain that the Bible is an incredible book and that even after reading it many times there is so much more to explore within its pages. It's as we read it and keep reading it that we can discover more about the great God we serve and fall so much more in love with him. If you have never read the Bible using a Bible planner, then go to my webpage www.nancygoudie.com and purchase one, it will be the best 50p you can spend. Reading the Bible changed my heart and I know it can do the same for you! Both my sons read through the Bible in their early teen years through using my Bible reading planner.

28

THE NGM YEARS – THE MISSION AND ARTS COMPLEX

Just before we left Malmesbury, we had begun to train other bands and individuals in the arts so that they too could see a harvest of souls won for Jesus. We wanted them to be effective in the mainstream as well as the church. Through the years we have trained many who are now 'salt and light' in the music industry, in theatreland, in clubland and in the media. We have also produced many youth workers, ministers and worship leaders in the church. God has done so much and the fruit coming from them all will only be fully known when we get to Heaven.

In 1994, 1995 and 1996 we held an event in the Colston Hall, Bristol called Shake the Nations. Each year we had to turn away many hundreds of people as we completely sold out of tickets. Many of our bands performed at the event and we also put a band together out of our artists to lead worship. We saw so many respond to Jesus and many people gave their lives back to God through this multi-media interactive event. It was at this event where I led the audience through a meditation on the cross and at the end people had discovered Jesus for themselves and transferred from darkness into the light. Ray and I hosted the event, I sang in the worship band and Ray spoke and many people responded at the end. It was such a joy to see so many turn to God.

When I look back at all God has accomplished through ngm, I can hardly believe it. Who would have thought that God would do so much? All it took from us was to be obedient to his call to keep our eyes on Jesus, to take his hand and to trust him to lead us through the many minefields that we would have to walk through along the way!

It was in Thornbury that over the years our work grew massively and it was here that God blessed us with not only with a bigger home of our own but also an amazing missions and arts complex.

For those of you who are parents of young children, you will identify with the wonderful feeling of a child's small hand in yours. When a child is insecure, fearful or just cautious, they will often come and take your hand. They know that you will protect and help them to deal with whatever is bothering them. They simply put their faith in you and in the love you have for them. God wants us to come as little children and put our hands into his, knowing that he loves us much more than we could ever love our children. We knew that if we listened, were obedient, and put our trust in him, he would lead us through each problem or 'death' into many fantastic new areas he had for us. We knew it could be hard, as we often didn't know where we were going, but as we kept our eyes on the Lord Jesus, he led us into an even more fruitful season. The seed had to die first before we began to see the massive fruit God had in store.

As the team grew, although we were so grateful for the offices and studio we had from the church, it became obvious that we needed a base of our own. During our personal times with God, the Lord told us he was going to give us a missions and arts complex.

We knew we were in for a big walk of faith; little did we realise how huge that walk of faith would be. We thought we were praying for God to supply around £200,000 in order for us to buy a house in which we could have our offices and perhaps change the garage into a studio. We thought we were thinking big as the most we had seen God supply in one lump sum previously was £15,000, but what we came to realise as the journey proceeded was that we were actually thinking small and it was God who was thinking *big*. Our journey of faith led us to believe God not for £200,000 but for £3million. If we had known at the beginning that our missions and arts complex would cost £3million, I am sure that our faith walk would never have started. God knew that it was best to let us see the picture bit by bit, and as we trusted him for one bit of the plan, he then led us to the next part.

If we had seen the whole picture at the start, I know we would not have had the faith to believe at that point for £3million.

Right at the commencement of our journey God told us, "not to worry about the money but to birth the project in prayer." It was good that he said that, because at that precise moment in time we did not have one penny towards our faith goal. I was pregnant at the time with Aidan, and my pregnancy became a prophetic symbol as to what God was saying. The fact that I was pregnant was a miracle in itself as I have already said. After all, I was 43 years of age! Because of this we knew that as we birthed this project in prayer, the outcome of this would be miraculous too.

We had early morning prayer meetings, late night prayer meetings and prayer meetings during the day, all asking God to show us where we could find our missions and arts complex. As we continued to pray, God continued to stretch our faith. As well as praying and fasting, we began to look to see what property was available in the local area. Without having any money in our bank account, we visited several homes that were up for sale for around £200,000 to see if we could find the property that God wanted us to own, but each one was either too small or too far out of town. Through our activity and our prayer sessions, God began to show us that he wanted to give us property within Thornbury itself.

One night, Ray and I received a phone call from two of our close friends, John and Rose Lancaster, who told us that they had heard from God and wanted to give us a donation towards our Caedmon project (the project was named Caedmon after a Celtic bard by that name who was known for writing songs that reached the masses rather than just the church. As this was our vision and desire, we felt this name was appropriate for us). We were excited and very encouraged by their phone call. We weren't sure how much they would give, we wondered if we dared to believe for a gift of £20,000 or more but when we heard that the donation was £1 million, we were overwhelmed. Praise God for people like John and Rose Lancaster who not only saw our dedicated prayers and understood our hearts but took time to hear from God, saw the vision, believed in it and were prepared to partner with us.

When I heard we had been given £1 million, I turned to Ray and said, "We could buy the whole of Thornbury for that!" I thought we would have no problem finding the correct place but I was woefully wrong. In fact, it took us years to find the right site.

You should have seen the ngm team when we shared the news of John and Rose's amazing gift. To begin with there was shocked silence and then a roar of joy as the news sunk in. One million pounds! We'd have no problem now – little did we know that we were only at the beginning of an amazing walk of faith which would end with a building that would be a testimony of God's amazing love and faithfulness.

Ray contacted many local farmers, asking them if they had thought about selling their properties. It seemed crazy to be phoning people we didn't know to ask if they wanted to sell their farms. The reactions from people Ray spoke to were varied. Some were bemused, others angry and annoyed thinking we were acting on behalf of estate agents; but most were just not interested. We did visit various farm buildings that were on the market to see if we could house our complex there, only to find that they were not suitable. We looked at numerous buildings in the centre of Thornbury but none of them were big enough for what God wanted to do.

After some time, I remember the estate agents telling us that the place we were looking for in Thornbury just did not exist. When we visited the planning department, they told us that even if we did find a place/land to buy, they would not grant us planning permission for a mission and arts complex. Then some church leaders told us to go to the north of England to build, because there was plenty of land there. At times like those we felt discouraged and went back to God in prayer: "Have we heard right Lord? Are you really telling us you will give us a missions and arts complex right here in Thornbury? Have we got this all wrong? Do you want us to look up north? Are the church leaders right, should we move our headquarters to the north of England?" Each time we went back to God in prayer, God confirmed again and again that he was going to give us a missions and arts complex and we would have it right here in Thornbury near the centre of the town.

At one point a good friend of ours, Wayne Drain, a pastor from the USA who has a keen prophetic gift, came to visit. Before he left, he gave us an encouraging prophetic word about our complex. He felt God say to him that the complex would be near the centre of town, surrounded by trees and set on a hill. We held all the words and scriptures that were given to us in our hearts and kept continuing to encourage each other to trust God despite the circumstances.

Throughout the years we visited many properties but we could not find the one that God had for us. I remember Ray getting into his car several times and praying, "Lord direct me like you did those Celtic saints of old when the wind blew their boats to the shores where you wanted them to go. Blow by the wind of your Spirit and direct this car to the property you want to give us." Often Ray would sit in his car and say, "Okay, Lord, which way do I go, right or left?" Even through our foolishness, we were genuinely saying to God, "We want to hear your voice and be directed by you." However, Ray could not find the property that was for us. We got the distinct impression when we prayed that God was saying that we could not see the property at present but that it did exist and that God would show it to us soon.

As I previously said, we felt my pregnancy was like a prophetic sign of what God was going to do and so when Aidan Jon Goudie was born on my birthday, Ray thought perhaps God would show us where the property was on that day, but again, we were disappointed when that didn't happen. Eventually, in 1997, we received a prophetic word from one of our prayer partners at our ngm open day that said, "The gates will open in 1998", and that was exactly what happened.

Through a remarkable set of circumstances, on Aidan's and my birthday, 27th February 1998, we found the right house. It was a beautiful old manor house which had fantastic gardens. It is set on a small hill, surrounded by trees, near the centre of town, right next door to a Tesco supermarket. When we stood in the building with our friends, John and Rose Lancaster, all four of us knew that this was the right place.

We had been unaware that this superb property existed. A high wall surrounded the property and the large wrought iron gates were boarded up by wood so no one could see through. The owner and his wife who had lived in this massive building did not want to encourage any visitors and so they made sure that the gates were always shut. No wonder Ray and I could not find it even though we passed its walls every day.

Our first contact with the owner was when we wrote a letter to him asking if he was interested in selling his property to us. He did not have the property up for sale, however he said that if we would meet his price then he would sell the house to us. We discovered on our first visit to see him that a firm of solicitors had also asked him if he was willing to sell and he had given them ten days in which to come back to him to let him know if they would meet his price. When we confirmed with him a week later that we would go ahead, he told us that the firm of solicitors had come back and said they wanted the house. However, as they had not come back within the allotted ten days, he told them that he had given us the first option. Despite the fact that the solicitors wanted to increase their offer, the owner stood by his word and by the grace of God we were able to purchase the building.

When we eventually got the keys to the house on 22nd June 1998, the first thing we did was to open the gates and remove the boards from behind the gates so that people could see into the driveway.

When God speaks and gives a promise, he will always fulfil it despite the many problems that may surround it. God will always find a way of honouring his promises. Some of you reading this book right now might be at a place where you are waiting for God to fulfil his promises. Can I encourage you to keep going and not give up because God will indeed be faithful to you! Do make sure again and again that God has indeed spoken and keep going back to him in prayer to find out what his instructions are. As I have said before, in any faith walk there are three ingredients that are vital: hearing, obeying and trusting. We must take time to listen to God's instructions, obey what he has said, and keep our eyes firmly fixed on him so that our faith will not waver. In Joshua 3:3-4 God told the Israelites to keep their eyes on him and on what he was doing because they had *never been this way before*. During our walk of faith, God constantly reminded us to do the same. We can so easily take our eyes off the Lord and put them onto our circumstances. When we do that, as Peter found out in Matthew 14:30, our faith flies out of the window and we begin to sink.

We needed to remember that when, a number of weeks after our offer had been verbally agreed I received a phone call from our estate agent who told me, "I am really sorry Nancy, to bring you such bad news, but the deal is off. The seller has pulled out." I was stunned. Ray was in Germany at the time speaking to a number of church leaders on the subject of faith. When I called him to tell him the bad news, he had just finished telling the leaders what God had done with us and had been encouraging them to keep going in their faith and to trust God no matter what. Neither he nor I could believe that the sellers had pulled out especially when our estate agent had told us that there seemed to be no reason for doing so. Apparently, the sellers had just decided that they no longer wished to sell. Ray and I agreed that we would pray and see what God was saying.

I called each of our ngm leadership team and asked them to come to my home to pray and fast with me. The four of us gathered together and prayed and afterwards I went for a walk on my own with God. I could not understand what God was doing. "Lord, did you not say that you would provide a missions and arts centre? Is this not the right place? God, what is going on? I don't understand." All the time I was praying I kept hearing these words in my mind, "*Why are you crying out to me? Tell the sons of Israel to move forward*" *(NIV)*. I dismissed these words and said, "Yes Lord, but what are you doing?" Eventually, after hearing these words from God so many times, I opened my Bible and looked to see where those words came from. I found them in Exodus 14:15.

Moses had been trusting God as he led the children of Israel out of Egypt. Things went well for a while and then suddenly after being careful to follow God's instructions, Moses found himself and the whole nation of Israel at the edge of the Red Sea. As he contemplated what God could be asking him to do, he suddenly heard in the distance the rumble of the Egyptian troops coming to murder and destroy them. There was no way forward and there was no way back. Right at that point, the children of Israel complained, grumbled and accused Moses of bad leadership. Moses cried out to God and the Lord replied saying, "*Why are you crying out to me? Tell the Israelites to move on.*" Exodus 14:15 (NIV).

As I read that story, I asked God, "Are you telling me that somehow you are going to open up the sale again? If you are Lord, would you also give that verse to Ray in Germany?" I phoned Ray and told him the Lord had given me a verse of scripture. He almost stopped me there and then, because God had given him the same passage of Scripture in Germany. We felt we should do what Moses did in Exodus 14:13 and *"Stand firm and see the salvation of the Lord"(EHV).*

Ray arrived home on the Sunday evening and on the Monday morning, I received a phone call from our estate agent, saying, "Nancy, you are not going to believe this, but it is all back on again." Before I could stop myself, I said, "David, I am not surprised!" When he asked me what I meant I explained to this man, who was not a Christian and yet had seen God move in many ways throughout this whole project, that God had spoken to us during Friday and Saturday and had told us that the deal would be on again.

When you go on a faith walk, you will discover that at times you will have to cling on to God's words despite the circumstances. In the natural it looked as if the deal was dead and we had lost the house, but looking at it through the eyes of God, this was not the case. It is not unusual to encounter problems and difficulties when you go on a faith walk. The question is how are you going to deal with them? Are you going to believe God, as Moses did and stretch your hand over the waters and allow God to make a way through the sea? It's very scary and I am sure you will appreciate a little of what Moses must have gone through. If God had not acted, Moses would have been dead and his journey of faith finished. Victory lay in his obedience to God's words. It says in Exodus 14:21, *Moses stretched out his hand over the sea, and all that night the Lord drove the sea back … and turned it into dry land (NIV).*

It is worth noting that when Moses raised his hand, the miracle didn't happen immediately, the Bible clearly says that *all that night the Lord drove the sea back (NIV)!* We live in such an instant world where we expect things to happen immediately. It is not always so in the Kingdom of God. Moses had to keep his eyes firmly on God and keep his faith and trust intact during that long, hard night. But as he did, God did a miracle. Even if at first we don't see anything happening, do remember that it's as we keep listening, obeying and trusting in God that God will do his part and we will see our 'Red Sea' open up! Keep trusting our great God through the long, hard and dark night. Our God is always good and is indeed faithful!

A number of weeks after we had purchased the house, we replaced the roof and had turned the house into our offices, meeting rooms etc., with the £1 million we had been given, we thought our journey of faith was over. However, God then spoke and said, "Now I want you to build your missions and arts centre on the grounds of this house." It's important to realise that sometimes when we think our faith journey should end, in fact that's when it is only just beginning. God was telling us that there was more ground to occupy. Our faith journey was to last another three years!

There was much joy when we moved into our new premises. We decided to hold a celebration each year on the day we received the keys, to thank God for all he had done for us. We felt it should be a celebration where we would tell the many stories of God's faithfulness to us, so that each new person in ngm would hear the stories of God's amazing grace to us. Every year on 22nd June, we have a fun-filled day for everyone in ngm. All of us, including our families, come and have great fun on the bouncy castles and the inflatable obstacle races we bring into our grounds. We supply food, drinks and ice-cream for everyone and we worship, we tell the stories, and we thank God for all he has done for us. It is a good way of reminding ourselves of the amazing adventure of faith that we have been on and what a wonderful, faithful God we serve.

In the Bible, God encouraged the children of Israel to tell their descendants of the amazing miracles that he has done for them. The reason for this is that God knows we so easily forget. At many points throughout the Bible we see the Israelites forgetting God's faithfulness to them again and again. We often imagine that we would never be like that, but it is so easy to do the same. We all need to be reminded of God's love and faithfulness to us even when we have, at times, lacked faith in him.

As we celebrated God's amazing goodness to us, we were also thinking about the road ahead that God was still asking us to walk on. What were we going to find there? How were we going to find the money that we needed for the next portion of our journey? And yet even before we had time to remind ourselves that God had said at the beginning of the journey, "Do no worry about the finance, just birth it in prayer," we were given a donation of £500,000 for the next phase of the building project from John and Rose Lancaster. What an encouragement those two have been to us. We praise God for their wonderful, generous hearts.

At that point we thought that £500,000 would complete the building that we were going to call Caedmon. However, when we went to our architects and builders, we discovered that we would have to see God provide another £1,500,000 (approximately) to complete our missions and arts complex. We continued to pray and small amounts of money from our supporters came in. Our trustees, Ken and Hazel McGreavy and Richard Collier-Keywood, were incredibly supportive and we valued the prayer, advice and wisdom that they gave us. Together with them, we agreed to start building the complex even though we did not have all the money to complete it. We had felt God say that we should put our faith into action and build as much as we could with the money we had. We split our project into two halves. It was estimated that phase 1 would cost us just over £500,000 and we knew that if we did not have enough for the rest of the building, then we could stop and wait until we had the finance to progress with phase 2. It was so good to know that in our board of trustees we had people of faith and integrity who were with us on the journey; their support meant so much to Ray and myself.

When we visited the local planning department and submitted our plans, we were told categorically that we would not get planning permission to build this building. The chief planner himself decided to oppose it. As always, with any opposition we encountered, we went back to God in prayer. We took our example from Nehemiah who encountered so many problems in the building work that God had called him to do, but each time he encountered a problem he first and foremost went to God in prayer. As he did so, God overcame each problem.

Eventually our planning application came up to the planning committee. The chief planner was given *ten minutes* to tell the councillors why this building should not be given planning permission. Ray was given *two minutes* to explain why he thought it should go ahead. We knew that without

God, the planning permission, which we needed, would not be given. All of us in ngm prayed and fasted and sought God for a miracle. In faith we bought champagne to celebrate afterwards and prayed like crazy that we would not need to keep it in the box. However, Ray came back to tell us that despite the opposition, God had won the day and the permission had been granted. The champagne was opened as we praised God that again he had shown us that when situations seem impossible, he is the God of the impossible!

No matter what you are going through, put your trust in our mighty God. He is able to do abundantly above all that you can ask or even think of (Ephesians 3:20). What seems impossible to us is no problem for him. How we needed to keep that promise in mind when the £500,000 was nearly all gone.

29

THE NGM YEARS – TWO MILLIONAIRES, ONE BILLIONAIRE AND NOT A PENNY!

At this point, in order to complete phase 1 of our building we needed God to provide approximately £120,000. Then once when we had completed phase 1, we would need another £1 million to complete phase 2. Over a period of months, we had been praying for God to supply us with what we needed for phase 1 and bit by bit donations came in, but we still needed approximately £100,000. The builders had given us a deadline but as each deadline approached, they would change the date and we would realise that we had another few weeks to see God answer our prayers. However, eventually the builders told us that a certain date was the last deadline and that they really needed the money by that time.

As we continued to pray there were times when our faith was low and we would despair as to where we could possibly find the money that we needed. I remember one time when the devil came and whispered in my ear, "You are going to have egg all over your face when God does not supply the finance you need." I even felt him remind me of a passage in Luke 14:28-30 which says:

'Suppose one of you wants to build a tower. Won't you first sit down and estimate the cost to see if he has enough money to complete it? For if you lay the foundation and are not able to finish it, everyone who sees it will ridicule you, saying, "This person began to build and wasn't able to finish"' (NIV).

We had a huge sign which had been put up by our builders on display at the gates of our property, advertising that there was going to be a mission and arts pop school (as they called it) built on the premises. The enemy took great delight in telling me that "Everyone in the area will hear what a disaster this will be." Time and time again we had to tell the enemy to get lost and declare that our faith and trust was in our God.

As the deadline crept closer, we got a phone call from two special friends who used to be in Heartbeat with us but who were now living in the States. Ian and Dorry Townend phoned to say that a millionaire friend of theirs would like us to come and visit him to chat about the work of ngm. Dorry told us that it seemed as though he and his wife were really keen on the Caedmon project and they were prepared to fly us over so that we could chat with them. She told us "You never know, this might be the answer to your prayers." As Ray was already going to the States to speak at an event called Worship Together, I decided to meet him over there and together we would go and visit Ian and Dorry and their friends.

On the Sunday evening when they invited us for a meal, we took all our leaflets and information on ngm with us. Although we had a fantastic night with some great people who were very interested in ngm and what our ministry was about, they did not seem interested in the Caedmon project at all. We left that evening wondering why God had brought us all the way to Boise, Idaho.

The next day, Ian and Dorry received a phone call from another couple that they had met just a few weeks previously. When they heard that we were visiting from England, they asked if we would go for a barbecue at their home. As we travelled to their home that evening, we were amazed to discover that this couple were millionaires as well. We immediately thought that perhaps this was why God had brought us to Idaho. However, even though we had an amazing barbecue and we had a brilliant time getting to know these people, not one of our prayers was answered. Although this couple were very interested in what we were doing and asked many questions about the Caedmon project and how much money we needed and by when, we left that night without having received a penny. We couldn't believe it, we had seen two millionaires in two nights and we hadn't been given anything towards our project.

On the Tuesday morning, we were flying to San Francisco to meet a church leader there. When we arrived at the airport, he told us that he had arranged for us to have a meal that night with a man and his wife who Ray had met before but I hadn't. Ray whispered to me in the car, "Nancy, he's a billionaire!" It seemed so unbelievable, but within three days we had met two millionaires and one billionaire! Surely, we would receive an answer to our prayers this time.

When Ray and I were praying before we went out for the meal, we both felt God tell us that he did not want us to talk about the Caedmon project to these people unless they asked us about it. Well, you can guess what I was praying about during the meal! "Lord, please get them to ask us about the Caedmon project" During the meal they asked us all about our work; all about our missions, our teams, our bands and artists and about what Ray and I were doing, but not once throughout that evening did he or his wife ask us about the Caedmon project even though they knew we were in the middle of a building project. The subject did not come up! After the meal was over, they invited us to go to their home for coffee. It was a great evening and we stayed as long as we possibly could to give God time to work, but it was to no avail. The subject of our building work did not feature in our conversation at all.

When we left that evening, tears started flowing down my face. "Lord, what are you doing? You know we need this money by Friday!" I cried. Ray and I were both confused and to be honest, hugely disappointed. We could not understand why God had not provided. We could not believe that God allowed us to meet two millionaires and one billionaire and yet we hadn't received one penny of the money we desperately needed. It was only much later when the whole project was over that we came to recognise that receiving no money from these three sources was in God's plan for us at that time. God was teaching us to keep our eyes on him despite the disappointments. The next morning as I picked up my Bible, I turned to my daily reading. As I mentioned before, since 1979 I have always used a Bible reading planner to read the Bible. That day, as I turned to the chapter I should read, I realised that it was a chapter I knew very well. In fact, I had taught on that very chapter (John 11) many times using the story of Mary, Martha and Lazarus.

I said to the Lord, "Are you telling me, Lord, that just as you did not turn up for the funeral of Lazarus, you are not going to turn up for us on Friday? Are you telling me that on Friday we are going to have to bury the Caedmon project?" Clearly, I heard God reply and say, "Nancy, I will tell you what I told Martha, *if you believe you will see the glory of God*" - John 11:40 (NIV). As Ray and I chatted together and discussed this chapter of the Bible, we knew we were going home with no money. However, we realised that what we had was better than money. We had a word from God.

When we arrived back in Britain on the Friday morning, the first thing we did was to call the ngm leadership team to our home. They were all expecting us to tell them how God had answered our prayers and provided at least £100,000. We explained to them that we did not have the money, but what we did have was a word from God. From there Ray went to a meeting with our project manager and the builders to tell them that we did not have the money to continue, and therefore they would have to stop working on the building. They listened to what Ray was saying and then explained that they had some work on site that would keep them there for another two weeks until the end of the month. They said that they would begin to close the project down, but if we received the money before the end of the month then they would carry on building. Obviously if the builders closed down the project, it would ultimately cost us even more to start it up again.

We called a team meeting where we told everyone in ngm what had happened. As Ray and I drove to that meeting, we had heavy hearts and wondered how the team would react. Our fears were that they would get so discouraged and disappointed when they discovered that God had not provided the money we needed. Our fears, however, were unfounded. When we told them the story of what had happened to us in the States and then asked them to join us in prayer, I was so encouraged by their prayers. I have to say that I have never been in such a faith-filled prayer meeting. Afterwards, as Ray and I drove back home, I turned to him and said, "You know, Ray, I've got the £100,000 – and not only that but I have the £1 million as well." Ray's response was, "I have too." For the first time, both of us received the money in our spirits. We did not know how God was going to bring the finances to us, but we were convinced that somehow, he was going to do it. At last we were experiencing real faith. In Hebrews 11:1 real faith is described like this: *Now faith is being sure of what we hope for, being convinced about things we do not see (EHV).*

As I have said before there is a huge difference between *hoping* that God will do something and having the faith to *know for certain* that God will do it. So many of us hope and then get disappointed when it doesn't happen, but faith is knowing that God has said it and therefore he will do it. We weren't just hoping that somehow we would get the money, we just knew deep within our spirits, with complete assurance in our hearts, that we had the finance needed to finish the project.

A few days later, Ray and I had a phone call from our friends, John and Rose Lancaster, who asked if they could come and see us. God had spoken to them so clearly through the Scriptures and they wanted to share what he had said. As we sat and listened, they told us that through something we had said a few weeks earlier God had begun to speak to them.

A few weeks earlier, John and Rose had given Ray and myself an amazing gift to help support us personally in our work. They were incredibly generous to us and we decided to put some of the gift aside as a pension fund for ourselves for the future. Throughout the years it had not been possible for us to put money aside for our future, there had always been such pressing needs, whether for ourselves, the team or for others we met and so we thought that some of this gift would go to our normal yearly support but a portion of it would go towards a pension. When we were wondering where the £100,000 would come from, we wondered whether we should try and cash in the money we had put aside as a pension pot. Before our visit to the States when John and Rose had visited us, we had asked them that if we felt it was right, whether they would mind us using some of the money they had given us to put it towards our Caedmon project. They replied that the shares they had given us were ours and that we could do what we wanted with them. It was only a two-minute conversation, however what we had said had really stuck in their minds. They had thought to themselves, "If Ray and Nancy are prepared to give out of the little they have, then surely we must go back to God and ask if we should give out of what we have." When they went back to God, he showed them through Scripture that they should again partner with us in the Caedmon project. They had come to tell us that if we were prepared to give our portion, then they would give whatever it took to complete the project. They told us that they knew when we went to the States that we would come back with nothing because they were supposed to give us the money! We decided to give our portion and they honoured their word and gave us everything we needed to finish the project. Praise the Lord for people who listen and respond to God's Word. God had done it – he had raised our Lazarus back to life. What a fantastic God we have!

Our building project came to an end in April 2001. What a celebration we had as we stood in the building with tears in our eyes and remembered God saying all those years previously, "I am going to give you a missions and arts complex." We never ever imagined that God would take us on a journey that would last five years and cost £3 million, and that after we had learned so many lessons about faith, he would provide two buildings that would far surpass all that we had asked for or even imagined (Ephesians 3:20).

Our training courses have been facilitated by our purpose built complex. We had two recording studios, a live room, two producer rooms, an engineer room, a media suite, a dance studio, a performance venue that can house around 120 people plus three separate training rooms that can each accommodate a band and in addition to this we have a large reception area. What a brilliant facility. Every time I walk through our buildings, I cannot help but thank God for his amazing provision to us. I often just stand and look at our miracle and thank God for his faithfulness to us. Who would ever have thought?

30

MY CALLING BEGINS TO WIDEN

It was after Heartbeat finished and before we had built our missions and arts complex that God began to widen my calling. First of all, Ray suggested to me that I write a book about my Spiritual Health Plans. For some years, I had been using plans to help people in Heartbeat/ngm hear from God for themselves. Some of the team used to ask me to pray and fast for them. I went away and prayed, fasted and sought God, whilst they went and watched television! After a while, I thought this is not right, I need to be teaching them how to hear from God for themselves. I suggested that they pray, fast and take a whole day out to seek God's answer but they told me they didn't know how to structure their time. So, I gave them a plan for the time they had set aside for God. It was filled with different creative ways of hearing from God. I gave them relevant passages to read, questions to ask themselves, verses to meditate on, prayer walks to go on, Bible studies to do, verses to memorise and times just to be quiet and listen to God's still small voice. I asked them to write everything down as they did each exercise and gave them rough timings for each task. When they came back to me, they had a written record of what God had said and immense joy in their heart that God had spoken directly to them. All I needed to do was to pray and rejoice with them. Ray felt that these plans could be the basis of a book that would not only help individuals hear from God for themselves, but would also help pastors, counsellors and mentors in their discipling of others. I dismissed Ray's suggestion as ludicrous. How could I ever write a book? My English teacher would die laughing! There was just no way that was ever going to happen.

However, the next time Ray and I met our record company about our albums, Ray suddenly raised the subject of me writing a book. Our record company was also a book publisher and without mentioning this to me before hand, Ray suddenly said, "Nancy has a great idea for a book. Nancy, tell them your idea!" I died inside! I couldn't believe that he had said this, but without batting an eyelid, I told them about my Spiritual Health Plans. They loved the idea and within a short period of time, I left that meeting with a book contract to write at least one book. I thought to myself, "What on earth has Ray done! I can't write a book!" However, when I started to write, I discovered that I had a passion and a love for writing.

My first book was about 60,000 words and I wrote each word by hand. There were no computers in those days! It was called *Developing Spiritual Wholeness* and was published in 1992. In 1995 I wrote my second book called *Nancy Goudie's Spiritual Health Plan* and this one was published by Hodder and Stoughton. I then combined those two books together and called it *Nancy Goudie's Spiritual Health Workout*. All three books were very popular and so with encouragement from many who had bought my books over the years, I updated the latest book and expanded it during 2015. In 2016 I released it as *Nancy Goudie's Spiritual Health Encounters* and many love and enjoy doing the programmes and discovering a deeper relationship with God through them. Through the years I have written 17 books and each one has surprised and encouraged me. Who would ever have thought? Certainly not my English teacher at school. I know if it hadn't been for Ray, I would never have known that the ability to write books was within me. As well as books, God gave me the desire and ability to create several meditation CDs using music and the imagination to take people on a journey that would lead them to know and hear from God. Also, I have created CDs using my voice along with music to declare scripture so that each of us would know and declare the truth of the word of God, after all it's the truth that will set us free.

Secondly, during the Heartbeat days, I had begun to speak publicly during our concerts. If you had known me before I left Scotland, you would have known that I wouldn't even pray publicly, never mind speak. People who know me now will probably find it difficult to imagine this, but you have to remember that I was brought up in a Christian Brethren church where women were not allowed to speak in public. To be honest, at the time I was very happy with this arrangement! Speaking or praying in public was frightening to say the least! However, after God began to change me, God began to give me confidence in him to pray out loud and also to speak a little in Heartbeat. When I was young my mum had sent me to elocution lessons and so I was experienced at speaking in public as long as I was saying poems or portions of Shakespeare. In fact, I have the letters ALCM (Associate of London College of Music) after my name to show that I am qualified to teach public speaking. Throughout the years, I have taught everyone who came on our training courses how to speak in public at a seminar, how to share from a stage to thousands of people and how to speak on radio and TV. I have also done the same for many national and local businessmen. However, firstly I had to learn to put all my training into practice not just in reciting poems and Shakespeare, but in speaking during some of our concerts and also on radio and TV. In the latter Heartbeat years, I began to preach rather than Ray, and then when Heartbeat finished, I began to get asked to do more preaching at churches and events in various parts of the UK. With each opportunity, my confidence grew. I remember God confirming his calling to me once Heartbeat finished. He told me to "Preach, preach, preach, preach, preach!" That word has often been my confidence, especially when some men have questioned my calling because I am a woman! I also received a prophecy from the Lord telling me that when I preach I have two angels with me. At times throughout the years, people have seen those angels as I have spoken. I have never seen them but that prophecy encourages me enormously to know that God is with me and that he sends his ministering angels too. I absolutely love speaking at events, conferences and churches where I can see that, through the words God has given me to speak, lives are challenged and changed. I live to see people transformed by God's love and power. If anyone had told me when I left Scotland that I would be a preacher or that I would have written one book never mind 17 books, I would have thought they were crazy. Who would ever have thought?

31

NANCY GOUDIE'S SPIRITUAL HEALTH WEEKENDS

In 1996, when Ray and I were in the States, God spoke to me and told me he wanted me to start a women's event in the UK. I told the Lord in no uncertain terms that he had the wrong woman! I didn't even like women's events. In those days, women's events were second class and were always held in what I call foostie (a Scottish word meaning stale) old conference centres where you have to make your own bed and wash your own dishes. It always seemed to be second class when you compared it to men's events. I had no desire whatsoever within me to start a women's event. However, the Lord then said to me, "But Nancy, what if you had a clean sheet of paper and you could do whatever you wanted. What would you do?" I thought about it and began to write. Well, I would hold it in a 4 star luxury hotel preferably with good leisure facilities. I would like a swimming pool, a jacuzzi, a sauna and steam room. I would have great teaching and brilliant worship. I would have optional sessions such as aqua aerobics, Pilates, strictly fun dancing or perhaps a gospel choir workshop. I would have a creative, God perfumed prayer room where people could go and pray on their own or with one of the ministry team. I would have pamper treatments where people could get a facial or a massage or a foot or hand treatment for free. I would have a banquet meal and afterwards have 5 star entertainment. I got really excited at what I had written and then the Lord said to me, "Nancy, go and do it" and so I did!

When I came home from the States, I visited a local hotel which was owned at the time by a Scottish firm. I told them I was Scottish and therefore I wanted a great deal. I told them what I wanted to do and they gave me a brilliant deal. I had booked a conference room for 60 people and within two months, without advertising, the place was full. It was after I had decided to go ahead with the very first Spiritual Health Weekend that I discovered that I was pregnant with Aidan. My first thought was, "How am I going to be able to speak several times and be on my feet all the way through the weekend whilst being 8 months pregnant?" My second thought was, "What if my baby comes early?" but then my third thought was, "God has told me to do this, so it will be fine." And it was! The whole weekend was so successful. Every year my Spiritual Health Weekends grew and every year we saw people saved, healed and set free. Eventually, I was attracting around 500 people and so we knew we had to do something to accommodate all the people who wanted to come.

I started to think about doing one up north and without my brother knowing what I was thinking he called me with an idea. He asked if I had ever thought of doing one of my Spiritual Health Weekends in Preston. My brother Jack, who together with his wife Susan, now lead a church in Preston and so they said if I took the step of holding one in Preston, they and their church would partner with me in any way they could. At this point I was using the biggest hotel in Bristol which was owned by the Marriott hotel chain, and so I approached the Marriott hotel in Preston never realising that this partnership would last 14 years. It was a beautiful hotel just off the motorway, and surrounded by stunning gardens. The management and the staff at this hotel were second to none, they were amazing and when we eventually decided to stop doing the weekends at that hotel, we were so sorry to stop working with them. Also, for a few years, I did a Spiritual Health Day in the Marriott hotel in Glasgow, Scotland. I really loved doing the one in Scotland but after three years it came to a natural end. I still have such a heart for my own nation, but only get the joy of speaking in Scotland about once or twice a year now.

I remember the difficulties I had in making the first weekend in Preston happen. My Spiritual Health co-ordinator decided to leave ngm just after I had decided to go ahead with the Preston conference. She was really good at doing her job and immediately my thoughts were, "Lord, how am I going to find someone who is able to do this skilled work?" Not only would the person need to learn the skills, but she would now have two conferences to co-ordinate. I knew I could not do it on my own. During the next few weeks, I asked two people in ngm if they would run the conferences together and both agreed. One of those people was Zoe Wickham. Zoe had started with us as a dancer, but it soon became apparent that she had other skills that we wanted to develop. After a year as a dancer/performer she moved into administration and through the years had gained vast amounts of experience in this area. She then began to work for Ray and myself as our personal assistant. During her early years in ngm, she also gained qualifications to be a fitness coach so that she could teach all our musical artists how to keep fit. In Thornbury we have a huge hill not far from our complex and so as part of their fitness routine, she used to get our teams to run up the hill. It certainly showed who was fit and who wasn't. I have to say just walking up the hill is bad enough! I also wanted Zoe to get her qualifications so that she could do some optional sessions of Pilates, aerobics and aqua aerobics at the Spiritual Health Weekends. These sessions have always been well attended even though they are held early in the morning. After a number of years, Zoe became our right-hand person when we put her into the position of being General Manager of ngm and Inspire. She then went through a course at the Institute of Directors and now has a Certificate in Company Direction.

During the first Preston weekend, Zoe mentioned to me that she would love to be considered to be the weekend co-ordinator. I was absolutely thrilled and felt this was a God-inspired suggestion and thus began a joyous working relationship that has lasted throughout the years. I have to say Zoe has been the best co-ordinator I have ever had because not only is she highly skilled at her job, but she is also faithful and loyal. We became great friends and our friendship is one of the most wonderful and special friendships I have. We get the joy every day of being able to work together as friends as well as colleagues and I think we make a great partnership. She has stood with me through all life's ups and downs. I praise God for her, her husband Tim and their wonderful children, Joseph and Bethany.

I can hardly believe that we have held these special Spiritual Health Weekends for 24 years. The next conference will be in February 2022 when we are going to celebrate 25 years of doing these special and unique weekends. It seems like only yesterday when God told me to go and do them. I have loved every one of them and God has done so much through them. Often some of the ladies who attend will say, "God did so much in me this year and so I thought to myself it can't possibly get any better, but every year it does!" More than ever, I want to see these weekends as a place where we see revival. I have always prayed that what God did with Heartbeat in the 80's, he would do again through the Spiritual Health Weekends. Through the years, we have seen miraculous healings, wonderful salvations and incredible transformation, not only in those who attend but also in their families when they go home.

One lady's children wrote to me many years ago and in the letter, they said, "Thank you for what you did for our mummy. She's a different mummy now and we wanted to say thank you!" That letter brought tears to my eyes.

We have seen in recent years more salvations than ever before. One lady who was into witchcraft became a Christian a few years ago. Her face was shining with Jesus. She couldn't thank me enough for all God had done in her. The following year she came to see me again and with the same shining face told me, "Nancy, I became a Christian last year and I'm still going for God." Another lady saw her partner commit suicide after threatening her with a gun. She hadn't been able to sleep because of the nightmares she was having. She gave her life to the Lord at my weekend and that night she soundly slept for 8-9 hours without any nightmares and she continued to sleep well after the weekend. We have had several people, who have been deeply abused and hurt through being involved in prostitution, give their lives to Jesus at the Spiritual Health Weekends. In 2020, so many ladies gave their lives to Jesus that we gave up counting!

One year a lady, who was a friend of someone in the team, came to the weekend and gave her life to the Lord. We then asked if her teenage son would like to come to our Summer School (a week long ngm event for teenagers who are interested in the arts), he did and he gave his life to Jesus too. Then her younger son came the following year and he too became a Christian. These are only a few of the stories of lives being transformed by finding salvation in Jesus.

We have also seen many miraculous healings. I remember one lady at Bristol got out of her wheelchair and together with the team member who had prayed for her ran around the outside of the building before coming back in to share her good news. Jesus had healed her! At Preston a lady who used a wheelchair and also crutches at times, was prayed for by one of the team and she ran up and down the aisle with great joy to show that she too had been healed. She spoke with me the following year and told me that she was still rejoicing in her healing God. Another lady who could not bend her knees was demonstrating how she could bend up and down with no problem at all. A lady who had a damaged rib and could not raise her hand above her waist asked the Lord if she could raise her hands in worship. After prayer, she was healed and raised her hands to God in worship thanking him for what he had done. Another lady who wanted to dance in worship but had to use a walking frame to walk, came walking and dancing into the room to demonstrate God had answered her prayers!

We have also seen some miraculous situations happen as God has moved during the Spiritual Health Weekends. A lady at Bristol cried out whilst I was preaching and some of the ministry team went to find out what was going on. They prayed for her there and then and also later in the prayer room. She had come through a very difficult time and God released her from a spirit of rejection. After she went back to her room, she changed for the banquet dinner that evening, and her clothes fell off her. She didn't understand what had happened but when she stood on the scales, she noticed that she had miraculously lost a stone in weight! She had to go out to the nearby shops and buy new clothes to wear. Another lady heard Ray give a word of knowledge about someone being in debt and that the Lord wanted to wipe their debts clean. She and her husband had been wanting to adopt a child, but because they were in debt they could not proceed with their application. She prayed and claimed that word of knowledge for their situation. The following morning her husband called to say that they had received a solicitor's letter which said that an unknown relative had left them thousands of pounds in their will. With tears in her eyes she told us that all their debt was immediately wiped out and they were able to proceed with adopting a child.

A lady who had scabs all over her arms came to ask myself and Dorry (who had come across from the USA to help as part of the ministry team) if we would pray with her. She had been very badly abused by her partner who had used her as an ashtray. She had burns and scabs all across both arms.

We prayed and the very next morning she came to show me that all the scabs were gone. Her skin was so silky smooth. In 2020, a group of women at Preston told me that because of the atmosphere of faith in the conference, they took it on themselves to pray for each other and lives were being transformed through their prayers. So exciting!

We also love to see the hotel staff affected by what we do. In Bristol one year some of the women from the conference talked to one of the hotel staff and after testifying of God's goodness and grace, they then led this young man to Jesus. Another girl who works at the Preston hotel is now attending church just because one person spent time talking to her about the Spiritual Health Weekend. Another worker at Preston was asking the team so many questions about their faith and he was seen to be staying in the conference room as much as he could to hear everything that was being said.

I just love what happens at the Spiritual Health Weekends, we always have masses of stories to share afterwards. The whole weekend is full of the Lord whether it's in the worship and teaching sessions, in the pamper sessions or even in the entertainment after the banquet meal. I remember one year that a lady was soundly saved during our performance of Broadway Live. There is no mention of our Christian faith at all in the show, but before and during each performance the team pray and ask God to release his Spirit through them in such a way that it changes and transforms lives. One lady's life was transformed by the love and power of God, not through the preaching of the word, but by the release of the presence of God through the show. Who would ever have thought?

My team and I pray for every person who books into the Spiritual Health Weekends every week so the earlier people book in, the more times we bring their name before the Lord. Also, in addition to this, I personally pray for everyone who books in and I ask God for a specific word for them. I simply put aside time each morning to pray and trust what God gives me. I then type it up and send it to the office where the girls put it on a card and then into an envelope. At the Spiritual Health Weekend, we open their envelope and read the word over them. The results have been incredible.

Many years ago, I got a word for a woman that said, "The Lord wants you to know that you are not small. You are not insignificant. The truth is that you are tall and that is how the Lord sees you. See yourself as the Lord sees you. You are not small, for God has made you 10 foot tall." The team member who was reading this over this woman could not believe her eyes for the woman was very small. She was only 4 foot something and as the word was read over her, she had tears in her eyes. She had always seen herself as small and insignificant, yet here was God saying that in his eyes she was 10 feet tall. The word encouraged her to remember who she was and how the Lord saw her. The Lord encouraged her to see herself as he saw her.

Another lady in 2020 told one of the team that she was not really a banquet type person, she would always just settle for toast. "Toast is fine for me," she said. In her word I told her that the Lord had prepared a banquet for her and she was not to settle for toast any longer. Another lady's word said that she had healing hands and a compassionate heart just like her Father in Heaven and that she was to remember that every day in life. I had wondered when I got this word if the lady was a doctor. It turned out that she was and had always wondered if what she was doing in life was worthwhile, and here was the Lord saying she was just like her Father in Heaven and that she was to remember that in her everyday life. There have been so many women over the years write to tell me what God had said to them through their word.

I remember one year being approached by my friend Louise Harris after she received her individual word. She let me know that she didn't understand it and actually didn't like what God had said. She told me that every year she loved her word from God and had kept every word I had given her. However, she felt that the word I had just given her was not something that she could identify with at all. The word told her that 'even if the worst should happen God would always be with her and that he would never leave her.' Her immediate reaction was that she didn't want the worst to happen and she told me quite clearly what she thought. I explained that I hadn't meant to upset her, but really felt that this was something she needed to hear whether it was for now or for the future. However, I did impress upon her that although I felt that God had spoken to me about this word, I could have got it wrong. She told me later that she put the card into her Bible and forgot about it. Around four years later and completely out of the blue her marriage fell apart and she was up all night crying out to God in complete shock and immense pain. She grabbed a hold of her Bible and out fell the card. She picked it up and read it and realised that God was speaking and this was a word she really needed to hear. The worst had happened and God was reminding her that he was with her and would never leave her. Who would ever have thought?

I find it really funny that in 1996 I told the Lord I didn't like women's events and now I absolutely love them. I also find it funny that at that time I had felt the women's conferences in my experience appeared to be second class compared to the ones I attended with the men (there were only about a handful of women at these conferences in those days). Nowadays, this has all changed for there are so many wonderful women's conferences in the UK but also recently I saw comments on Facebook from men saying, "Why can't we men have a weekend conference like the women have where you get built up and encouraged and told you are amazing!!" It was great to realise that women's conferences are no longer second class!

32

NANCY GOUDIE'S SPIRITUAL HEALTH WEEKEND BURSARY FUND

During 2009 the full effects of a recession were being seen in the UK. My Spiritual Health Weekends were usually full many months before the event actually started, but this year was a little different. The bookings although initially had been good, began to slow down as the year went on. By the autumn, I was concerned. Ray and I went to God in prayer and Ray saw a picture of an iceberg blocking the way of a ship and felt that God was saying that we needed a different ship (a different way) to cut through the ice of recession. We prayed and we sought God and by faith we cut through the ice and as we did, someone felt that generosity was the key. I put out an email and encouraged our mailing list to pray and believe God for their own finances whether they were coming to the weekends or not. The result was that my inbox was flooded with emails. Some were saying that they really wanted to come to the weekends, but couldn't afford it this year and were asking if we could pray for them? Their stories broke my heart as they told us about their dire financial problems. Others wrote to say that as they joined with us in prayer, fasting and seeking God, their faith in God had increased and their circumstances had changed. One lady told us she could not come to the weekend because she had lost her job, but within weeks of praying with us, God had totally changed her situation. She wrote saying, "Nancy, I'm coming. I've booked in." So many women up and down the country were seeking God and seeing God change their circumstances. It was wonderful, but I kept thinking that God wanted to do more.

One day whilst talking to God I was reminded of the word about generosity and also felt that God gave me a word which said, *Go to the highways and the byways and compel them to come in.* As I talked with the Lord it became clear that we should go to some people who were financially poor and also spiritually poor and invite them to come. I sent out another email giving people an update on what was happening and also mentioned that we felt generosity was a key. We contacted a few people that we knew were struggling financially in a big way and had the pleasure of telling them they could come to the weekend for nothing. Each person was astonished and broke down in tears at the generosity they were being shown. We didn't have the money at that point to pay for these ladies, but we felt we should go ahead and do it and then take an offering from among our team. We did that, but it was still not enough to cover all the places we had given away. But then something miraculous happened. Gifts of £10, £30, £40, £170 started to arrive at our office. One lady even sent in £1000 so that others who were struggling financially could attend the weekends for free. The more places we gave away the more money came in. As well as this, some people who were already booked in called us to book their friends in, telling us that God had told them to pay for their place. In the end we received over £3,000 to pay for free places. Over 82 people that year were allowed to come to the weekends because of the generosity of others.

We then began to work with various organisations who work with those who are poor, abused or marginalised, like Christians Against Poverty. We struck up partnerships with those who work with prostitutes and those who are recovering alcoholics so that we could compel them to come in. The results down through the years have just been incredible. Every year we raise over £20,000 from trusts, individuals and from our team to allow those who are hurting to come to the Spiritual Health Weekends for free or at a reduced cost and we are always amazed at what God does. Many are saved, healed, set free and transformed by the love and power of God. One lady wrote to us saying, "I have spent all my life trying to accept that God loves a wretch like me and to feel part of God's Kingdom. ngm opened my mind, my heart and my soul to not just understand God's great grace and love, but to finally accept it for myself; to accept my salvation. I went hoping for God to speak to me personally, to feel that connection that I have been searching for and I am so blown away by the mist clearing in my brain. At every turn, from the first hour of arriving and throughout the next two days, God spoke to me so many times in every session...I am so blessed to have spent a beautiful weekend with God's children and to finally be certain of my place among them." Since the weekend, this lady regularly attends church and has attended Alpha. On Easter Sunday after the weekend, she felt ready to share her story with the congregation at her church. Praise God for his love at work in her life.

Another lady said, "I went to the Spiritual Health Weekend searching for the meaning of life! I found Jesus in a remarkable way whilst I was there. In one of the meetings I heard God's call on my life very clearly...yes, I found Jesus!"

One of the highlights from the Preston weekend in 2016 was to hear of a young lady attending the weekend with special permission from the prison service. This had never happened before and the organisation who brought her to the weekend told us that they were so surprised that the prison authorities had agreed to this. She came straight out of prison to the Spiritual Health Weekend and after the conference was over, she returned to the prison. However, she went back a different person. Her life was transformed during the weekend and her face just glowed with the presence of the Lord. At the weekend, during the worship sessions, she learned a song called Good, Good Father. When she went back into prison, she not only told the other inmates about her incredible weekend, but taught them all to sing this worship song. She told us that she feels completely different inside. God had obviously done something really special with her and she couldn't help but tell everyone she met.

Here are some more comments on the Spiritual Health Weekends – each of these ladies came on a bursary funded place. You can tell each person has been transformed by the love and power of God.

"It was awesome – the experience of a lifetime. I know that God healed me of my depression and restored my appetite. My son noticed there was something different about me when I got back."

"It was spiritually uplifting – the best gift you could have given. My daughter became a Christian at the Spiritual Health Weekend."

"The most amazing weekend! Thank you so much – it was brilliant."

"It was a joy, a pleasure, just what I needed to hear – to be filled with the joy of the Lord."

"Enjoyed the talks and enjoyed Nancy – very warm and understanding, very calm and enjoyable. Have grown in my relationship with God and am eager to continue growing."

The leader who had arranged for these ladies to attend said this:

"It is clear that these weekends leave an indelible impression on almost all of the women who attend them. In the main, these are women who, in their daily lives, face a constant struggle to manage, so the chance to get away from the day-to-day pressures and just spend time together in the presence of the Lord is a true blessing. For many of them, it proves to be a liberating experience, so once again, can I thank all at ngm for providing such a wonderful weekend and for enabling so many of our clients to attend."

In 2020, we raised enough money to allow 135 women to attend. Many of them came from very poor, broken and difficult circumstances. Some of them were prostitutes and many of them gave their lives to the Lord Jesus. We heard recently that when they went back home, these women left their former lives behind and discovered love, truth, acceptance and freedom in the Lord. What a joy to rejoice with the leaders as they saw so many of their clients give their lives to the Lord.

One bursary lady told me that before she came to the weekends, her partner had pulled a gun on her. He pointed it straight at her and she thought her life was over. He had been very controlling, not allowing her to see family or friends and not even giving her access to her own bank account. However, instead of pulling the trigger on her, he turned the gun on himself and committed suicide in front of her. She was absolutely traumatized and hadn't been able to sleep soundly since. She responded in one of the sessions and gave her life to the Lord. That night and since she has slept soundly. What a joy to see God do so much in her life and also in so many of the others who came on a bursary place.

One lady who became a Christian at the Spiritual Health Weekend in 2018 came back in 2019 with her mum and her mum gave her life to the Lord too. In 2020 she came back, this time with her niece and she too became a Christian. A few months after the weekends, the niece called us to say that she had started to pray with her children and God is transforming their whole family. This is so encouraging. What we saw in the Heartbeat days, we are now seeing in the Spiritual Health Weekends. It is just so wonderful.

It's sometimes really hard to raise the finance to allow people to come for free or at a reduced price, but stories like these make all the hard work so worthwhile. We praise God for the trusts, the churches and the individuals who stand with us to believe God for well over £20,000 each year.

33

NANCY GOUDIE'S SPIRITUAL HEALTH WEEKEND IN SPAIN

As the years went on, I received a number of prophetic words from Carl Wills (a prophetic speaker) that my conferences would expand abroad. To be honest I could see no way of how this would happen, but I told the Lord that if he wanted me to do this, then he would need to show me how to do this. It was one of those words that didn't leave me, but sat with me for years. I had invitations to do these weekends in the USA, but despite pursuing these, none ever came to fruition. I left the prophecy in the Lord's hands. It was in 2017 that God gave me an idea of doing a Spiritual Health Weekend with a difference in Europe.

A good friend of mine, Rosemary Conley, author and broadcaster on health and fitness, had done retreats in Austria and so I wondered if we could do something similar with the Spiritual Health Weekends. I called her to learn everything I could about doing a similar type of event. She was full of wisdom having done these types of events for many years. Zoe and I then prayed about where to go and we felt drawn to Spain. We chose a few places in the Costa Del Sol and flew over there to see them. The first hotel we visited was in Malaga, but the more we saw of this hotel the more uneasy we became. The other hotel we visited was one Ray and I had been to for many years. We had stayed in this hotel when Ray was recovering from his burnout and I knew it was a place of peace and rest. When we arrived at this beautiful resort, we knew it was the right place to hold my very first Spiritual Health Weekend in Spain.

It's a five star luxury resort with incredible facilities; three outdoor swimming pools, one indoor swimming pool, fitness room, sauna, several Jacuzzis, a beautiful beach, etc., but the most important thing was that not only were the staff so incredibly helpful, but it was still a place of peace and rest. It was the perfect place to hold the first Spiritual Health Weekend Spain. In January 2018, I released the news of my first weekend abroad knowing we could only take a small number of people and so in May 2018 the first Spiritual Health Weekend in Spain was born. The prophecy had begun to happen. During the weekend we had some main worship and teaching sessions, individual prayer and pamper slots, aerobics on the beach and delicious meals out. There was also plenty of time for people to rest and enjoy the sunshine in such a beautiful location. The individual prayer and pamper slots were so important for everyone and God did so much. During one of our main sessions, one lady burst into tears as God was working deeply in her life. She told us during the session that God had completely set her free from a problem she had carried for 20 years. We saw people set free and some individuals were healed too. Each person who went to this weekend told me that they had been impacted by the love of God and that given the choice, they would love to come back again. Who would ever have thought from the word God gave me that God would do so much! We held another weekend in Spain in 2019 with similar, incredible results and now have plans to do another one in 2021 as well as perhaps do some smaller retreats in the UK too.

On 30th June 2020, I held my first Nancy Goudie's Spiritual Health Breakthrough Session online. The reason for these sessions is contained in the title. We want to see breakthroughs in people's lives as they join us online. We are praying for deep and incredible transformations every time we hold one of these sessions. The sessions are open to men and women of all ages. I'm so excited at all the possibilities for the development of these in the future. The first one was so incredible. We saw around 76 households join us and the feedback was so wonderful. Some people said, "This was just what I needed!" Others told us of breakthroughs as they processed what God had done. Another lady said, "I needed this so much. It was such a blessing. We all need to be reminded of who we are especially at the moment when we are isolated." The team worked hard and each of us were so thrilled at the results. God has done so much and we can't wait for the next one. We all love to see lives transformed by the truth of the word of God.

I would never have imagined that from one instruction from the Lord whilst I spent time with him in America, that so much would be accomplished in so many ways as I heard, obeyed and trusted. Who would ever have thought?

34

THE NGM YEARS – NEW GENERATION MARRIAGES

After we had moved and were settled in Thornbury, the number of people working and training in and through ngm grew hugely. At one point we had 120 people working full time in ngm and had eleven teams working in eight locations. We planted many youth churches in various parts of the UK and sent teams to work in those areas for a number of years. We all met together at various points throughout the year at our complex in Thornbury. I remember looking around our performance venue at one point with the place absolutely packed with ngm people and thinking to myself, "Where did all these people come from?" When we left Scotland in 1980 there were only two of us, when we left British Youth for Christ in 1983 there were only 6 of us. When the Heartbeat chapter closed and we moved our offices from Malmesbury to Bristol in 1993, there were only ten of us! When we began to pray for our own premises in 1996 there were only around 40 of us. After we had moved out of the buildings of Bristol Christian Fellowship, we rented an office in the centre of Thornbury, but there were so many of us that we could not have everyone in the offices at the same time. Once our missions and arts centre was completed in 2001, we began to grow hugely and we could hardly contain the whole team in our performance venue which holds 120 people. We didn't have enough room for everyone to have a seat so most of the team sat on the floor. I looked around the room marvelling at what God had done. As the one seed died, God produced many seeds. Who would ever have thought?

Also, during those years, romances started and many met their lifelong partners in ngm. We had 6 weddings in one year and the following year there were 7 weddings. There was hardly a year that went by without at least one or two weddings. There were so many marriages happening that we joked we should have been called New Generation Marriages rather than New Generation Music/Ministry. A few years ago, Ray and I counted how many marriages there had been where the two people had met because they were both in ngm and off the top of our heads we quickly counted over 40 marriages within minutes. We joked that if we had advertised ourselves as a dating agency, we would have made a fortune! To be honest, Ray and I loved the fact that many people found their wife/husband in ngm. What a blessing!

Another thing that encouraged us was that many discovered lifelong friendships in ngm that have even lasted since people left ngm to do other things. In a world where people find it difficult to have good, loyal and solid friendships, ngm was providing a place where this was a real blessing.

Throughout this time of growth, we continued to make sure prayer was always a priority. Ken McGreavy encouraged Ray and I to have personal intercessors, people who would commit to pray for Ray and myself and our family at least once every week. Over the years, we have built up a number of people who have faithfully prayed. Every month I send each intercessor a confidential list of things to pray for. Many of them have been with us for years and we are so grateful to each of them for their regular prayers for us. They pray behind the scenes but when they get to Heaven, I know they will share in the rewards. I can't stress how important prayer has been in our 40-year journey. One of our intercessors had an interesting way of remembering to pray. She called her cat Nancy and bought her cat a toy mouse which she named Ray, so that she would not forget to pray for us. How clever and funny is that?

35

RAY'S 50TH AND 60TH UNIQUE BIRTHDAY PRESENTS

When my husband reached his 50th birthday in 2001, I was concerned that I might not be able to think of a present that seemed special enough for him. So, I thought I would consult the greatest mind in the universe and ask him what to do. He gave me an idea. The idea was to give Ray a present each month of the year so that rather than making one day special, his whole year would be special. I spent ages thinking through what presents to arrange for him. Some months the presents were big, like a trip to Paris and other months the presents were small like breakfast in bed served by the lovely Nancy. Some presents were trips to see special friends we hadn't been able to see for years like Ian and Carol White in Scotland or dinner with Rob and Liz Marshall, both of whom had been in the Dave Pope band with Ray. I knew Ray would love to see them but because of our busy schedules we hadn't been able to do that. It took ages to put his present together as there was so much to arrange, but I loved it. When everything was organised, I wrote on each card what the present was for that month. When I wrapped his present the night before his birthday, those 12 little cards didn't seem a lot, yet there was so much planning and prayer had gone into each one. I really hoped he would like what I had done.

I still remember presenting the present to him. Normally when any of us in our family have a birthday, we would have quite a number of cards and gifts on our table for them. However, this year, Ray only had a couple of presents to open. Suddenly I was troubled inside. I wondered if I had done the right thing. As I handed him a small package that contained the 12 cards, I said to him, "This is your main present. I really hope you like it." As he looked at it curiously, I was thinking, "Oh maybe I should have given him something else." He opened it up and began to read what he was to receive each month throughout his special year and I could see he was visibly moved. Tears came to his eyes as he told me it was the most special present he had ever received. He could hardly speak. I was so relieved. For years to come Ray would tell people about his 50th birthday present and when people heard they would turn to their wife and say, "Please do this for me!" I can't take any credit for the idea, because it came from the Lord; he planted the thought in my head. Every month Ray received a new birthday present and when the last one was given, he told me he was really sad there were no more to come. He had thoroughly enjoyed being blessed each month. When it came to his 60th birthday, I did it all again, except this time it was the deluxe version – in other words, the presents were even more special. I don't know who enjoyed it the most, Ray or myself. Despite all the hard work in arranging everything, I loved putting all the surprises together and discovered again just how much joy there is in giving! I love it!

36

THE NGM YEARS – REVIVAL IN NGM

During 2003 we had a mighty move of God in ngm. We are still praying for a great awakening to happen in our land but what happened to us in 2003 was the closest thing I have ever seen to revival. Ray and I were getting up in the morning as usual to pray and seek God before starting our work, but the Lord prompted Ray to get up even earlier. The Lord told him he had something to tell him. Ray responded by waking earlier and went to his study with a pen and paper ready to write down what the Lord was going to say. He thought God was going to give him more vision, instead God told him, "You are my beloved son in whom I am well pleased." These precious words wrecked Ray as he fell face down in his study before the Lord. Tears poured down his face as the Lord visited him with his love again and again.

A couple of weeks later we went on holiday to Minorca. I had seen the change in Ray and so I decided to get up before anyone in the apartment was awake and go and sit beside the pool to spend quality time with the Lord. I was at the pool even before the sun had risen properly. The attendants were there cleaning the pool and the chairs, but no one else was outside, everyone was still asleep! Those times were so special. After two hours I went back to the apartment to go with Ray, Daniel, Aidan and a friend who was with us on holiday, for breakfast. I kept telling them day after day that those two hours were just not long enough. Ray and I had fallen headlong in love with the Lord all over again. We just couldn't spend enough time with him. When we came home the hunger in our hearts for the Lord kept us getting up very early every morning. Life had changed in the Goudie household. It wasn't business as usual; we were so desperately hungry for him.

Upon our return to ngm, we shared with the leadership team what the Lord was doing in our lives and how we were crying out for more of him and less of us. God met with us and we all ended up on our knees crying out for God to do something deep in each of our lives. Ray and I then shared with the rest of the ngm team at our church meeting. I will never forget that night. It was incredible. What happened was like scenes from the revivals that we had only read about in books. This is what we had prayed and longed for. After Ray and I spoke that night, we stood to the side to see what God would do. Never in our wildest dreams did we ever think we would see what we saw. We left a microphone at the front and said if anyone wanted to pray or say what God was doing with them then to come and use it. That night and for three years thereafter we saw God move in revival. Streams of people came to the front to say how much they had been impacted by God's love through what we shared. They expressed their love and desire for the Lord. Others came and with tears in their eyes openly confessed and publicly repented of secret sins. People were getting free in an instant from stuff they had struggled with for years. Many were lying flat on their faces before the Lord and the floor of Caedmon was literally wet with puddles from the tears of those repenting. This didn't just happen one night, but it happened night after night. It felt as though the Lord walked into the room and brought his deep and wonderful presence. We all changed hugely. Daniel, who was a teenager at school at that time, after his casual work in a local restaurant, used to run down the road with his mate so that they would not miss the meeting, such was the desire to be there. Here are a couple of extracts from our ngm newsletter in 2003: *Each one of us is spending more and more time in the secret place with Jesus early in the morning and as we do our hunger for him seems to increase like never before. As Ray and I lead the meetings, we often just don't know what to do. We are not in control anymore! God is and often we just watch as he moves deeply in the meetings. Ray and I would often look at each other and say, "What do you think we should do?" and often our answer is, "I don't know!" and then we laugh because we'd realise once more that God is doing something really special. We realise that it is all about him. Our cries of hunger for him are disturbing Heaven and he is coming and bringing his presence.*

We couldn't keep quiet about what was happening. In our conversations with those who did and didn't know the Lord, our love for our God just spilled out. One of our guys was shopping in Tesco next door and got into a conversation with a girl who worked for Tesco. He told her about what was happening at ngm and invited her to come to one of our church meetings. She came and was transformed. She said as she walked through the gate between our property and Tesco that it was like walking into Narnia. The difference between what she knew and what she saw was incredible. As she walked into our premises, the presence of the Lord hit her. She eventually gave up her work and came to be a part of the ngm family.

At the same time, we were working with pupils that were excluded from school because of their behaviour. The education committee asked if we could try and help these young people. We began to befriend them and train them in the arts and suddenly their behaviour changed. The first time one of them walked into our premises, the presence of the Lord opened them up and they began to tell our youth worker things they hadn't told anyone before. Other people, teenagers and adults, when they entered into our Caedmon complex were overwhelmed by the Holy Spirit and began to say to us, "What is this place? It feels like church!" Our building does not look like a church, it's an arts complex, so their comments were obviously relating to the presence of God in the place. Others told us that the place was covered in peace and they just loved coming into our buildings because of the peace they experienced. We just loved what God was doing and we prayed and longed for not just a visitation but a habitation.

I remember one day sitting in my study preparing to speak at a church, when I thought I heard Ray shout from upstairs. I was aware that Ray needed to leave the house shortly as he was taking a session at ngm and so, as I was in the middle of preparing a preach, I ignored him thinking if he really was shouting for me, then he would shout again. He did shout again and so reluctantly I got up from my desk, a little annoyed that he didn't think to come down and see me as he knew I was busy preparing. As I entered our bedroom, I saw Ray lying on the floor obviously having fallen in our small en suite. I ran to him saying, "What's happened? Have you hurt yourself?" Ray assured me that he was fine, but that God had overwhelmed him and he now could not move, he was pinned to the floor. He was completely drunk, not from wine, but instead from the Spirit of God. He couldn't get up! I lay down beside him laughing and said, "Hey this is not fair! It should have been me! I'm the one preparing for a speaking event. It's me who needs the anointing and refreshing of God." We were all so desperate to receive anything God had to give. I had to call ngm and let them know that Ray would be late in arriving for his session as the Lord had filled him so full that he was drunk! It was hilarious!

As we travelled throughout the UK, we discovered so many people had secret sins in their hearts, especially those in leadership. They felt they could not let anyone see the stuff that was keeping them in chains. They were supposed to be free from these secret sins and not the ones who needed to experience freedom. Many didn't feel they could tell anyone what was happening in their lives. Fear of being rejected or exposed meant that these secret sins kept many people in bondage and no matter how hard they tried they could not experience true freedom. The enemy likes to tell us that there is no one as bad as you and that you had better keep your mouth shut, because if they find out how bad you are then you will not be accepted either by them or by God. Instead, the truth is that as we confess our sins to God, he will lead us into freedom. Ray knew this was so true for himself. It was when he confessed to me that he had a pornography problem all those years ago that God began to set him free. It didn't happen in an instant but instead, as he kept himself accountable to me and confessed every fall he had, God totally set him free. There came a day when he did not have any desire to watch a sexy film or read a pornographic magazine ever again. This would never have happened had he not confessed what was going on inside his brain. The enemy wants to keep us in chains, the Lord Jesus wants to release us and bring us into freedom.

As God moved in revival through us, we discovered things that we didn't understand. Some people didn't like the intensity of what was going on and decided not to attend our church meetings. Some of those in leadership found it so difficult that God was highlighting others instead of them. Although God was moving in revival power, we found that it raised issues that were difficult to deal with. We began to read about God moving in the past in a similar way and saw that they too had experienced similar problems. We didn't want to stop what God was doing and so we kept saying, "Lord have your way!" I would never have thought that a deep move of God could ever raise such problems and issues. We were learning every day how to continue to love Jesus and love people despite the issues that were being raised. However, no matter how many problems there were, it was wonderful to be living with a supernatural move of God moving through in ngm.

37

THE NGM YEARS – THE BIRTH OF LUV ESTHER – THE MUSICAL

In the year 2000 we had been in full time ministry for 20 years and so Ray and I went on our first sabbatical. We went for three weeks to a place in the Algarve in Portugal. We took our boys with us and also the girl who was there to help us with Aidan so that we could rest, recover and be revived. As always when on holiday we expected God to speak to us about the future, but especially during this sabbatical, we wanted to know what the future held for us both. Never in a million years did we think that as Ray was reading a book by Tim Rice, that God would suggest that Ray should write a musical. He had never written a musical before. I remember him leaning over to me and saying, "Do you think that God could be calling me to write a musical?" It sounded such a huge vision, but we really didn't have any idea as to how big a vision it was going to be. Tim Rice said that when you write a musical there are three things you need. 1) A good story, 2) A good story and 3) A good story. Ray felt that the story of Esther was not just a good story but an extraordinary one!

The story of Esther is filled with drama, fear, courage and hope. It tells a compelling story which is full of love and beauty, and yet hatred and ugliness is never far away. It's the story of how one seemingly insignificant orphan girl overcame her fear and saved her nation from complete destruction. Who would ever have thought that God would use someone so young and inexperienced to become Queen and make a huge difference at government level? Who would have thought that a book that has no mention of God should even be among the 66 books that make up the Bible? God may not be mentioned by name in the pages of the book of Esther, yet God's presence is felt on every page.

It was a few years later that John and Rose Lancaster took Ray with them to visit some of the poorest places of South Africa. One day he began to pray about the abject poverty and the awful situations he had seen and wondered if ngm could somehow help. He turned to Rose and said, "Do you think that my new musical, luv esther, could carry a heart for the poor and needy? Do you think we could use the vehicle of luv esther to get the message out and make people aware of what is happening here in Africa? Rose immediately replied and said, "Ray, I was just about to say the same thing to you and if you do, then John and I will help to fund it."

John and Rose have been so faithful to us throughout the years. They were the major funders of our two new buildings and here they were again saying they would help us to produce the musical luv esther and see it tour throughout the UK. We have so often been astonished by their amazing generosity. They have been partners with us in the gospel. They have given so many gifts over the years and today they still give to ngm.

They have also blessed Ray, myself and our family. If it wasn't for them, Ray and I would not have been able to afford the home we bought in 1998; they provided the extra we needed to make the jump from our previous home to the one I still live in today. Without their generosity, we would never have experienced a beautiful family holiday in Mauritius. They called us up one day and asked us if we would like to attend John's 60th birthday party. We told them we'd love to, not realising that his birthday party was in Mauritius. He wanted to take us and our family along with their own family to the island of Mauritius for a ten-day holiday in a five-star luxury hotel. If it wasn't for them, we would never have flown in a Learjet. We flew to see John and Rose in their home in Switzerland; we arrived on an Easyjet flight and flew back with John and Rose in their Learjet. When we arrived at Bristol airport, a red carpet was put out on the tarmac by the Bristol airport authorities to welcome Ray and I off the plane. I think they must have thought we were famous! They would have known that was not the case however, when two friends from ngm picked us up in their old car! They had been told by the airport authorities to drive their car on to the tarmac right to the plane, so that we could walk from the plane straight into the car! We have had so many different experiences because of our precious friendship with John and Rose Lancaster. As I said earlier in this book, we knew them when they had very little money and with the little they had they were always generous and now they are multi-millionaires, they are still mega generous. Also, they are such great people – so full of life, love and laughter and Ray and I always found their friendship such a tonic. Throughout the years we have laughed and cried with John and Rose.

The journey to see luv esther become a reality, however, was such a long and hard journey. From the time God released the vision, it took five years before we got the show on the road. At times, it seemed like we would overcome one problem only to experience another. It felt like the enemy did not want this musical to succeed. Ray and I had many sleepless nights because we were concerned about how to overcome the latest problem. Have you ever noticed how in the middle of the night the problems always seem worse? Sometimes the anxiety of the luv esther journey was just too much for us. One night after hours of needless worry, with my brain sore from thinking through the many issues, I said to Jesus, "I give you all my concerns just let me lay my weary head on you." In my imagination I saw myself rest my head on his chest and as I did so, my body relaxed and I fell asleep. When I woke in the morning, all the issues were still there, but I knew God was with us and he would overcome all the problems we had. I could rest on him at any time. It's wonderful to know that God has all the answers when we have none. When you are feeling overwhelmed, use your God given imagination to rest your weary head upon his shoulders and let the Lord give you rest on every side whilst he takes the strain.

Every problem was eventually overcome and after an exciting time of re-hearsals the show was ready to be premiered. Ray had co-written the show with Murray Watts and Ray also asked him if he would direct the show as he absolutely loved working closely with Murray. Ray and Murray became close friends and both had such fun putting this great show together. I wrote a book on the story behind the journey of luv esther and in it told the story of how God took us all deeper into intimacy and revival. We hired the Colston Hall in Bristol and prayed that the 1800 tickets would sell. It was amazing! We sold so many tickets that we had to hire the Colston Hall for a second evening in order to accommodate everyone who wanted to attend. On the first evening we had over 100 specially invited guests. Some of these were friends and families of the cast, others were national Christian leaders.

However, on the day of the premiere, we were experiencing problems again and again. The crew had started early in the morning to set up, but it wasn't long before the problems got so bad that Ray thought that he may have to cancel the show. The show worked together with a combination of music, singing, acting and dancing as well as back projection and video. It all had to work together to portray the full beauty of the show. Eventually every issue was sorted and the show was ready to begin. When the audience gathered, we all sat down to see this great show. Everything was going really well, when suddenly the house lights came on. Just as Murray and Ray were going to find out what was happening, the lights went off. We concluded that someone from the venue had turned on the house lights by mistake. But when a few minutes later, the house lights came on again, we knew there was a problem. This happened several times. We praise God that the cast showed their professionalism and continued with the show despite the lighting issues. We discovered afterwards that it was the fault of one of our hired technicians. He had, by mistake, programmed the house lights into our system so that they came on and off many times. Ray and Murray were furious! It could have destroyed the whole show. This was a hugely stressful day for Ray as producer.

The audience, however, absolutely loved the show and the response and comments coming back from all who attended were superb, apart from two people who were very vocal in telling Ray that he was an abomination to the Lord. They took offence at some of the outfits that the dancers wore. A few weeks later, Ray received a letter from someone who didn't give their name but who told him, "You are the runt of all runts and as for that Murray Watts he is just as bad!" Ray immediately put the letter in the bin where it belonged. Someone who doesn't sign a letter that contains such a horrible message shows something of their own character. From the Colston Hall, Bristol, the show toured various theatres in the UK to many sold out audiences and raised over £100,000 for the poor and hurting people of Africa! Ray had produced a brilliant musical which was the first of its kind. Who would ever have thought?

38

THE NGM YEARS – THORNBURY MISSION: TEN/12

It was around this time that the Lord began to prompt us about what was happening in our own town of Thornbury on a Friday and Saturday night. We live in a lovely market town near Bristol. It is not as beautiful as Malmesbury, but it has been a lovely place to live for the last 28 years. However, each weekend not many people would dare venture into the town on a Friday or Saturday night because of the level of crime. The drug squad and the police were often in Thornbury. The shop windows on the high street were often smashed by drunk young people coming out of the pubs. Ray and I wondered if we at ngm could help in some way. When we explained to our leadership team what we wanted to do, one of the leaders in particular was very vocal against it. I could see he was full of fear. We prayed together and felt we should, despite the fear, try and bring the presence of God into our town centre every Friday night and so we launched an outreach called Ten/12. The idea was to try and befriend those coming out of the pubs and bring them along to a café style event. We asked the Methodist Church if we could use their hall as our base, whilst our teams went out into the streets. We brought people to the church hall where we held the café style event. Some of our artists performed at various points throughout the night. We gave out free hot chocolates, coffees, donuts and cookies and invited the young people to sit and eat at the tables we had brought from our complex. Our teams chatted with the young people and got to know them first before sharing with them about our faith in God. We also had a prayer room where we could take some of them when they asked for prayer or wanted to become a Christian. Although our intention was to hold the event from 10pm – 12midnight, hence the name, we often didn't finish until 1 or 2am.

At times, some of our team would have to go with people in an ambulance to the hospital. Many of them needed help with alcohol or drug abuse. We funded the whole event ourselves with a little help from some of our supporters. This event became the highlight of our week as we saw so much happen. We sent some of our teams to the local Mundy playing fields where a lot of drugs were sold and taken and befriended those who were there. We would invite them to the café and many came. After a number of years of doing this we began to see a difference in the town we were living in. Every Friday night we would clean up the sick that had been splattered around the toilets in the church hall.

At one point the church told us we could no longer use their building as they discovered someone had been sick in it. We were gutted. Ten/12 was seeing so many lives transformed and the church which is situated in the middle of the town centre was obviously the perfect place to have our base. We knew that had John Wesley been alive, he would have loved what we were doing in reaching those who would never be reached by the established church services. Ray and I were thrilled when the Methodist leadership called us to say they had changed their minds and we could start using their building again. Praise God for people who had vision and who heard from God.

We did Ten/12 for years until it became obvious that the whole atmosphere in the town had changed. In fact the Police, who had at times given finance towards our event, thanked us personally for all we had done and told us our job was done.

39

THE NGM YEARS – BURNOUT: "MY BODY IS SHUTTING DOWN!"

It was during the latter part of our work with 10/12 that Ray began to get ill. I noticed in 2005 that there were little signs that Ray seemed to have less grace and energy to cope with the pressures of everyday life. Ray and I had always lived with pressures but throughout the years we had carried them lightly. I remember my mum asking me how I coped with all the pressure of having 120 people working with us, with all the problems that could cause, and I told her that because we carried it lightly, we didn't feel the pressure too much, but all this was about to change. Throughout the latter part of 2005, I could see that life was hard for Ray and the pressure seemed to be getting to him. He had been showing signs of irritability which for him was unusual.

One night when we had a couple coming for dinner, Ray suddenly said I should cancel them as he didn't think he could cope. As we didn't know this couple very well and because I thought they would be on their way already, I explained to Ray that I didn't think we could do that. After a few minutes, our simple discussion turned into an argument. Suddenly and without warning, Ray exploded in frustration and then for several minutes acted as though he was having a complete mental breakdown. As you can imagine I was shocked and frightened. What was going on? What I didn't realise at the time was that this was the beginning of two years of what felt like hell on earth for us and our family.

At the end of 2005 it was obvious that Ray was so tired and weary. Occasionally he would tell me he could not attend another meeting or deal with another problem, but then would just get on and do it. Ray was due to speak at the last ngm meeting before we took our usual two weeks off at Christmas. Some of the leaders felt it should be a light hearted meeting and others felt that Ray was carrying something so deep that we needed to impart it before Christmas. Ray felt a nudge from the Lord to make it light hearted and preach his message in January, but because of pressure from others and with him not being sure of what to do, he was persuaded to preach the message anyhow. So instead of Ray coming away feeling God had done something wonderful, he came away feeling completely drained and realised that he should have listened to the gentle nudge from God. As soon as our church meeting was over, we travelled by train to London to meet with our Trustees. After this meeting, Ray and I went to our hotel to sleep and he said something I had never heard him say before. He said that he felt that his body was completely shutting down. This was a phrase that I was to hear several times in the next few weeks.

Christmas as usual was spent in Scotland seeing our elderly parents so it was difficult for Ray to relax and recharge his batteries. He was still not feeling right and was continuing to experience bad acid reflux. When Christmas was over, we had our annual ngm conference where again God gave Ray extra strength to cope. We had an amazing conference where God did so much, but in my heart, I knew something was not right.

A few days after the conference we again experienced a few intense days of meetings with quite a number of issues. That night Ray came home collapsed into bed and didn't get out of it for weeks. He was diagnosed as having a very bad chest infection as well as acid reflux which was burning his insides. However, as time went on, we began to realise that he was also experiencing burnout. We had no idea what burnout was, but in the weeks and months to come we would come to realise that it was the closest thing to having a nervous breakdown. Little did I know that Ray would not be in ngm for the next nine months and that it would take a whole two years to see him fully recover. I have written about Ray's journey into burnout, depression and ill health in a book called *Treasures of Darkness*. It's a very naked and honest autobiographical account about the struggles we went through during those next two years. It was Ray who encouraged me to write this book and when I started, he told me, "Nancy, tell it all, warts and all!" We wanted this book to be a book that showed people that sometimes leaders don't have all the answers, but that God does!

Sometimes we go through things that we don't understand but it's often in those times that we discover how strong our God is and how much we need to trust in him. Many leaders cover up their tough times and don't let people see or know what they are going through, but people can learn so much from watching how we deal with the hard things in life. Ray wanted people to know how hard it had been and what we had learned through it. Many people, including many leaders, told me that they have found this book to be so helpful in their own journey through pain, sorrow, depression and also being misunderstood. When all else fails, God does not fail. He stood with us even in the darkest times and we discovered a friend who is faithful and who never leaves us nor forsakes us.

Ray went through such a tough time, but some in ngm did not understand what was happening to him. One particular person could not understand why Ray could not see him to mentor and pray for him. Ray was not able to get out of his bed, never mind spend time mentoring and praying for someone else. Instead it was him who needed prayer and understanding, but because Ray had always been there for this guy, he didn't understand.

We had always been very pleased with our mentoring programme in ngm. When someone joined ngm we would always make sure that they had a discipler/mentor who they could go to if they needed prayer and counsel. It worked really well and many people loved the love, care, advice and prayer support they received. However, we began to see that perhaps, for some people, it had fostered a dependence on the mentor that was never meant to be there. We all benefit from being mentored and discipled, but we need to be able to find strength, comfort and help from the Holy Spirit. Unfortunately for that one person, when Ray was removed because of ill health, he couldn't cope.

Many in ngm sent words of encouragement and cards to say they were praying for us but two couples stood out in their love for us during that time.

Tim and Zoe Wickham, rather than demanding time from us, gave us a gift of love every month. Some months it was a bottle of Champagne or a box of chocolates. At other times it was everything we needed for a night in – a DVD, some candles and some snacks. It really didn't matter what it was; it was what it said that meant so much to us. To us it said, "We're with you. We are for you. We love you and no matter how hard this journey gets we will continue to show you love and care. We are in this with you until the end." The other couple were Neil and Tanya Wilson. Neil was so pastoral and caring whilst Tanya kept us laughing with her infectious personality and incredible sense of fun when we had nothing to laugh about. We will never forget their kindness and also the many other faithful friends who prayed and helped in any way they could. When someone goes through tough times, don't hurt them even more by giving them your wisdom about the situation, especially if you have never gone through it yourself. Instead, show your love like Tim and Zoe did by making sure they know you are there for them.

When people go through depression, the Christian church can make it worse by saying that Christians shouldn't suffer from depression and if they do then they must have done something wrong. To be honest that thought was in our minds too. What did we do wrong? Why were we experiencing this? We went through our lives and confessed to God anything and everything we had done. We asked him to forgive us for anything we had done wrong but eventually the Lord told us, "You haven't done anything wrong, just trust me. I am in the boat with you!" God wasn't saying we were perfect, we do make mistakes and I know we have made many throughout our lives, but Jesus was saying that this storm hasn't come on you because you have done something wrong, just trust me in the storm. Ray and I learned so much in this storm. I really wish we hadn't needed to go through it, but life is like that at times. As I said before, Jesus told us, *"In this world you will have trouble, but take heart! I have overcome the world"* (NIV). As we went through this horrible time, God was indeed with us and he brought us through this horrendous storm much wiser people because of it.

It was comforting to know from scripture that others had gone through similar things yet had not lost their faith, but they had come through it stronger in the end. David shows us his thoughts and feelings in many of the Psalms. Psalm 119:28 says, *my soul is weary from sorrow; strengthen me according to your word* (NIV). Psalm 116:3 says, *the cords of death entangled me, the an-*

guish of the grave came over me; I was overcome by distress and sorrow (NIV). Psalm 13:1-6 says, *How long, Lord? Will you forget me forever? How long will you hide your face from me? How long must I wrestle with my thoughts and day after day have sorrow in my heart? How long will my enemy triumph over me? Look on me and answer, O Lord my God. Give light to my eyes, or I will sleep in death, and my enemy will say, "I have overcome him" and my foes will rejoice when I fall. But I trust in your unfailing love, my heart rejoices in your salvation. I will sing the Lord's praise, for he has been good to me (NIV).*

Then Jeremiah says in chapter 15:18, *Why is my pain unending and my wound grievous and incurable? You are to me like a deceptive brook, like a spring that fails (NIV).*

Habakkuk says in chapter 1:2-3, *How long Lord must I call for help, but you do not listen? Or cry out to you, "Violence" but you do not save? Why do you make me look at injustice? Why do you tolerate wrongdoing?* (NIV) Yet in chapter 3:17-18 he declares, *though the fig tree does not bud and there are no grapes on the vines, though the olive crop fails and the fields produce no food, though there are no sheep in the pen and no cattle in the stalls, yet I will rejoice in the Lord, I will be joyful in God my Saviour (NIV).*

There were so many times when we prayed, "Lord take this storm away; remove it from us," but the heavens were silent. Ray had prayed many times especially during the first few months of being ill, "Lord I commit my sleeping time to you. Help me to have good peaceful dreams," but then in the night he would have nightmares where he would be chased by someone who wanted to kill him. At other times he cried out to God to send an encouraging word. He pleaded, "Lord, please get someone to text or email me a word that will let me know that you love me." Nothing happened! He asked God for a hug and got silence. It's when you do not understand why your simple prayers are not being answered that you then have a dilemma. Does God not exist? If he does exist, why does he not answer? Does God not love me? If he does, then why does it seem as though he doesn't?

I love the story of Shadrach, Meshach and Abednego who stated so clearly to the king, "*The God we worship can save us from you and your flaming furnace. But even if he doesn't, we still won't worship your gods and the gold statue you have set up."* Daniel 3:17-18 (CEV). They decided that even if God did not answer their prayers, they were willing to die rather than disobey God's word. They put their faith in God and God took them far beyond their time frame. I'm sure they were praying that God would answer their prayers before they had to go into the furnace, but God didn't. Instead he stood with them in the fire. They were saved, but they were saved *in* the fiery furnace. When they came out of the fire, there was not a hair of their head singed; their robes were not scorched and there was no smell of fire on them. Hallelujah!

I remember Ray preaching on this story years later and saying that when we come through a tough time, it is important that we too have no smell of the fire on us. It's important that we don't come out of our fire with the smell of bitterness on us. It's important that we don't have our hearts scorched with unforgiveness of any kind or lack of trust in God in our spirits. Ray and I wanted to come out of our storm with the smell of Jesus on us and not the smell of cynicism, disappointment or any kind of unforgiving heart towards others.

God stood with Shadrach, Meshach and Abednego in the fiery furnace; right in the middle of the worst experience they had ever had in their lives and he will do the same for you and for me. He promises no matter what the circumstances, that he will never leave us nor forsake us. Jesus never said that life would be easy, but he did promise that through each situation of life he would be with us. The great thing about God is that he never breaks his promise. Psalm 145:13b says, *The Lord is trustworthy in all he promises and faithful in all he does (NIV).*

Ray recovered from his chest infection after several weeks; the acid reflux took several months, but his burnout took a lot longer. During that time, we received many words from God through our intercessors which said that we should go away on a three-month sabbatical. Around the same time, we also received a word from one person who was praying for us saying perhaps Ray should think about working voluntarily for another organisation or perhaps even work at our local supermarket in a job that would not give him any responsibilities. She also said we needed to ask God if it was time for us to leave ngm. We tested each word we received and submitted them to our trustees who are godly men and women. They all felt that it was right for us to go on a three-month sabbatical, preferably to a country that was blessed with sunshine and that we should not make any decisions about our future until we had come back. We didn't know how we were going to afford to go away for three months, but God provided every penny we needed mostly through our intercessors, our financial supporters and those who believed in us. We will always be so grateful to the many who gave so sacrificially to us at that time. When the person who had suggested to us that perhaps Ray should work in Tesco heard what we and the trustees had decided, she wrote a month or so later to say that she was disappointed that we had not received her words with the openness she would have expected and therefore she no longer wished to pray for us and was stopping her regular financial support to Ray and myself. Again, just at the time when we needed understanding and help, it was withdrawn. Ray didn't need a job in a supermarket or anywhere else, he was ill and what he needed was encouragement and healing.

I realise that it is easy to make judgements when you are standing and looking from afar. I have done this myself at times. When I was standing on a beach in Majorca many years earlier, in the days of our band Heartbeat, God spoke so clearly to me about this issue. One morning when I was walking and talking to God, the Lord said to me, "Nancy what do you see?" I said, "Lord I see a beautiful beach with amazing golden sand and a calm blue sea. I see the cliff rising steeply on the far end of the beach and Lord, it is wonderful - what a view!" The Lord then instructed me to walk to the other side of the beach and when I had done so he asked me to tell him what I saw. I said, "Lord the view is still amazing! However, this time, I don't see the cliffs, (as they were behind me) but what I see as well as the beautiful sand and sea are many yachts and boats tied up at the side of the bay. The view is different, Lord, but it is still amazing." The Lord then asked me to walk to the centre of the beach and sit facing the sea. When I had done that, he again asked me what I saw. I said, "Lord from here I see both sides of the beach. I see the cliffs and I see the yachts; however, I don't see as much of the golden sand as I saw before because a lot of it is behind me, but Lord the view is still so wonderful." Then the Lord spoke to me and said, "Nancy, I want you to remember this: Truth is multi- faceted. It depends which side of the beach you are on as to how you see things. You might view things differently to someone else, but it is the same beach; it is the same truth. You will also hear people saying, "I can see it from both sides," but actually they don't, for even if you sit in the middle and you see both sides, you will not see the exact same view." The Lord went on to say, "only if you are standing in the same position with the same circumstances will you understand what others are going through."

When God said all this to me, I was in Heartbeat. I had always stood up for the truth and could not understand how people could perceive a truth differently to me. When God spoke these words, I knew he was asking me to apologise to the others in Heartbeat for being so dogmatic that my view of the truth was correct. When I came home, I sat with the others in the band and with tears in my eyes apologised for the times when I hadn't loved them enough by thinking my way of looking at situations was the only correct way. It's important to remember that we all perceive the truth through our own circumstances.

Even though Ray had been so ill with burnout, depression and ill health during 2005-2007 he never stopped spending time with Jesus. He loved the Lord and so he spent time alone with him. We also continued to bring the Lord into everything that happened in our lives. Our deep relationship with the Lord is the reason that Ray and I came out of this storm sane. If you want to read the whole story of these two years then you can do so by reading the book: *Treasures of Darkness.*

It was during those years that Daniel left school and went to BIMM (Brighton Institute of Modern Music) as a drummer. I remember the day he left our house to drive to Brighton to stay in the home of some friends of ours. From there he would travel each day to go to college. I cried as Daniel left. I was one of those mums who didn't cry when he first started school, but I couldn't help crying when he left to go to college. He was leaving to start a new phase of his life, but never in my wildest dreams did I imagine that the Lord would give him a clear calling to come back to work in ngm. In fact, when he suggested that this was where the Lord was calling him, Ray and I both quizzed him to make sure he was not just choosing the easy option. However, we discovered that he had a clear call of God whilst playing keys for worship leader, Paul Oakley, at a festival. One day whilst playing in the band, one of the speakers prophesied over him that his music would go into the mainstream and affect a generation of young people. He gave him some very clear guidelines to follow and prophesied that God was calling him. From there he went as a delegate to Soul Survivor and two different people picked him out again and prophesied the same words over him.

After his time was over at Brighton, he came back home and began to work for ngm as a drummer in a band called Thundershock. Many a time, Ray and I went into the clubs in Bristol to support the band at some of their early gigs. Daniel was in ngm for 5 years and gained a lot of experience in our studios before he and another guy who had come through ngm plus someone they met in the music scene in Bristol felt a call to go to Los Angeles to work from there. They didn't know anyone in LA. It was a real step of faith, but God honoured that step and I am so proud of what they have achieved. Daniel is fulfilling the vision of ngm about reaching a new generation and being salt and light in the mainstream over in the States. Many years later, Aidan too felt a call to ngm, but that comes later in the story.

40

THE NGM YEARS – EXPANSION AND PRUNING

At one point during the next number of years, when we were speaking to God about our training, he told us to go to the other side. We didn't totally understand what he was saying, but we began to pray this word through with our leadership team. We felt the Lord was saying that we should train people who weren't necessarily Christians, but we couldn't see how this would work. How could we put people who did not share our faith through our discipleship course? Did God want us to do something that we had never done before? Was there a different way of training? We asked loads of questions and prayed for a very long time, but we couldn't see how it would work. So, we said to the Lord, "Lord we don't know what to do, but you do, so if this is you, then you do it."

During these years, we started another charity and called it The Inspire Arts Trust. This charity was set up so that we could work more freely in the mainstream. We would run courses in the arts called Pop School during the summer and invite local people to be trained in the arts. We wanted to bless and encourage those in the arts locally whether they were Christians or not. We saw about 20 – 30 people attend Pop School.

One of our Trustees, Richard Collier-Keywood, mentioned a weekly arts course which was going on in his area and suggested that perhaps we could consider doing something similar through The Inspire Arts Trust. As we continued to pray, we felt we should start a course called Bristol Academy of Live Performing Arts (BALPA). Over the years this grew massively. Most of these young people are not Christians, and it's wonderful to see the difference in them after they attend our courses. We run courses in dance, vocals, musical theatre, drums and keys.

Every year, we have two events where we invite the families of those attending the courses to come and see what they have learned. We have to put on three shows to be able to accommodate all the people who want to come. The parents' comments are so encouraging. Many tell us that their child has grown in confidence hugely because of all the encouragement they receive from their tutors (most of whom have gone through training at ngm). Some pupils have special needs and their parents are amazed and thrilled that their child really enjoys coming to BALPA as they have tried other arts courses, but their child had ended up not wanting to go back. We want every single life to be transformed by the love and encouragement given. We love hearing about the difference in each child as we pour our love into them. We cannot preach with our words, but we can preach with our actions, especially our love and encouragement.

It was during these years that the Lord told Ray that he was going to prune ngm. And prune us he did! The number of Christians coming to us for training began to diminish slowly over the next ten years. Churches were beginning to do their own arts training and therefore there was not the same support from churches. They obviously were encouraging their people to do the course in their own church. As I previously said, we had around 120 people working with us before our numbers began to dwindle.

Ray and I had a small leadership team of six and a wider leadership team of 20. When Ray and I fully returned in 2007 after Ray's burnout, several of our leaders began to leave. Most of them left through the front door so to speak, but two left through the back door! In other words, many left in the right way, being called by God to other opportunities, but a couple left in the wrong way causing pain and difficulties in their relationships with us/ngm. Some people left to work with the church and others to work in the mainstream. Even though we knew it was right that they moved on, it didn't mean that we didn't miss them as friends and colleagues. Some of these people had been with us for over 15 years. We had always wanted a 'Billy Graham type' leadership team who would love each other and grow old together. Our dream of this happening seemed to be ruins. However, we kept reminding ourselves that when a vine is pruned, it is always pruned for greater fruit. Our romantic dreams might be in tatters, but God's dream for us was not!

Over the years our Christian training gradually diminished to virtually single figures but at the same time BALPA increased and now we have around 160 young people coming into our premises every week

It was only in 2017 that I realised that God had answered our prayers. We didn't know how to change our training around. We didn't know how to train those who weren't Christians, but God had done it. Our ngm training course has now finished, but BALPA is still flourishing. When we didn't understand what God was saying, we didn't close the door on God's promptings, instead we gave him permission to do what he wanted to do and we didn't fight against his will. Sometimes, we can only see in retrospect what God is doing behind the scenes. One of the things I have learned through the years is that you can trust God even though you don't understand what is going on.

A friend who visited us during that time told us that after he had pruned his garden he looked around and realised that he had pruned it so severely that he was concerned nothing would ever grow again. It looked so bare, however, within a year the fruit he got from the garden was huge, much more than he had ever seen before. God had told us again and again that greater fruit was on its way. Back in the 80's we saw many, many people saved and healed through the work of Heartbeat/ngm and just before this pruning started, God spoke and said that we were going to see much more fruit than we had ever seen before. God told us that what we had seen in the 1980's would be just a small reflection of what he was going to do. When we were pruned, at times we wondered whether anything would live, but as time went on, we began to see not only BALPA expand hugely, but also other areas in ngm were expanding too, like my Spiritual Health Weekends. God was moving in great power in various different ways. It was just so encouraging.

ngm has changed so much since the move of God in 2003, not just in numbers but in our hearts. We had always been a passionate people for God, but something in our hearts was changed forever. We could no longer settle for anything less than his presence. We often said at the beginning that if God ever left us, if his presence did not keep coming as it did at first, then we could not go back to where we'd been spiritually, good as it was! We had tasted something of the depths of God and we could not settle for anything less.

In the following years we had several separate visits from preachers (David Reidy from Hillsong; Rolland Baker and his team from Iris Ministries, Barry Woodward from The Proclaim Trust and Carl Wills from Pioneer) and each of them said that they sensed God was doing something special at ngm. They told us, "You have to know we travel to many different places and what you have here is very special. God's presence is here. We are not seeing this kind of hunger for God everywhere. God is obviously preparing you at ngm for something amazing." The truth was that we were and still are so hungry for God; our hearts yearn for more of him. We want him more than anything else. We will not settle for being comfortable, our hunger for the deeper things of the Spirit means that we keep pushing on into the deep. We have so much further to go, but we have determined to go as far as he will take us.

Barry Woodward wrote to us and said while he was contemplating the atmosphere of ngm, God took him to a scripture in Genesis 1:2 where it mentions the Spirit of God brooding over the waters. He then went on to say, "This is what I sensed, there is a 'brooding' of God's Spirit at ngm." Wow, how exciting! The word for brooding in my Bible is hovering. This reminded me of a story I heard that Duncan Campbell told about revival in the Hebrides. After a particularly dry meeting, an elder in the church turned to Duncan Campbell, the evangelist and said, "Don't worry, Mr Campbell, God's Spirit is hovering here and is about to break out at any minute." At that moment, God's Spirit fell on those walking home from the meeting and they fell flat on their faces before God and cried out for the Spirit of the living God. At the same time God's Spirit visited many homes on the island and many people started to weep and cry out for God. They started to congregate at the local churches and that night and afterwards many gave their lives to Jesus. This was a spontaneous move of the Spirit of God and how we long for God to come and do it again!

Another area that grew so much during those years was what we were doing in the mainstream. Ray began to expand his vision for his musicals, more of that story to come, and our artists began to step out of ngm and trust God for work in the mainstream industries. Our vision has always been to see lives transformed in the mainstream as well as the church and so our training had always been geared towards both those areas. It was wonderful to release many of our artists to fulfil their greatest potential. We are proud of every one of them who have truly been salt and light as dancers, musicians, singers, performers, speakers and management personnel in the media world, in the music industry, in theatre land, in clubland and as youth workers and worship leaders in the church. However, there were others who, when they left ngm, kind of lost their way which really saddened Ray and I. It was obvious that their relationship with the Lord was not secure enough to be able to succeed without having a strong community of Christians beside them. At the end of the day, it's our own relationship with the Lord that is most important. If we are relying solely on others to feed us, rather than being fed by the word of God and if you only meet with friends who love Jesus and never meet with the Lord and gaze into his eyes for yourself, then when all else is stripped away, what will remain? We all need a personal relationship with the Lord in order to grow strong and secure in him. We can only do that by sitting at his table and hungering after all he wants to give us. I so love the Lord, he is my everything. I fell in love with him when I was six years of age, but as every day has gone on, I have grown more and more in love with him. I could not have lived my life without him; all I have seen is because he has been so faithful and so incredibly wonderful to me. He took two fresh-faced young people from Scotland with hardly any experience of the work we were being prepared for and did so much through us. Who would ever have thought that God would use us in the way he did? Keep reading though, for I have so much more to tell you of the faithfulness and love of God. The truth is that if he can do this with Ray and myself, he can also do it with you!

41

THE NGM YEARS – SHOCKING NEWS

One morning in December 2010 whilst Ray and I were talking, my telephone rang and on the line was our good friend Karen Collier-Keywood. She called to give Ray and I the shocking news that our precious friend, Ken McGreavy, had died. He had a fatal heart attack that morning as he sat in his chair. We couldn't take it in. It was totally unexpected and I know it was a huge shock to Hazel, his wife, and to their precious family. Ken was only 65. It took a while before Ray and I could really believe it. We made plans to go to the funeral to stand with Hazel and her family in their incredible loss.

We went to London the night before the funeral and our friend and Trustee, Richard Collier-Keywood, said he would take us in his car to the funeral. However, Ray never made the funeral. Just before we were due to leave the hotel, Ray received a phone call to tell him that his mum was not well and wasn't expected to live. Ray quickly made plans to fly to Scotland to see if he could get there in time to say goodbye to his dear mum. Ray got the next available flight to Glasgow and from there travelled to Ayr, but unfortunately, she passed away about twenty minutes before he arrived.

What a day! Our hearts were so heavy with emotion. We had lost two people who were so special in our lives within a short period of time. We knew we'd see both of them again one day, but we also knew that we would miss them greatly. I went to Ken's funeral where we were all able to lay hands on his coffin and spend some time praying. Karen prayed for me that I would receive a double portion of what Ken had. I eagerly opened my heart to receive that! He was a remarkable man, a great teacher, an incredible man of God and a very special friend. After the funeral, we went to his celebration in the centre of London. It was special being able to celebrate Ken's life and thank God for the way he had invested so much in Ray, myself and the ministry God had given us. It was a day filled with celebration, grief and many tears.

At the end of the celebration, I had to quickly leave to try and get to Paddington station in time to get the train home. It was only when I got outside that I realised that the weather had taken a turn for the worse and all the trains had been cancelled because of snow. I didn't know what to do. Aidan called me saying he wasn't well and was very upset on the phone. I knew that I needed to get home, but didn't know how I was going to do that. I called Ray and he told me, "Nancy you need to get home, so see if you can get a taxi to take you to Bristol." I said, "Ray it will cost a small fortune." He said, "Don't worry about what it costs, just get home." It was difficult even getting a taxi, but I eventually managed to arrange for a black cab to take me. I was sitting waiting in the Hilton Hotel, which is situated at Paddington, for the cab to arrive when I saw someone I knew. One of the guys who used to be in ngm, Tom Fowler, walked through the front door of the hotel. He saw me and came over to speak with me. He had been at Ken's celebration and was going home. I asked him if he was going to try and get a train, because as far as I knew all the trains were cancelled. I told him that I had a taxi arranged to take me to Bristol and asked him if he want to share it with me. I wasn't keen on travelling alone in a taxi for two and a half hours and was so glad of the company. Tom told me it was a brilliant answer to prayer for him. He had already gone through the Hilton Hotel on his way to Paddington station and discovered that the trains were all cancelled. He didn't have any money and didn't know what to do, but the Lord told him to walk through the hotel again and that's when he met me. The taxi arrived and somehow got through the snow and managed to take us both home safely. What a wonderful answer to prayer. God was watching over both of us.

42

THE NGM YEARS – THE BIRTH OF
THE PRODIGALS

Just before I finished writing the book *Treasures of Darkness*, Ray began to pray about whether it was right to write another musical. He needed to know if this was just a good idea or if, in fact, this was on God's heart for him at that time. He had been spending time alone with God early in the morning as normal, when he got down on his knees and asked God to confirm if he wanted him to write another musical. He had been feeling that it could be right to write a musical inspired by one of the greatest stories ever told by Jesus, the Prodigal Son. His first musical, luv esther, was a message primarily for the church, but should he write this one for the wider community? He has always had a strong calling to be prophetic to the nation and so he asked God to tell him what he wanted him to do. He said that morning, "Lord, I only want to do your will and I don't want to get ill again. Please tell me if this is right." He then went on to say, "Perhaps Nancy and I could go to a conference and you could get a speaker to pick me out of the crowd and prophesy over me and confirm your will for me!" He then got off his knees and he and Aidan went to church in Bristol. I was not with them as I was speaking at a church in Reading, England that morning. As Ray's musical, luv esther, was on again at the Colston Hall in Bristol a few weeks later, the church played a DVD that morning to advertise the event.

Later in the service a visiting speaker called Mal Fletcher got up to speak and in the middle of his sermon, he stopped and asked if there was anyone connected to luv esther was in the building. Ray put his hand up and Mal immediately recognised him and said, "Your name is Ray isn't it?" He then went on to say, "God wants you to take your musicals into the market place. He has given you favour before, but he is now going to greatly increase his favour on you. Like Joseph in the Bible who went from prison to prime minister in an instant, God will raise you up and give you great influence. You will not only have a tremendous impact on the audiences who see your musical, but you will also have an influence on the producers/directors and people working in the West End in theatre land and in the music/media industry." What a wonderful answer to prayer. Ray had asked for a confirmation word from God and he certainly got it that morning. It was full steam ahead into what was to become The Prodigals – a man with two sons.

After Ray received that word from God about taking his musical into the marketplace, he realised that there was only one person he knew who worked in the West End, a friend we had known from our early days in the 1980's called Sean Cavanagh. Sean was and is a West End set designer who has been so successful through the years. You will find his name on many of the shows in the West End. He is a director and artistic associate of the acting company called Riding Lights. Heartbeat used to work with Riding Lights in the 80's and that is how Ray and I came to know Sean all those years ago. When Ray co-wrote luv esther with Murray Watts, Sean became the set designer for the show. Ray loved the wisdom that Sean had given him in the past and so it was with excitement and some trepidation that he sat down to talk with Sean about his call and ideas for The Prodigals.

At that time, we were doing a luv esther show in a theatre in the heart of London and so Sean invited West End General Manager, John Dalston to come and see the show and meet Ray and myself afterwards. John told us that he didn't particularly like luv esther but agreed to begin talks about The Prodigals. Sean, John and Ray began to meet and discuss the way forward. The first thing we felt we needed was a director, so Sean and John put forward two people that they thought would be perfect for the job. One came from RADA (The Royal Academy of Dramatic Arts) and the other was the Director of all the Agatha Christie plays in conjunction with Cameron Mackintosh. We approached both and after initial talks we suggested that they come separately to our base in Thornbury for an interview and discussion with Ray and myself. We could see how it would be a privilege to have either of them as director but after much prayer and discussion we felt we should invite Joe Harmston to be the director of Ray's new show.

We went on to work with RADA over the years. Some of their courses were included and taught as part of our ngm training programme so in actual fact we got to work with both of them in the months and years ahead.

Joe began to co-write the story with Ray and thus started a wonderful friendship that has lasted down the years. Ray realised that for Joe to work the long hours he did, it meant that he would miss seeing his wife and children and so out of the blue we sent a gift to Polly, his wife and also included some gifts for his children. We later heard how Polly had in no uncertain terms been complaining about those 'bloody awful people' who were taking her husband away and then a few minutes later the doorbell rang and she received a gift from us for herself and her children. She was completely blown away. Polly is so lovely. I got to meet her in Scotland some time later when the show was about to be released.

Ray wrote most of the lyrics for the songs for the show and worked with various song writers on the melodies. Daniel, our own son, wrote or co-wrote about eleven of the songs.

Ray and Joe had over 1000 people applying to be auditioned for The Prodigals, one of whom was from ngm. Emma Franklin (now Fentiman) expressed an interest in being part of the cast and Ray encouraged her to put her name forward. Emma had joined ngm in 2007 as a dancer in luv esther. Ray knew she was an excellent dancer but he also knew that she had to apply to get into the show the same way as everyone else. She also has an amazing voice, although when she came to ngm she told us all that she didn't sing. Ray knew she could sing and so encouraged her to use her voice too. Through the training, experience and encouragement she received, she became someone who had what they call in the business the triple threat (being able to sing, dance and act). Emma ended up not only on the short list to be auditioned, but also got picked to be one of the cast for the show. J.John's son was also auditioned and he too got into the cast. There were 11 cast members of which only three of them were Christians and Ray had only known one (Emma) beforehand.

The idea of the Prodigals started in 2008 but that idea became a reality in 2011 when, after a month's rehearsals in London, we took the show to the Edinburgh Festival Fringe in Scotland. Joe, Ray and myself shared a small apartment in Edinburgh with some of the cast and Polly came to stay for some of the run at the festival. Ray and I loved Polly from the minute we met her. She is a very clever and wonderful woman with so many incredible talents.

The run at Edinburgh lasted almost a month at the Gilded Balloon, which was one of the most prominent theatres at the Festival. Some of the shows were well attended, but others were poorly attended. We were an unknown show and so we had to somehow grab the public's attention. We asked the cast to go and perform a small part of the show on the streets of Edinburgh and every time they did, crowds would gather. During and after these performances, we would all hand out leaflets and engage in conversations with those who had watched a small snippet of the show. I loved being in Edinburgh with Ray. It's not only a beautiful city, but it was so good to support him in what he was doing and help in any way I could to see his dream become a reality. Daniel and Aidan also travelled to Edinburgh to join us during the month.

Although it was an amazing month, it was also a hard time and Ray just needed to get away at times from the small and crowded apartment we were living in. One of those brief respites came when John and Rose visited Edinburgh to see the show. They booked themselves into a very nice hotel in Princes Street and they booked us a room so that we could also stay in the hotel with them for a couple of days. What a joy it was to have the peace of that hotel and also to be spending time with our dear friends.

John and Rose had been invited by one of the largest banks in our land to go to a meal at the Edinburgh Castle and then to watch the Edinburgh Tattoo and so they invited us to go with them. We met some very rich and influential people. The bankers who had arranged this were obviously looking for business and when we arrived for the meal, we were led to a table where we were all split up so that their people could talk to us about how their bank could help us with our investments! Each of us were targeted including Ray and myself as it was obvious that the bankers thought that because John and

Rose had included us in their party that we too had money. Little did they know, we had none. I told John and Rose later that we already had our bank account with that particular bank and that if they looked at our account, they would see how very little we had and realise it was laughable that they would want to help with our investments! We had no investments! In fact, we only had about £100 in our bank account at that time! It was hilarious. We still laugh about this today.

After our delicious meal they took us into the arena and not only did they give us great seats at the Tattoo but also gave us wool blankets as a gift to use in case we were cold. We had an amazing night. The next morning as we walked out of our hotel, Peter Andre was walking in. I did tell you it was a nice hotel. We went with John and Rose to see a brilliant show that Murray Watts had written and directed and then we took them to see The Prodigals.

Whilst in Edinburgh, some of the cast decided to go to a church service and take a few of the other cast members with them. One of the cast members listened intently to the speaker and at the end of the service when the invitation was given, she responded and that night started a relationship with God.

So many great things came out of our time in Edinburgh. We got some amazing 4 and 5 star reviews from The Edinburgh Guide, The New Current, The Times and What's on Stage. Not only that, but we were nominated for Best Production. What a great start to The Prodigals!

When the run was over and once we had all recovered from the intense month, Ray, Joe, Sean and John met again to discuss the way forward. It was agreed that a run in The Belgrade Theatre in Coventry would be the next thing to do. We had raised thousands to put the production on at the Edinburgh Fringe during August and here we were again needing to raise even more funds to have a run in Coventry.

J.John was amazing and introduced us to many of his contacts who could possibly help financially. I must say, Ray and I have never enjoyed asking people to help us financially, but this was part of the job description of being a producer in the theatre world. We emailed a friend who we knew from our past and asked if we could meet with him. I guess it was obvious why we wanted to see him and so he told us that he was not interested in investing in The Prodigals. J.John encouraged us to write back, so we did and said that we understood his decision, but asked if we could still meet him as we would value his advice. He agreed to meet us in a small café in London. He bought us a coffee and we talked. We shared the vision and asked for his advice. We hadn't mentioned the budget. He then asked how much we needed. We told him we had been given an investment of £50,000 from another trust but we needed another £50,000 and more! He then told us out of the blue that he would match the other investment. He gave us £50,000! As we left him, he laughed and said that it was the most expensive coffee he had ever bought. The first person we called with the good news was J.John!

We raised enough money for the run in Coventry to go ahead. We managed to secure the Belgrade Theatre and prayed for many to attend the shows. We visited many churches in the area asking if the congregations would help support the show by buying some tickets and bringing their friends. There were posters all over Coventry and even the buses had posters on them. We were sitting in the theatre café one day when we suddenly saw a bus with The Prodigals advert on it. We were so excited and so we all ran out and got our photos taken beside the bus. People came from all over the UK to show their support of the show, but there were still many days when the audience was small. It is really difficult to launch a new show especially when you don't have a named person as the lead.

We had a press night which was very well attended and the response from the papers and the critics was really great. We got 4 stars from the Birmingham Post and the Coventry Telegraph. We got 8/10 from the Leamington Courier who said, "This is a show and cast that surely deserve a shot in the West End." However, what we appreciated the most was the audience reaction. Grown men and women were coming out from seeing the show in tears and telling us that the show was brilliant. The story of the prodigal son was affecting them emotionally. Some of the twitter responses said: "Still thinking about the wonderful show I saw in Coventry. So powerful. I would love to see it on tour!" "Can't wait to see what happens to this show. We'll be at the front of the queue for tickets." "I've had the song We Are One from The Prodigals in my head all day. Please release a soundtrack!!" "Just back from tonight's show – thought it was absolutely awesome!" Many were asking about the story behind the show. There were so many wonderful, encouraging and interesting conversations about the show over and over again.

However, in amongst all the positive and encouraging comments, there were also many difficult situations that we had to deal with. Personally, although there were great and wonderful outcomes from Coventry, and although the show was stunning, I found the emotional roller coaster quite difficult to cope with. Every day there were new and difficult challenges, on top of all the normal challenges of trying to get an audience into the theatre. For me personally, it was a relief to be going home at the end of the month.

When the show was over and the reviews received, we had great and positive interest from several people about the show. One of those came from a mainstream touring company who absolutely loved the show and who were keen to tour it in the UK and also put it on in the West End. Throughout the coming years and even still today, we are having talks about taking the show to the next level. Do I think it will ever happen? I don't think it will now that Coronavirus is here, but you never know. All of us would absolutely love to see it happen.

43

MY 60TH BIRTHDAY AND OUR 40TH WEDDING ANNIVERSARY

2013 was a big year for us. Not only was it the year when Aidan turned 16 and I turned 60 but it was also the year when we were going to celebrate our 40th wedding anniversary. We decided we would love to celebrate it with some friends. We decided to have a meal for a number of our close friends in our performance venue in Caedmon. Ray organised most of it and insisted that he take me to London to pick out a dress. We looked at many dresses but none seemed right until he took me to Harrods. I had never shopped in Harrods before and I never imagined for a moment that we would find a dress at a suitable price. However, we did find a beautiful white fitted dress and Ray encouraged me to try it on. It fitted me perfectly and was so beautiful. He was insistent that it was the right dress and so we bought my first and only dress from Harrods. I had no idea that the colour was part of the reason that the dress was right.

On the night we had our meal to celebrate my birthday and also our 40th wedding anniversary, I arrived at our complex to discover my husband had hired someone to play the saxophone to welcome everyone to the event. I thought to myself, "This is perfect!" as I love to hear sax solos, but I didn't realise just how perfect the night was to become. After an amazing meal with 50 of our friends, Ray took me up on the platform, got down on one knee and proposed to me! He had never properly proposed all those years ago and so he decided he would put that right and do it on our 40th wedding anniversary. I was so stunned for a few moments that I could not speak. I seemed to lose the ability to form words! I was so shocked! Then, with tears in my eyes I said, "YES!" He then told me that he had written a song for me. He had asked Neil and Tanya Wilson to write the melody and he wrote the words. On that evening, he asked Neil and Tanya to sing it for me. These are the lyrics that Ray wrote:

Lullaby of Love (A Song for Nancy)

How can I give my thanks to you?
For all these loving years
I cannot find the words to say
You fill my every day
I remember our first kiss
The way you held me close
To hold your hand was such a thrill
My love, I feel it still.

You ask me my desire
I love you, I love you
My heart beats my reply
I love you, I love you.
Forever in my life
I'll sing this lullaby
I love you, I love you.

Here is my song of love to you
To say your beautiful
Your love has made my dreams come true
With everything you do
You will never be alone
For always we are one
And when the bells ring it is time
My love, you'll still be mine.

© 2013 Lyrics: Ray Goudie. Music: Neil and Tanya Wilson.

Even as I copy the lyrics of the above song into this book, it still reduces me to tears. What a special moment and a great memory! That night was so very precious; it was almost as though we were getting married all over again. That was why he wanted me to wear a white dress. He then took me on *honeymoon* to the Caribbean, somewhere I had always said I wanted to go, not to an island but to Mexico. What a romantic thing to do and what precious memories we made during that time!

44

THE NGM YEARS - MORE EXPANSION - 2014-2016

One of the things the Lord told me, was that I was going to travel much more than I had ever done and so in 2014 invitations to Germany, USA and South Africa came into my inbox. Ray loved to see the ministry I was doing increase and so we decided that I would travel to the States with him, I would travel by myself to Germany and travel to South Africa with Zoe. We had preached in the USA many times and so it was good to be going back again. I loved being in Munich, Germany at Hope church to do my very first talk on my Laughter Tour. I had written a book called *The Gift of Laughter* and then toured the UK speaking at various events and churches on the subject of laughter. Whilst in Munich, I immediately made friends for life with Kevin and Marty Brogan. They are both pastors in the church. Kevin is Scottish and Marty is a rock-chick with an amazing voice. She leads worship in the church and also plays in a number of mainstream bands in Germany. Every year since, Kevin and Marty have invited me back to speak at their church and Marty has come a few times to my Spiritual Health Weekends. We regard each other as family. I had a brilliant time with them and I just love the church they are building in Munich.

I absolutely love South Africa and so to have an invitation to visit that country again and minister at a large church over there was wonderful. I discovered that the pastor of the church I was speaking at was the great, great grandson of Smith Wigglesworth. Whilst there, I also met the great granddaughter of Smith Wigglesworth. She and I became good friends and have remained in touch with each other through social media. I loved her inheritance and could see God was doing so much through her. What a privilege it was to speak at this incredible church. There were over 1000 people at the women's conference I spoke at and well over that number when I spoke at their two church services. I loved praying and talking to people at the church and the conference and loved seeing the response as many stood to say that God had spoken to them.

It was while we were in South Africa that Zoe began to feel very itchy. We were staying at a beautiful hotel and had two gorgeous rooms that the church had kindly paid for. We were being treated like royalty. The lady assigned to look after us even took us, at her own expense on her birthday, to a spa day outside of the city. We were treated to a massage, a facial and foot treatments. It was incredible. At the same time, Zoe thought she had an allergic reaction to something she had eaten, but no matter how many anti-histamines she took it got worse. Eventually we discovered that she had been bitten by bed bugs. Her bed was covered in them. We and the church were mortified. The hotel eventually changed the mattress. Zoe was worried that the crew on the flight home wouldn't let her on the plane thinking that she had some infectious disease. However, she and I got the flight and the first person she saw when she came home was the doctor. He said he had never seen a body so badly bitten by bed bugs! There was hardly a spare inch of skin that was not covered in bites.

I have often said that I should write a book about our adventures on mission, some of the stories are crazy like this one, but not anyone's fault (other than the hotel), but many are hilarious, like the one where our host asked us before we went to bed what we would like for breakfast in the morning. Before we could answer she said, "I have bought bacon and eggs, but I wondered if I could keep it for ourselves to have at another time!" Fortunately, we only ever ate toast in the morning! Or another time when our hosts asked us before going to bed if we would like a hot water bottle. I was embarrassed to say, "Yes please", so decided to decline. However, since I had a hot water bottle in my suitcase, I filled it with hot water from the tap. In the morning when we left our host's home, we thanked them for their kind hospitality. However, I realised later that I had forgotten to remove the hot water bottle from the bed! I couldn't write and ask them to send it back to me! How embarrassing! Or another time when we were in Heartbeat and Ray had been asked to play drums for a well-known choir in Scotland. They needed a drummer for one of their gigs in England and so asked Ray if he would play drums and could I play the tambourine? We agreed to do so and they said they would put us up in host accommodation. When we arrived at the host's home, they took us into their lounge and asked us how long we had been in the choir. We explained that we weren't a part of the choir, we were just helping them out on this one occasion. The hosts then clearly told us they were so upset that we were not in the choir and were so disappointed not to meet two of the choir members. They said they had told the organisers that they specifically wanted to meet two of the choir members.

They brought in something for us to eat. Before they poured a stew like soup into a bowl, they noticed a spider in the bowl and threw the spider into the fire. They didn't clean the bowl before pouring the stew into the dish. When we went upstairs to our room, we noticed the floor had not been vacuumed for many months and the bed was literally wet from the dampness in the room. We should have left, but we were young and we didn't have any money to stay in a hotel, so we stayed, prayed and laughed about it together. We didn't take our clothes off and put a covering over the bed and lay on top. Sometimes you just have to laugh. Many people are great at hospitality, but it was obvious that it was not this couple's gift. Our friend Ishmael told us that he used to keep a book (similar to a visitors' book) that he would ask his hosts to sign with their name and address in it so that if he was ever in that area again, he could ask to stay with them. Obviously only the good hosts got a place in his book.

45

THE NGM YEARS – "NANCY, I'VE MET AIDAN'S WIFE!"

I will never forget the day when Ray came home after a day of auditions in ngm and told me that he had met Aidan's wife! My son was only 17 and he didn't have a girlfriend so Ray's words were astonishing to say the least. I spurted out, "Ray, what do you mean? How could you have met Aidan's wife? He's not even got a girlfriend!" He then told me he had auditioned a young girl from Scotland and when she sang the anointing of God fell in our performance venue. He said he immediately knew in his spirit that this girl was Aidan's wife. I said, "You can't say that Ray! How can you possibly know that she will be Aidan's wife? Do they even know one another?" and then before he could answer, I added, "And by the way, please don't mention this to Aidan. You can't tell him!" He replied, "I'm not going to tell him, but mark my words, I have met Aidan's wife!"

What neither Ray or I knew was that Leanne already had her eyes on Aidan. They didn't start their romance until 11 months later, but we could see months before that their friendship was growing. Aidan had just finished college in Bristol where he trained to become a fitness Instructor. As I have said earlier, he was always very keen on sports, so it was a massive surprise when he came and told us that he felt called to join ngm. During his last year at college, he went through our discipleship programme and then in the following year, he joined ngm as our fitness coach and also helped with our social media.

We got used to seeing this beautiful and talented girl in our home for meals after they became an item. In December 2015, they got engaged but it was over six months later, just before Ray died, when Ray eventually told them how he knew at Leanne's audition that she was the one God had picked for Aidan. Ray always was very prophetic. Ken McGreavy would often say that we were both intuitive, but really all we were doing was listening to God and asking for his wisdom and even to this day, I still do the same. Throughout our 40 years, church leaders have often said that we have an apostolic and prophetic ministry and have called us pioneers. We didn't see all of that ourselves to be honest, we were just ordinary Christians who spent quality time with the Lord and listened to his voice. Isn't that what everyone does? We heard, obeyed and trusted what the Lord said and then taught others to do the same. Our vision and heart has always been to transform our culture and release God's word to those who would listen.

Ray could see the potential in people before they could see it in themselves. There have been many who have come through ngm who would not be in their ministry today had Ray not encouraged them and told them prophetically what he could see. He saw that although Aidan was not a musician, that he had talents in leadership, an ear for music and skills within him that needed encouragement to be brought out of him. Ray could see a great talent within him and so he was going to train and mentor Aidan in ngm, but this was cut short really before it had started when Ray got ill.

46

THE NGM YEARS – THE END AND THE BEGINNING

It was at the end of November 2014 when Ray began to experience an unexplained pain in his stomach. Through December, Ray continued to feel unwell but the doctor told him that the pain was probably severe wind in his stomach.

At the beginning of January, we had arranged for our senior staff in ngm to go away together for a day or so to Wales to talk, plan and pray for the next season. However, as we spent time together it was obvious that Ray was not very well and we ended up calling 111 as he was in so much pain. From that phone call they arranged for Ray to go to a hospital in Newport to see a doctor. He was examined but was told again that he was probably experiencing some severe wind pains and really there was nothing to worry about. However, to me it was obvious that there was something really wrong as Ray could not eat without feeling pain. When we went home, he went to his local doctor again and this time he referred Ray for an endoscopy. After the endoscopy, we discovered he had a blockage in his duodenum. The blockage would explain why Ray was finding it difficult to eat but what was causing the duodenum to be blocked? He was then sent for a barium meal, an ultrasound scan and eventually a CT scan. Each scan came back clear.

Ray had already lost about 10lbs in weight because of a lack of food and we were keen that he didn't lose any more. Ray and I had built up over the years a group of people who were committed to pray for us personally on a regular basis and therefore we had been keeping them up to date with Ray's health situation, but I knew we needed more prayer for Ray. I felt I should personally do a 21-day Daniel fast for Ray but at the same time I felt I should try and mobilise more prayer support by posting our situation on Facebook and asking people to pray. Something was wrong with Ray and at the beginning we didn't know what it was!

When I posted on Facebook to ask people to pray for Ray, what happened was extraordinary! A huge army of people were stirred by God to pray for Ray. Throughout the journey thousands of people from all over the world prayed for healing. Some of these people knew Ray, others didn't. I posted every day and for some months I posted twice a day asking people to pray. My posts were shared by many and soon I began to receive emails and messages from people I didn't know, encouraging me to keep on posting as my posts were encouraging them in their walk with God. People contacted me to tell me that they had become a Christian through following our story. Others said that their faith in God had been restored through what they were reading. It was incredible. I wasn't able to speak at events or churches during this time, but here I was reaching many by the posts I was putting on Facebook. It was so wonderful. Many people were praying for Ray in many different parts of the world. We even had a prayer group in Pakistan praying for Ray! None of them knew us at all. It started as a cry for help because I knew how much prayer and faith in God could change Ray's circumstances. I needed an army of people praying for my beloved husband and this is what happened. Thousands of people from all over the world began to pray and intercede. At times when things were really bad, and believe me they got really bad, I had the comfort of knowing that somewhere in the world someone would be praying for Ray even whilst I was asleep.

We knew that our God was good and kind and that we could trust him whatever the outcome. It was in April 2015 that Ray could not cope anymore with the pain and told me that he had to go to hospital in Bristol. Something was wrong. It was almost midnight when we arrived at the Bristol Royal Infirmary (BRI) and through a random blood test which no doctor had previously thought to take in the many medical appointments he had had, we were told that there was a problem with Ray's liver and gallbladder.

On Saturday 4th April 2015, Ray and I were told the worst news possible. Ray had pancreatic cancer. The whole remarkable story is told in my book called

Our Greatest Adventure. It was the hardest journey that Ray and I have ever been through. It was a journey filled with courage in the midst of pain, peace in the midst of sorrow and trust in the midst of confusion. It was a journey filled with many miracles, but just not *the* miracle we wanted to see. We went through many highs and many lows. He survived a 12-hour life threatening operation. He was told he could not go through chemotherapy because his weight was so low, but God helped him to gain enough weight after the operation in order to start the treatment. He was told he would have to stop the chemotherapy treatment at some point along the journey as everyone experiences loss of weight, but he gained weight every week. With every miracle we rejoiced and praised God and with every problem we prayed and sought God's answer.

Both Ray's dad and my own precious dad died during 2015 and unfortunately we could not attend either funeral. Ray was going through chemotherapy and we were advised that neither of us should be in crowds at that time. I know both our dads would have understood, but we desperately wanted to be there to celebrate two men who meant so much to us both. Ray wrote something about his dad to be read out at the funeral and sent it to his brother, Derek. My brothers asked if I could send something about my dad which could be read out at the funeral, which I was only too pleased to do. I was so thrilled when my brother Jack sent me texts and pictures from my dad's funeral so that I could feel included. My father was a special man who loved his Lord Jesus and loved his family. He missed my mum so much and now he would be reunited with her. The same is true for Ray's dad. Both Ray and myself had great parents who loved Jesus.

After 6 months of chemotherapy, Ray was told he was cancer free – we rejoiced so much. The doctors then advised him to go through 5 and a half weeks of radiotherapy and listed all the problems he would encounter. However, the Lord told him he would sail through it, and he did. He even wrote worship songs and had intimate times with the Lord as he was receiving the treatment.

We eventually went on holiday to Spain in May 2016 to recover in the sun and stayed there for a month. Aidan and Leanne came out and joined us for a week and it was brilliant to make some wonderful and special memories with them. Although Ray wasn't feeling too good on a few of those days, Aidan and his dad shared a great deal of fun. During this holiday, Ray sat on our balcony and expanded and re-wrote luv esther. I can still remember the time when he was struggling with lyrics for one for the songs and suddenly said, "I've got it – listen to this!" Out came another brilliant, heavenly idea from my husband's mouth. He absolutely loved re-writing the show and came back from Spain with the idea of touring the show again in the UK. My husband was never short of vision and great ideas.

It was towards the end of our holiday month that Ray began to show signs that everything was not good with him physically. He was experiencing pain again and so when we came home, we went to the hospital and we were told that Ray had two days to live! The shock of hearing that prognosis was so hard. We were on holiday just last week! How could things change so quickly? What was God saying? We turned to him again for help. Lord, hear our cries!

Again, Ray defied the doctor's words. The whole story is in my book, but eventually after a month or so he was told that he was too well to stay in hospital and he could go home. When he came home, although he was still ill, he began to come off all his drugs! He had what is called a driver in his arm which fed him all sorts of drugs during the day. But with the help from the doctors, because all these drugs had terrible side effects, Ray began to cut down the number of drugs he was taking. Slowly bit by bit he came off all drugs and at that point was only receiving 5ml of morphine through the driver. One morning when he woke up, he told me he was so tired he just wanted to sleep. When the nurse came to the house to remove the driver from his arm, he asked her if she could do it tomorrow as he was just too tired, but tomorrow never came.

After he had slept for a number of hours, I decided at 2pm that I should wake him as I was worried that he hadn't had anything to eat or drink. However, when I woke him, he was promptly sick. Once I had settled him again, he took my hand and said, "Nancy don't worry about me. I'm fine! Just stay around. Come in and out of the room but honestly I'm doing fine love." Those were the last words I ever heard my husband say. I sat beside him all through the day. There were times when I was really worried about him and so I would go outside the room and call several friends asking them to pray. When I came back, he was still asleep.

At 7pm that evening, Zoe arrived with my meal. She had said she would cook a meal for me that evening. Before I left him, I looked at him and he was still fast asleep. About 10-15 minutes later, I walked back into my bedroom to discover that my beloved husband was gone! He basically slept into the arms of Jesus.

I panicked, I cried, I prayed, I commanded the spirit of death to go. I did everything I knew to do, but he was gone! Nothing changed. I was inconsolable. This was not in the plan. This was not supposed to happen. I hugged him. I told him I loved him. I asked the Lord to bring him back. I was devastated. Sobbing, I called the nurses and they immediately said they would come to the house. Then I sobbed down the phone to Zoe asking her to bring Aidan home. I didn't know what to do with myself other than cry out to God. Ray was my best friend, my lover, my husband, my confidante. He and I were co-leaders. What was I going to do without him? "God, my great and wonderful God, help me! I can't cope with this!"

When Aidan, Leanne and Zoe arrived, I hugged Aidan and told him while sobbing, "He's gone! He's gone!" The worst that could ever have happened had just happened. We all cried together. Still today as I write this book, tears are pouring down my face as I remember the pain of losing Ray. We lost so much. The world had lost a good man but we had lost a dad, a husband, a co-leader and our best friend. That morning before Aidan went to ngm, I randomly asked him if he had said goodbye to his dad. So, before he left, he spent a few minutes with his dad and me. As he walked out the door of our bedroom, Ray said, "Have a good day, love you son!" None of us ever anticipated that those would be the last words he would ever speak to Aidan.

I asked Aidan, Zoe and Leanne if they wanted to see Ray and they all did. Aidan spent time on his own beside his dad praying and asking God to bring him back but also saying goodbye. I called Daniel and through my sobs told him that his dad had gone. Daniel had only left to go back to the States about a week or so beforehand. When I told him, he did not say a word. We were all so shocked. We didn't expect this to happen at all. It was not in our minds at all that Ray would die. Yes, I had been worried. Yes, I had been concerned, but I expected a miracle. I expected Ray to be raised to life. So many people said that they believed that Ray would live and not die. Daniel got on the first plane from Los Angeles.

Aidan was only 18, yet he was so kind and supportive to me even though he was hurting deeply himself. His dad was not just his dad; he was his mentor and he was his best friend too. Yet despite what he had lost, here he was comforting me. Aidan reminded me that Ray had constantly said, "I will not die a day too soon or a day too late." He had often said, "Cancer will not kill me, instead God will take me when the time is right!" He always told me, "If I die, Nancy, don't allow anyone to say that I died from cancer. I won't die because of cancer but because it's been my appointed time to die." He also said, "Nancy if I die, then you have to know that it's my time to go." After Ray died, those words brought me great comfort.

I will forever be grateful to Zoe and Tim. Zoe came as soon as she got my phone call and despite her missing Ray and being devastated at his death, she stayed beside me each day, helping me to make decisions when I needed to do so. She called the funeral directors and they came and took Ray's body away.

If you read my book Our Greatest Adventure, you will discover that all sorts of questions went through my mind. How could this have happened? I thought the Lord was going to heal him? He was only on 5ml of morphine and not on any other pain killers. This isn't how someone with cancer dies! What was going on? What about the verses of scripture that had been given to me? What about all the prophecies that said he would live and not die? The enemy said to me, "God has turned his back on you. Turn your back on him!" I have to say for a moment or two in the midst of my confusion I thought about it. Was God not real? Was everything I believed in just a load of rubbish? Why hadn't God turned up for me?

That night before I went to bed, I stood beside the bed where my beloved husband had died and spoke out loud to the Lord. I said, "Lord I don't understand what has happened. I have so many questions. I was not expecting this Lord, but I want to tell you that even though I don't understand it, I want to tell you that I trust you. I know I'm not called to understand everything in life, but I am called to trust you and trust is what I am going to do."

I decided to trust even though I didn't understand everything. Trusting in God when you are on the mountain top is easy, but trusting him when you are going through a dark valley is essential. God asks us to trust him when you are feeling alone, afraid, confused or when you think life has not been fair. It's at that point when you need God so much. So many people turn away and blame God and therefore miss the comfort he brings. Don't turn away from him at your greatest time of need. Turn to him and tell him, despite what you are feeling, you trust him. I didn't understand why our prayers had not been answered in the way I thought they should be, but I chose to turn to him and trust him anyhow. Is God good? The answer is always, "Yes." If he is good, then he can be trusted. There are things that will happen in life that we won't understand and we may never understand until we get to Heaven. That's where trust comes in. We trust in our good and faithful God. Bill Johnson, speaker, author and leader of Bethel Church in Redding, California says it like this, after talking about losing his beloved dad to pancreatic cancer, "I refuse to sacrifice the revelation that God is always good on the altar of human reason because of my need to make sense of my seemingly unanswered prayer."

That night as I lay in bed breaking my heart, the Lord gave me a gift. I physically felt it come on me. It was the gift of a peace that passes all understanding. I had peace in the midst of grief. I didn't understand it. It didn't make sense, but I knew God had given me an amazing gift of peace. It didn't stop me crying or mourning for Ray, but there was an underlying peace through it all and dare I say it, a joy! I could feel a spring of joy within me. "How can this be?" I asked myself. I had just lost my husband, but not only did I feel this incredible peace that I could not even begin to describe, but I also had a bubble of joy within. I didn't understand it, but I was so grateful. These wonderful gifts have never left me. They continue to this day.

I don't know when I fell asleep that night, but through the tears at some point sleep eventually came. When I woke in the morning, I thanked the Lord for his gift of peace. I thanked him for his presence with me. I prayed for strength for my family and myself to get through the first day without

Ray. I placed everything into the hands of God and told him I loved him. I told him through many tears I would never stop loving him.

At some point throughout that day, I physically felt God walk into my bedroom and engulfed me in a hug. I felt it happen. Actually, it was more than a hug, it felt like he completely surrounded me and became one with me. I felt completely overwhelmed by his presence. Psalm 34:18 says that *The Lord is close to the brokenhearted (NIV)* and I know that to be true. He came and embraced me in my sorrow and he can do the same for you too. His presence became even more real to me that day and the wonderful truth is that his presence has never left me. I feel his presence in our home. So many people tell me that they feel such peace in my home. His presence feels so tangible. I know he is with me and in me. I remember going out to speak at various places a number of months after Ray died and on my way home, I would feel so excited about being alone in my home with the Lord. His presence in my home was and is so wonderful. I often walk around my home telling the Lord how grateful I am. I am so grateful for his love, his peace, his joy, but mainly for his presence with me. I live alone but I am never alone. He is with me all the time and I am so grateful. If he does this for me, he will do the same for you.

It says in the Bible that God will never leave you nor will he ever forsake you and I have found that to be so true, not just in the last few years, but throughout the whole of my life. The truth is that he is always there whether you feel him or not. People often accuse God of doing something wrong, so it's important, as I have said before, that we know that God is good – always! He is good when things are going well for you in life and he is good when things are not going so well. Life is full of ups and downs; life can sometimes suck, but that is not God's fault, that's just life. We all make choices in life and those choices can affect us and others either positively or negatively. God sent his son so that we could experience life to the full, but he didn't promise that life would be a bed of roses all the time. He told us that he would be there when the road was tough, but when we shut him out, we don't get the help that he has for us. I could not have gone through what I went through without having God at my side. I would not have survived. He has been my help and my strength; he has given me hope in the midst of pain and intense sorrow.

When it came to the funeral, I made sure that one of the songs we sang was The King of my Heart which has a chorus that says, You are good, good, oh, oh. I wanted people to know that despite what had happened to me, my God is good. I also wanted them to know that as the song says, You're never gonna let me down! I knew that as I walked into the future, a future without my man walking beside me, that God would never let me down and I wanted people to know that despite the many challenges life would bring, I had put my faith and trust in God.

I discovered in the days, weeks, months and years to come what I already knew to be true from the Bible, that God's presence is always with me. His love, peace, joy and his favour rests on me even in the middle of the darkest valley. There is a book in the Bible called Lamentations; the word Lamentations means 'sad thoughts' and this book is full of sad thoughts, suffering and pain. Jeremiah, who most people think is the author of this book, had an amazing calling to be a prophet, yet his life journey was often full of difficult and sometimes terrifying circumstances. When Jeremiah found life hard and painful it says in Lamentations that he had hope when he called the truth of the word of God to mind. *I remember my affliction and my wandering; the bitterness and the gall. I remember them well, and my soul is downcast within me. Yet this I call to mind and therefore I have hope: Because of the Lord's great love we are not consumed for his compassions never fail. They are new every morning; great is your faithfulness.* Lamentations 3:19-23 (NIV). God's love is there for each of us no matter how dark and difficult our lives can sometimes be. He will not fail us; his mercies are new every morning!

Many people have told me that I am the strongest woman they have ever known, but I know in my weakness that it's God who has made me strong. Any strength that I have and that people can see comes from above. It's supernatural.

When someone dies, you often feel as though the whole world should stop but it doesn't, life goes on. Minute follows minute, hour follows hour, day follows day. Time speeds by and everything within you screams for time to stop! There's so much to process and take in but you feel as though you haven't enough time to do so. My brain was muddled. I didn't know what day it was. I got out of bed each day but couldn't get my brain to function in the normal way. I was drowning in sorrow, but the amazing gift of peace continued throughout it all. I was and forever will be grateful to Zoe Wickham, my best friend, who stood with me every moment of every day. She and Tim were and are so wonderful to me. Zoe took control when I didn't know how to do even the simple tasks of life. She went through everything that needed to happen. She contacted everyone who needed to be contacted. She came with me to register Ray's death and to sort out the bills. She spoke with the funeral directors. I would not have coped at that time without her practical help and without the goodness of God. I asked her recently how she knew what needed to happen when someone dies, she told me she didn't know. What she did was call her dad and ask him for advice as he used to be a Baptist church minister.

We restricted the funeral to our family, the ngm family and to close friends, but still there were no free seats at the funeral. Around 250 people attended and many more across the world joined through a live skype feed. Facebook was filled with tributes about Ray. At one point I thought Facebook would collapse at the amount of tributes that had been posted. Many told their stories of how Ray had impacted their lives.

We also held a celebration of Ray's life at Edge Church in Bristol on 16th September 2016 and around 450 people attended. I was so grateful to everyone who came to stand with me and my boys in acknowledging the life of a wonderful husband and great dad, but as I look back at that day, I cannot remember who was there and who wasn't. My memory of that day is very patchy. However, it was wonderful to celebrate a man who was described recently as "such a bundle of electric joy and purposefulness."

Hannah Lindsey who was in ngm for a few years and who was Esther in Ray's musical luv esther posted this on Facebook the day before we celebrated Ray's life:
"Some are born great. Some achieve greatness, and some have greatness thrust upon them." - Shakespeare: writer, artist.
"The greatest among you will be your servant." Jesus: GOD.
Is one born a servant of humanity? Can one achieve true servanthood? Or is this higher calling thrust upon you?
I don't know how it happened in this case, but certainly if greatness is con-

nected to serving your fellow man, then by those standards, (and perhaps by the only standard that truly matters) Ray Goudie was a GREAT MAN. A man whose life has been unrelentingly poured and lavishly, lovingly spent in service to the *Greatest Servant* of all, and in service to untold numbers of deeply grateful artists.

I feel honoured to count myself among them.

I'm sure I speak on behalf of dancers, actors, graphic designers, producers, directors, musicians, singers, MCs, speakers, DJs, presenters, costume designers, sound & lighting technicians, stage managers, writers, lyricists, coaches & choreographers, those up and down the country, and in nations that canvas the globe, when I say, "Ray, from the bottom of our hearts, THANK YOU.

You taught us how to be artists. How to be servants. How to be the men and women God dreamed for us to be.

We know how to create & to craft, because you taught us.

We know how to wait & to woohoo, because you helped us.

We know how to love & to lie down, because you showed us.

We know how to believe & to BE, because you believed in us.

And not just because you believed in us, but because you believed, with an unshakeable faith, in the Greatest Man, the Greatest Servant, the Greatest Artist of all.

May your love affair become ours.

Tomorrow, as we come together, whether in body or in heart, to celebrate your life, I hope that from your window in glory you see us, and the impact you made on our lives for all eternity.

Ray Goudie, we are your legacy and we love you and miss you VERY much." - HANNAH LINDSEY

Hannah is now a performer in London's West End. I am so grateful for her lovely, encouraging words.

Ray left a huge legacy behind and we, his family recognize this more than anyone else. He invested so much into our two boys, Daniel and Aidan as well as myself. We and countless others will never forget him. His fun, his laughter, his passion for music, the arts and creativity were infectious and he always inspired us to go for excellence rather than settle for something second rate. Having said that, it was obvious that his love and his passion for God were always his first calling. Ray and I were always a double act – a team called by God to pass on to our family and to many others who crossed our paths our love, passion and gratitude to our God, who loved us even before we loved him. We became who we were, because of who God is.

In the middle of something so sad, something so beautiful happened. Many of those who had been in Heartbeat and ngm through the years came to the celebration of Ray's life. Two of these were Jackie Harding, the first lead singer of Heartbeat, and Colin Vallance, our first bass guitarist. Colin's wife, Sue, had died a number of months beforehand. He had been an amazing husband who cared and looked after his wife for many, many years through a difficult and troubling illness. Jackie had been divorced from her husband for many years and throughout her life had accomplished much for God. They recognized each other, even though they hadn't seen each other since Jackie had left Heartbeat in 1982. They sat together during the celebration and afterwards decided to keep in touch. A friendship started and then a romance that eventually led to them getting married in a beautiful part of Italy.

When they got engaged, they immediately contacted me and said they wanted me to come to the wedding which was going to be held in Ravello on the Amalfi coast. I said I would definitely go but after I came off the call, I was a little concerned about going to Italy by myself. However, I needn't have worried. God provided the ideal partner. When a close friend of mine, Louise Harris, heard about the wedding and how the two of them found love through the celebration, she contacted me saying, "Do you need company when you go to the wedding and by the way I speak Italian?" I called her immediately and said, "Please come with me!" We decided to make it into a week's holiday and that was the first of a number of wonderful holidays abroad together. Jehovah Jireh – my provider!

47

THE NGM YEARS – GOD'S PROVISION CONTINUES!

Now that I am on my own it's important that I continue to trust and rely on God for everything I need to not only survive but to thrive in these days. I have a great family. I am so grateful for my two boys and their wives and also for my brothers and their wives too. I am often in touch with Jack in particular, but all three of my brothers and their wives have been so supportive. I have many really good and wonderful friends. I've already expressed how much Tim and Zoe mean to me, but God has given me many special friends throughout my 40 years. Just the other day, I praised God for the many dear friends who call me or write to me or support what I do financially or in any way they can. One friendship that has lasted since we were children is my special friend, Elsie Good. Elsie and I have known each other since the age of 7. We both went to the same church and as youngsters we developed a way of communicating with each other during the church service which could be considered to be an early texting system! We were always close through the years. When we were teenagers we were in the same crowd and Ray and her husband Richard were part of that crowd too. In fact, Richard played bass and was in the band Unity with us but even before that Ray and Richard were in another band together as well. Something that many will not know is that Ray occasionally sang from behind the drums. He didn't possess a world class voice, but somehow found himself singing in a band at one of the largest concert halls in Glasgow. He sang a cover version of A Whiter Shade of Pale by Procol Harum and changed the lyrics to fit the occasion. However, before this I remember he and Richard playing in a band in a church in Glasgow. Ray was playing the drums and singing a song called Heaven, I'm Going There. The chorus went like this: I'll meet my father and my mother, my sister and my brother and reign throughout eternity, but best of all I'll meet my Saviour and share his blessed favour, this is why I want to go. While he was singing this song, Ray forgot the lyrics. Richard recognised this and tried to mouth the words to him, but Ray ended up singing, I'll meet my father and my father, my father and my father and reign throughout eternity, but best of all I'll meet my father and share his blessed favour, this is why I want to go. Elsie and I were in the audience and we were under our chairs with laughter. It was hilarious.

When Ray and I got married Elsie was one of my bridesmaids. We always had such fun with Richard and Elsie. Through the years when Ray and I went back to Scotland to visit family, we always made sure we had time to see Richard and Elsie. We have so many wonderful memories with them.

When Richard was diagnosed as having pancreatic cancer, we began to intercede for them, never thinking that a couple of months later Ray would be told that he too had pancreatic cancer. Elsie lost Richard about nine months before Ray died. We spoke often on the phone encouraging each other through the toughest time of our lives and we still do today. At my earliest opportunity, I went to Scotland and stayed with her before going on to preach at various churches. We have also had two brilliant holidays together, one in Israel and one in Mexico and I pray that God gives us the time and opportunity to go on other holidays in the future.

A few weeks after Ray died, Aidan and I went to Italy to get away for a short while. It was a beautiful yet very difficult time. We were both in such pain at losing our best friend. Before we went, Louise Harris contacted me to say if I ever needed some time away then her home was always open to me. Although I had known Louise for years, we didn't have as close a relationship then as we do now, but when I got the invitation, I immediately felt urged by the Lord to go. So, when I came back from Italy, I took a train to York. As you can imagine, I was quite vulnerable but staying with her in her home, just outside of York, was the perfect place. She was so very kind to me during that long weekend and our friendship became so much deeper. She came with me to Colin and Jackie's wedding in Italy the following year. During 2018 we went back to Italy for another holiday and then in 2019 we went to Greece together.

John and Rose Lancaster invited Louise, Gill Riley and myself to spend time with them in their home in Switzerland as well as their home in the Lake District. I am indeed a very blessed woman. I am so grateful for the many friendships God has given me. I have been on holiday with Aidan and Leanne and I am always so grateful for their company. I have also been on holiday by myself to Jersey and also Portugal. I chose hotels where Ray and I had been before where I knew it would not feel too awkward to go there on my own. People tell me I am strong to be able to do that, but to be honest, without God's presence with me, I know I wouldn't be able to cope. I enjoy my own company, but if I had a choice, I would much rather go on holiday with friends or family where we could have a good laugh!

Many years ago, I remember worrying about our future. Would God provide for us when we were old and perhaps no longer able to do ministry? For 36 years (40 now for me!) Ray and I lived from day to day asking God to provide for our every need, and I am here today to tell you that God has been so faithful. He taught Ray and myself so much as we continued to depend on him for our finances. All those years ago, as I began to worry about our old age, I did what Philippians 4:6 tells us to do and prayed about my concerns and when I did the Lord spoke to me so clearly from 1 Kings 17:14: *For this is what the Lord, the God of Israel, says: "The jar of flour will not be used up and the jug of oil will not run dry until the day the Lord sends rain on the land"* (NIV). God spoke and said, "Nancy, the jug of oil will not run dry. You do not need to worry about your latter years." After 40 years of living by faith and now I guess at the beginning of my latter years, I can tell you that the jug has certainly not run dry. He continues to supply what I need so generously. I am constantly amazed at the way he blessed Ray and I, and now I am a widow, I can testify to the way he looks after me and ngm. He has sometimes not delivered in my time frame, but he has never let me down.

About a year after Ray died, a good friend of mine, Sammy Lole, gave me a gift of a two-night bed and breakfast stay in a beautiful hotel in Skipton. I was overwhelmed by her generosity as Ray and I had stayed at that hotel before with John and Rose Lancaster, so I knew what a great hotel it was! When my two special friends, Louise Harris and Rose Lancaster realised that I would not be far from their homes, they decided to book in to the hotel to be with me for one night. On the first night, we had a gorgeous meal together at one of the two restaurants in the hotel and Rose kindly paid the bill. The restaurant we ate in was a very lively and busy place and so on the second evening, I made a reservation in the other restaurant which I thought, although it may be more expensive, it seemed easier to eat there on my own. I had decided that I would only order a main course and therefore the total cost of the meal would be less. When I arrived at the restaurant, they led me into the bar and asked me if I wanted a drink whilst I looked at the menu. When I opened the menu, I nearly died! There were three options and each one was expensive. The first choice was a 3-course tasting meal, the second choice was a 6-course tasting meal and the third choice was a 9-course tasting meal. My idea of only having a main course suddenly went out of the window. Who would ever have thought that there wouldn't be a normal menu? If it hadn't been so serious, I would have laughed. Instead, I panicked and prayed! "Lord, what do I do?" My first thought was maybe I could just leave before anyone came back, but then I knew they had my room number! My second thought was maybe I could tell them that I have changed my mind, but I reckoned that would have been very embarrassing. As I was thinking through what to do the Lord spoke. He said, "Nancy just relax and enjoy your meal." I thought, "Really?" After a few moments, I said, "Okay Lord I will and I will trust that this is the right thing to do!"

I chose the three-course meal and ordered a jug of iced tap water together with a glass of wine. When I got to my table, there was a bottle of still water on my table. I immediately called the waiter and told him that I ordered a jug of iced tap water. I didn't want to pay for a bottle of still water when a jug of iced tap water would have been sufficient. You can tell I'm Scottish! I was making sure it wasn't any more expensive than it needed to be. He apologised, but returned saying that as they had given me the wrong item, I should just keep the bottle of still water and he would take it off my bill. I ate a gorgeous meal and at the end of the evening I asked for the bill. He came back and told me that there was no need for me to sign a bill as he would just allocate it to my room.

The next morning, as I checked out of the hotel I asked for the bill. Obviously, my accommodation for both nights had been paid for by my friend, and so the receptionist told me that I had only a small amount to pay and handed me the invoice. I looked at it and the only item on the bill was my glass of wine from the previous night. They had definitely taken off the bottle of water, but my dinner was not there. I told her that the invoice was incorrect and I had eaten in the hotel restaurant the night before and my meal was missing. She went away and checked it all and then returned and told me that there was no record of my meal from the night before. I told her that I definitely had eaten there and asked if my friends could have paid for it. She went away and checked again and said, "I have no way of telling you that as there is no note of your meal at all in our system. The only thing you have to pay is the glass of wine!" I was confused but relieved! I left thinking Rose or Louise must have paid the bill. I wanted to thank them and so I texted both of them and asked if they had kindly paid my bill. They both replied saying that they hadn't paid the bill for me. I don't know what happened to the cost of my meal, but God does and I am so grateful. I went home praising God for his provision for me and knew that no matter what, he would provide.

Ray and I often said that our 'employer' is so much more generous than any earthly employer ever could be. We have had opportunities that we would never have experienced had we stayed in Scotland. We've had many holidays given to us. As well as the one in Mauritius, we also had a skiing holiday in Colorado in the States and a holiday in the Algarve in Portugal. As well as flying with John and Rose in a Learjet, we've also had several journeys in their helicopter. We have visited various countries of the world including South Africa, Mexico, USA, Belgium, Holland, Ireland, France, Canada, Germany, Spain, Portugal, Israel, Dubai and Thailand to minister or to have a holiday. We've played, sung and spoken in all the major theatres and venues in the UK including the Royal Albert Hall. We've appeared on television and radio many times in this country and also in the States. These are just a few of the incredible things that we have experienced as our heavenly employer has blessed us. I am incredibly grateful for all he has done over the last 40 years as we served him and I know that as I trust him, he will provide for me even in my latter years of life.

48

THE NGM YEARS – OUR SONS GET MARRIED

When Aidan and Leanne got engaged in December 2015, they had asked Ray if he would marry them. He joyfully agreed to do so. However, after his dad died, Aidan asked me if I would step in and marry them. I was honoured to be asked, and although I was no substitute for Ray, it was a joy and a delight to marry my son and his beautiful bride.

We had an amazing day at the Marriott Hotel in Chepstow. The hotel itself looks a bit like a castle and has many amazing places for photos to be taken. We had 120 guests and Aidan, Daniel (the best man) and myself all brought Ray into the day through our speeches. At the end of the day, I thanked God for the privilege of not only seeing my younger son married to his princess but also having the joy of marrying them. Ray and I had often prayed for the right princess for each of our boys. We never for a moment imagined that Aidan would get married before Daniel as Aidan was almost ten years younger.

During the wedding, Rose Lancaster spoke to Daniel and she asked if I had been over to Los Angeles to see where he lived. He told her that his dad and I had planned to come over in August, but unfortunately that was now impossible. Rose told Zoe that when I was ready to go to see Daniel, she and John would pay for my airline tickets. When I heard, I was so grateful but when I realised that she wanted to pay for me to go first class I was overwhelmed. I had never flown first class in my life.

When I arrived at Heathrow airport, the car I was in was directed to a special entrance where upon arrival five people came out to welcome me and carry my bags. As I only had one large case and one small cabin bag, most of the Virgin representatives were redundant. I went inside and checked in at the desk. I was the only person there! I was then shown through fast track security and before I knew it, I was in duty free. I had been told to make sure I spent some time in the Virgin lounge and so I immediately made my way to discover what it was like. Well, I could not believe it. Inside the lounge, I discovered my wish was their command. It was incredible. You could order whatever you wanted and all for free. There were even massages and nail treatments on offer. I could not believe it. I was so pleased that I had arrived at the terminal early and gone straight to the lounge so I could enjoy the many treats on offer. Eventually I heard an announcement that my flight was going to be delayed, but instead of complaining, I rejoiced as that meant I had more time to enjoy all the delicacies at my disposal. I hadn't left the airport and yet I felt I had been on a 5 star holiday.

When I got on the plane, the amazing treatment continued. I was asked if I would like something to drink. I asked them what they had on offer and she told me I could have whatever I wanted! So, after ordering a glass of champagne, I sat down on my luxurious leather seat to choose my meal and to watch a film on my large TV set. When my meal arrived, it was like dining in a 5 star restaurant. When I wanted to go to sleep, they came and changed my seat into a bed. They made my seat go flat and covered it with a sheet, gave me a proper pillow with a proper duvet and then asked me if I would like a pair of pyjamas? I could not believe it! A pair of pyjamas? I said "Yes please." Then I took them to the toilet so I could change. Most of you will know what a toilet is like on a plane! It's a small space where you can hardly turn around, however this toilet was nothing like that. I walked into a bathroom where besides the usual toilet, sink etc., it had a long length mirror, a chair in which to sit on with a huge space beside it. Changing in this bathroom was a real joy. I got into my bed in the sky and thanked the Lord for such a wonderful experience. I absolutely loved my gift from John and Rose. What a way to travel.

I got to see where Daniel worked and lived in Hollywood, Los Angeles. It was wonderful. It was lovely knowing that when I came home, I would be able to imagine him at work and at home. We travelled to Bethel church,

Redding where Bill Johnson is the main leader. Daniel absolutely loves his Uncle Bill as he always calls him. Ray and I had visited Bethel with Daniel previously and very much identified with Bill and the ministry that comes from that church. Zoe and Aidan joined us at Bethel for the leaders' conference. I had booked an Air B&B, which happened to belong to Danny and Sheri Silk, which meant that all of us could stay together in their beautiful home. It also had a swimming pool and a hot tub which we loved. I spoke at Bethel's Conservatory of the Arts and had a wonderful time with the students there. When our time at Bethel was over, Daniel and I went back to San Francisco and I flew on to Boise, Idaho. Aidan and Zoe left the day before to go back to England. I was booked to speak at various places in and around Boise and of course I got to see my special Heartbeat friends, Ian and Dorry Townend. My trip to the USA was so special even though it was my first time there without Ray. After a number of days in Boise, I went back to LA and then back to England, flying first class all the way! As I went home, I thanked God so much for a wonderful time with Daniel and continued to pray for his princess.

It was some time later when Daniel started to mention a girl he had met called Veronica. Ray and I had prayed that both our boys would marry girls who they not only loved, but also who shared their faith. I was delighted to discover that Veronica was not only in the music industry in LA but also that she loved the Lord Jesus and shared Daniel's faith. Daniel had always said he would not marry a girl who didn't know the Lord and God gave him (like Aidan before him) a beautiful godly girl. He brought her to England so that we could all meet her and when we did, we all fell in love with her. It was the first time she had been out of the USA and I had fun showing her what it was like to live in the UK. We had a spa day together as a family in Wales, we showed her Bristol and Bath and all of us had a meal at Thornbury Castle. She loved it all.

It was during another visit that Daniel asked me if I knew that I had a line down my television screen. I told him I knew but that the TV still worked and you only saw the line in certain colours. The next day I opened my front door and was astonished to see a man with a very large box. I was about to say that he must have the wrong house as I was not expecting a delivery and certainly not one so huge when he said, "Delivery for Daniel Goudie."

He pushed it into the hallway and left me staring at it. My first thought was, "How is Daniel going to take this back to the States?" Then I noticed writing on the box that said 50 inch. I thought, "Surely he has not bought me a television?" He had. He bought me a beautiful TV. I was completely overwhelmed by his generosity as I knew he didn't have much money. What a wonderful surprise! He set up the TV for me and we gave the old one to Aidan and Leanne to use until it dies.

A number of months later, Daniel began to talk about getting engaged. He had chatted to her dad and asked for her hand in marriage. Veronica called me to ask if I would give my blessing on the marriage as well. Of course, I was delighted. Daniel then arranged, without Veronica knowing, for his friends to pick her up on his birthday and bring her to a meeting point. She thought she was going out for Daniel's birthday with his friends, but instead, Daniel had arranged to propose to her and then take her on a helicopter to an island off the coast of California. She had no idea that it was going to happen. What a truly special day!

In December 2018, Aidan, Leanne and myself flew over to Los Angeles for Daniel and Veronica's wedding. Aidan was a groomsman and Leanne was a bridesmaid. I was asked to read a portion of scripture that Daniel and Veronica had chosen in the wedding service and was also asked to give a speech at the reception. What a joy to see both my boys married to their princesses. God had honoured our prayers and I know that Ray would have loved to have been physically there to see this happen, but I'm sure he was watching from Heaven.

When I arrived in LA, Daniel explained that he was really missing his dad as he needed help to choose an outfit for the wedding and asked if I would help him. What a joy it was to help him choose what to wear at his wedding. One of Ray and my favorite shops just happened to be in LA, and this was one of the shops that Daniel wanted to shop in. I had such fun helping him to pick his outfit. It really was very special.

I have two incredible sons, both so similar in many ways and yet so different. I absolutely love them both and love my daughters-in-law too. What a blessed woman I am! My two daughters-in-law are kind, beautiful and amazing girls who both have incredible voices. They are both singer/song-writers and to be honest it is such a shame they live so far apart because they get on so well. Leanne had the joy of knowing Ray and knowing that he loved her. Daniel said in his wedding speech, "I know if my dad was here today, he would love Veronica, because they are like two peas from the same pod." Ray was so creative in many ways but particularly with what he wore. Veronica is just the same. She is amazingly creative and I absolutely love the clothes she wears. She's different and Ray loved being different. She looks like a pop star and Ray too was regularly asked by strangers if he was famous!

Wherever Ray and I would go we would get stopped in a restaurant or even just walking along the street and asked if he was famous. We were mistaken in the States at one point for Paul and Linda McCartney. We were told that Ray looked like Davy Jones from The Monkees but often we didn't know who people thought he was. In a restaurant in Spain once, the waiter came to our table and said, "I'm sorry Sir, I should have recognised you. I have seen you on many television programmes. I should have known who you were. Please do forgive me! It's a pleasure to serve you tonight." Then he walked off leaving us dumbfounded. In the same restaurant at another time, we were having a meal together with Neil and Tanya Wilson. We were laughing so much that night, but we laughed even more when the man on the next table leaned over and said to Ray, "Who are you? I know you are someone famous, but I just cannot place you!" Ray told him he wasn't any-one famous. The man then said, "I know you are famous, and so if you don't mind, I'm going to take your photo." As we laughed out loud, he did indeed take several photos. At another restaurant in Portugal, a waiter put a piece of paper and a pen on our table and said to Ray, "I'm sorry sir, but my daughter thinks you are amazing and I wondered if you would mind giving me your autograph for her!" He then walked away. Ray said to me, "What name do you think I should sign?" He was always mistaken for someone famous and I'm sure Veronica will find the same!

As well as being a singer/songwriter, Leanne has recorded her own ep and has also just recently written a book. I had been praying for some time that someone in ngm would write other than me, but never in my wildest dreams would I have imagined that my daughter-in-law would be the one to do just that. When I realised that she had a desire to write, I gave her as much help and encouragement as I possibly could and also edited the book for her. The book was and is a great success and almost sold out within a few months. I was thrilled as I had prayed that she would have more success with this book than I had seen with mine. I hope she will be inspired to write many more books.

About a year after Ray died, something so weird and so awful happened. First of all, Aidan got sick. He was very ill with severe stomach problems and was in immense pain. At first, we thought it was something he had eaten and that it would pass, but it soon became apparent that he needed help. I went to see Aidan in his apartment and I could see he was quite distressed with the pain. We called 111 for help and advice. We were told to take him to Southmead hospital where he could see a doctor. When we arrived, the doctor examined him and after some discussion, he admitted Aidan to hospital. He was put on a drip, blood tests were taken and pain relief given. He was taken for a scan and then we waited for the results. As I sat beside his hospital bed, it brought back memories of doing exactly the same with Ray. You can imagine how we both felt as we realised that Aidan was going through the same tests, scans and procedures as his dad had a couple of years before. They thought Aidan had appendicitis and that they might have to operate, but in the end the tests showed that he had severe viral gastroenteritis. He was eventually allowed home before the end of the day, but it took him about ten days before he began to improve.

About a week later I was in ngm speaking at our training course, when in a break, I received a phone call from Daniel. He was extremely upset and was in hospital. He had exactly the same symptoms as Aidan had the previous week. I could not believe this! What was going on? Both my boys in serious pain going through the same tests for appendicitis and both being told they would have to go through an operation. Daniel told me he needed me and so I said I would get the next available flight. I had never heard my son so upset and in such pain before. The doctors took the same blood tests, put him on a drip and took him for a scan. In the meantime, while they waited for the results, they gave Daniel some morphine for the pain. When I next called him, he told me the minute the morphine began to work, he felt so much better. He was eventually told that he did have appendicitis and that he would go through an operation that day. He insisted that I didn't need to travel out to be with him as he would be out of the hospital and back in his home that evening. He wasn't married at that point and lived with a couple of guys in a shared house and so it was impossible for me to stay with him in his home. I discovered that I couldn't get a flight for a number of days and so Daniel persuaded me to stay in the UK. Veronica was his girlfriend at the time and so she kept in touch with me during the operation and also during Daniel's recovery at home. What a nightmare! I found it so hard that I could not be with him as I had been with Aidan. I was so grateful for Veronica keeping me up to date with his progress, especially during the night (UK time) whilst the operation was happening. I found it incredible that they released him home after such a short time after his operation, but that's the way it seems to be over there. I couldn't believe that both my sons were ill with the same symptoms, both suffering severe pain, both admitted to hospital, both going through the same tests that their dad had gone through, although the outcome was different for them both. Aidan didn't have appendicitis but Daniel did. Still to this day, we cannot believe that this happened, but I am so grateful that God brought my two boys through this trauma. Who would ever have thought that this would happen?

49

MOVING INTO THE NEW – LUV ESTHER TOURS AGAIN

After Ray died, I decided to continue the work that Ray and I had started back in 1980 and so I asked God to give me a double portion of his Spirit. I knew there were things we could not do without Ray, but one thing we could do was to continue to see lives transformed. My heart for revival in our land has never changed. I and my family and those in ngm miss Ray so much; he was such a creative man with many brilliant and prophetic ideas, but his life lives on in and through our two sons in particular and also in many of the spiritual children he had through the years in ngm.

We knew from what Ray had prophesied in January 2016 that God was moving ngm into the new and so it was essential to keep our eyes on him because, like the children of Israel thousands of years before, we had never been this way before. We were excited about the new, but never realised just how much of a change would occur. Neither did we realise in early 2016, that the new would be without Ray. This was a new journey for me, my family and for all at ngm. Ray and I always loved change but we have always known that for others it can be a bit of a challenge. Our last Summer School was held in 2017 and what a brilliant week we had with a number of young people aged between 12-20. Actually, that Summer School was particularly amazing! We saw many young people come to know the Lord and again we saw many signs of revival as these young people lay flat on their faces before the Lord. So many of them were changed forever. It was sad to lay it down, but it was right to do so. We also stopped our Christian training courses in 2019. We had known since 2017 that this was the right decision for the training, but it took a while before the end actually happened for many different pastoral reasons. When it eventually happened, Zoe and I were so relieved. It was the right thing to do. Our training was one of the most brilliant things we had done and so much has happened through those who were trained at ngm, but we knew it was so right to lay it down. The culture had changed, our world had changed, ngm had changed and BALPA had arisen.

It was difficult to do some things without Ray. Ray had rewritten and expanded the new luv esther and although we knew it would be tough to bring his vision of seeing luv esther tour again, Zoe and I knew we wanted to make sure it happened. Some of the journey was great fun, but some of it was so tough. We asked Murray Watts to be the director and Emma Fentiman to be assistant director. For years Ray had been training Emma to be his assistant director, so she was the obvious choice. I took on board the role of producer and Zoe worked as the general manager. We never anticipated the journey of putting the show on the road would be so tough. It was littered with issues and problems, some easy to deal with and some very difficult to deal with. We incorporated all Ray's ideas and creativity and managed to buy LED screens, something that Ray had always wanted in his shows and also in ngm. We had a great show in the end and it was worth all the pain, hardship and difficulties to see it happen.

The places that luv esther visited were so positive in their praise of the new show that Ray had written. It was right to put it on, but afterwards both Zoe and myself said, "Never again!" The cast, crew, and all of us on the production team missed Ray. We missed his leadership, his creativity, his wisdom, his infectious joy and his godly character. We missed him and although the show was great and the audience reaction was really good, it just wasn't the same without him. His creative juices were running through the show, his brilliant ideas really worked and the new set design by Sean Cavanagh was spectacular but without Ray actually being there in person, it lacked that certain something. I was both sad and glad to see the tour come to a natural end.

50

MOVING INTO THE NEW – THE 21ST SPIRITUAL HEALTH WEEKEND

In 2017, I held my 21st Spiritual Health Weekend. I wanted to mark it by seeing God do so much more at the weekends than ever before, and although this did happen, what I didn't realise was that behind the scenes Zoe had arranged something to mark the occasion that I had no idea about. She and the rest of the team, Jill Kemp, Derek and Ruth Tiffany and Leanne Goudie wanted to make it extra special for me and so they asked the ladies if they wanted to contribute gifts for me. Zoe gave people ideas of what to get, and what happened was that they were inundated with gifts as people's love overflowed. Of course, I had no idea. They kept it completely quiet and I never suspected anything at all. At the Bristol weekend, I was on stage with Zoe just before the meal on the Saturday evening, when she suddenly announced that they wanted to mark this occasion as it was the 21st. I was so surprised, but when the gifts were brought on stage, I was overwhelmed. Three of the guys on the Spiritual Health Weekend team brought on to the stage three large baskets overflowing with gifts. In the baskets were gifts of perfume, body creams, bath oils etc., make-up, candles, vouchers and gift cards for my favourite shops and so much more! There is a video of it all happening and you can see that I was overwhelmed. I started to cry and could not speak. I tried to get a few words out to say thanks, but it was difficult. On top of that, all the women gave me a standing ovation, I was a blubbering mess! I was completely overwhelmed with this outpouring of love towards me. Zoe said she was surprised that I had no idea as this had taken her and the team months to organise. But I had absolutely no idea whatsoever! She is an amazing and beautiful friend and we have an amazing team working behind the scenes. I am still enjoying some of the incredible gifts I was given. What a wonderful surprise.

As I continued speaking at churches, events, conferences, on TV and on radio, everywhere I went I kept getting the same prophecy. God kept saying through various people and leaders that God had great expansion ahead for me. People would prophesy that God was going to raise me up and I would see so much more than I had ever seen before. Many said that God would expand my influence in my own country and across the globe. When I was out on the road and someone started to prophecy, Zoe and I would look at each other and smile, because God was giving me the same commission and the same encouraging words again and again. I obviously needed to hear it many times and to be honest I still do.

One time when I was in Dubai visiting my friends, Mike and Olenka Aspinwall, I received a prophecy from Shawn Boltz at a conference. Shawn is a very accurate prophetic minister. He asked anyone to stand if they had a birthday on 27th February. I nervously stood amongst the 500 or so people who were there and he prophesied that my life was going to have a national impact and that God was going to activate his wisdom over me on how to do what he has called me to do. He told me that a higher-level prophetic function would come on me. He said it had been there from time to time, but it would come on me in such a strong way that it would be shocking to me. He said that I was going to be shocked by my own ministry because of what God does through me. There were many other things that he shared which were so special and so encouraging that I wondered if he was really talking about me. He said that I had been faithful and loyal and that I had never fainted, but that I was strong. He said that although I had grown tired at times, I had never allowed myself to weary from doing good. He said I would mount up like on wings of eagles like it says in Isaiah 40. He said he could see that eagle picture had been quite consistent in my life. Since he gave me this, I have had prophetic words about rising and soaring on eagles' wings again and again. I believe part of this prophetic word has perhaps been outworked during the coronavirus pandemic, but that story is still to come!

I hold this and other prophecies I have received, close to my heart, not really knowing how God will outwork it all, but I am leaving it for God to do as I keep close to him. In the late 80's we changed our name from Heartbeat to New Generation Ministries. During the years when the music side of our ministry changed, we again made a slight change to the name and called ourselves New Generation Music. Then before Ray died, we changed it to New Generation Music/Ministries – and using whatever name was appropriate. More recently we have been using New Generation Ministries again as a lot of our music side, especially the Christian arts training, has finished. The mainstream training we do through BALPA is carried out through our second charity called The Inspire Arts Trust. Ray and I used to laugh because people used to think that ngm stood for Nancy Goudie Ministries. When people saw me speaking at my weekends and saw the name ngm, they mistakenly thought that's what ngm meant. Recently however, people have suggested that Nancy Goudie Ministries would be more appropriate as a major part of what ngm does now is what I do. I've always hated promoting myself. Ask Zoe and she will tell you; it's always been something that I struggle with, I always find it difficult when part of my work highlights me. I'd much rather highlight others and leave all the limelight to God. ngm will continue to stand for New Generation Ministries because it's not just about me, if it was then when I die the ministry would surely die too. The truth is that it's about everyone in ngm and ultimately, it's about God and what he wants us to do.

51

MOVING INTO THE NEW – EMBRACING CHANGE

I asked God one day how to reach more vulnerable women and he told me to go to the prisons. I contacted my friend Barry Woodward (who has worked in prisons for many years) and he opened up some of his contacts to me. I ended up visiting a prison in Wakefield and absolutely loved my time there. In the morning, before I left for the prison, I heard the Lord say that I should be prepared to be the only speaker on that occasion. There was supposed to be another lady speaking as well as me, but when I heard the Lord's words, I thought through in my mind what I would do if I had to speak for longer than my 20 minutes. When I got through security, I was told that the other lady had turned up, but the prison had not admitted her as she did not have the right paperwork to get in. I was asked if I could expand my talk. I was so glad the Lord had spoken to me beforehand. The response from the inmates was amazing and so many of them responded at the end of my talk. It was wonderful to have an opportunity to pray and chat with some of them. Out of that one visit I received two invitations to go back, but then COVID-19 arrived and the visit had to be postponed. Apart from one visit in 1994, I hadn't been in a prison since the Heartbeat days, but it felt good and right to be back.

I feel I have so much vision for the future, but don't at present have the capacity to do it all. As there are so many other issues with buildings, finance and personnel, it means that much of the vision is not able to be carried out. Zoe and I felt this was not right and so we began to ask God if there was more change that needed to happen. Zoe and I spent a day praying and laying down everything we were doing and asking God to give us the wisdom to know what was on his heart and mind for us. We only want to pick up those things that he wants us to do.

Shortly after this I listened to a T.D. Jakes podcast where he was talking about what he had to lay down and leave behind in order to do what was his heart and vision. In his talk he asked, "What are you prepared to lose in order to gain what God has for you?" His words jumped out of my computer at me and suddenly I knew God was speaking. I told the Lord, "I am prepared to lose whatever it takes in order to make sure that the vision of seeing lives transformed and the vision of seeing revival in our nation become a reality." Immediately I knew what God was saying! We had to lay down Lancaster House, one of the buildings that he had given us in 1998.

A number of weeks later, I listened to my good friend, Marty Brogan, a church leader in Munich, Germany and as she was talking, God spoke again. She said that in the season we are in, that sometimes God asks us to let go of the good in order to come into the best. She went on to say, "God sometimes says this was good for the season we were in, but is not good for the next season." Again, I knew God was speaking. Lancaster House which was named after John and Rose Lancaster, had been so brilliant during the last 22 years, but now it was becoming a burden rather than a blessing and that in order to move into everything God has for us in the future, we need to leave this building behind. When it was suggested by Ray a couple of years before he died and then again at our Trustees meeting about a year ago, that perhaps we needed to think about selling this building, my immediate reaction was, "No, this is a building the Lord has given us." But now the Lord was showing me that in order to move forward into all the great things God has for us, we sometimes need to leave good things behind.

We no longer need the space that Lancaster House provided because the season has changed. After talking it through with Zoe, I then asked my two sons what they thought as they understood and knew the vision. Then after discussing it with our Trustees, I spoke with John and Rose Lancaster because they had provided the money for the building in the first place, but also because I valued their wisdom and support in it all. Everyone I spoke to agreed that the time was right to sell it and move on to the new fresh things God had for us. As we began to think through the plans for moving everything over to Caedmon, we began to get really excited about the future. There's a lot to do before we can proceed, but we feel God has spoken and that enables me to move forward now. Previously I had found it very difficult to even think about selling this property as God had so clearly given it to us, but once I had a word from God, I could begin to move forward. I told the Lord with tears in my eyes, "Yes Lord, I will do it" and suddenly I was free.

God has been speaking to us about moving into the new since January 2016 and every change has been a good and positive step, even though at times it's been sad to leave some good things behind. However, here we are in 2020, with more change about to happen. It's so important not to hold on to the past if the Lord is moving on. Instead, we continue to use the past to propel us into the future knowing that as we follow the Lord the best is always yet to come. So, as I write this book, we are getting ready to put the beautiful manor house on the market and move our offices into Caedmon. As we do, we are keeping our eyes on the Lord and making sure we are only doing what he wants us to do.

I have never understood over the years why it's difficult for people to follow what God is calling them to do. He only has good things for us. As we lay our lives down, he gives us so much peace and joy. Many people settle for less and make do with the good, when God is offering them the best. Ray and I left our homes, our jobs, our house (with a mortgage on it), our families, our friends and our church to obey what the Lord had told us to do and we never regretted that decision once. We could have settled for what we had in Scotland, but as good as that was, it was important to trust God for the best.

As I have said earlier in this book, whatever we laid down, God has given us more than we could ask for or even imagine. Yes, there were times when it was scary and the enemy would whisper his lies into our ears, but as we stood on his word and kept our eyes on him, he led us through every problem, every dark night of the soul, every trial and tribulation, even the valley of the shadow of death and brought us through victoriously. God can do the same for you if you, like Ray and I, take time to hear, obey and trust him. I want every day of my life to be in tune with the sound of Heaven. I don't want to discover when I get to Heaven that I missed out on the more that God wanted to do in me and through me because of a lack of trust. It's his will I want and not my own. I only want his ways and his thoughts. I want my eyes to rest on his wonderful face every day. Even in the midst of fear and problems, I want my heart to hear his voice more. I want to be captured by his amazing love in a way that nothing else even comes close. One thing I have learned is that hearing, obeying and trusting is the only true way to live an exciting adventurous life in God. Are you ready to join in on the fun of living dangerously?

I discovered over the years that as you hear from God, he then takes you step by step so that obedience becomes a joy. Once you have obeyed, then he often tests you to see if you will move to the next step of trusting him. At that point, many people cannot find the strength to trust God for the journey. God has been the best employer that Ray, myself, Zoe and many of those who've come through ngm's door have ever had. We would never have had all the opportunities we had, if we had not heard, obeyed and trusted God to move from my homeland of Scotland across the border to England and see the work of Heartbeat, ngm, The Inspire Arts Trust, the Spiritual Health Weekends, luv esther, The Prodigals and many other incredible and wonderful visions come into reality. Can I encourage you to trust him so you too will be able to say with me, Who would ever have thought?

52

LIVING IN THE NEW – CORONAVIRUS

While I was writing this book, we saw something so incredible yet so awful happen. As you will know we saw a deadly virus called COVID-19 travel throughout the whole world. It was like watching the scriptures come alive. The streets emptied as people were told to isolate themselves at home. An unseen virus began to kill thousands of people all over the world. People began to be filled with fear and panic. At first people didn't really think it would affect them, but slowly this virus showed its deadly strength. Governments and leaders all over the world are now dealing with issues they have never had to deal with before in their lives. Many thousands of people were and still are infected. Many described it as feeling as though a snake was around their throat and it was squeezing tighter and tighter. They then went on to say that they felt as though an elephant was sitting on their chest. Many thousands worldwide lost the battle to breathe. I heard on the news stories of people telling their loved ones on the phone, "I'm sorry I'm not going to make it!" Many had to die on their own without their family around them. At first, we thought it was only the elderly and vulnerable people with existing health conditions who would die and mainly at that time it was, but when we began to see healthy, strong people who had no health conditions dying, people began to get so very scared. Nations all over the world went into lockdown, meaning you were only allowed to go out for food, medicine and in some countries for one daily walk/run. The whole world became silent. The streets, the skies, rivers and oceans were empty as the human race disappeared from view. It's like living a life we have never experienced before.

I was so encouraged when other nations began to have a National Day of Prayer and so I decided to write to our government, asking our Prime Minister if he would initiate a day of prayer, but got no response. I also wrote to our Queen, reminding her of what her father, King George VI did in World War II. During the war, it looked like we were going to be beaten by the Germans, but King George VI called the nation of Britain to pray. A National Day for Prayer was initiated and the churches were packed all over the country as people cried out to God in their fear and panic. What happened was incredible. Many miracles occurred and as a result the war was turned around. What seemed impossible became possible. God moved because people prayed. I asked the Queen to ask the Government to initiate a National Day of Prayer in this time when again our people are so fearful and so afraid. I eventually got a lovely letter from her telling me that she had taken careful note of my views that I had expressed regarding the particular importance of prayer at this time, but still no National Day of Prayer.

At one point the Archbishop of Canterbury initiated a day of prayer, but it seemed so low key that not everyone knew it was going on. Before it had happened, someone saw one of my posts on Facebook and asked me if I would propose a day when everyone could pray. My first thought was, "Who am I that I should initiate a National Day of Prayer", but then knowing God was with me, I took up the challenge and on 20th March 2020, interestingly enough the first day of spring, I initiated a National Day of Prayer. I received so many encouraging emails, texts, messages and posts telling me how much people valued the prayer points I had written. Then two other people asked if I would organise a National Day of Prayer every Friday, and so every Friday I began to release up to date prayer points for people to follow, as we all cry out to God to heal our nation and cleanse our world. Each week I spend time asking the Lord what I should say. I often feel so inadequate, but every week, God gives me the words to say to inspire and encourage people in the UK and beyond to pray for our nation and indeed for our world.

Our government asked people to wash their hands properly to help eradicate the virus. They suggested everyone sang the song Happy Birthday twice so that they cleansed their hands for 20 seconds. I decided to ask people to sing the chorus of the song that our band, Heartbeat had recorded in 1986 called Heal our Nation and make that time of washing their hands (which we all have to do frequently) into a time of prayer. Many people all over the UK did so and they continue to do so. I've had so many wonderful emails, messages and posts telling me that people all over the world are singing our song Heal our Nation as well as praying for our God to bring so many to know him through this crisis. Slowly, we began to hear of people being naturally and supernaturally healed of coronavirus.

Churches were no longer allowed to hold services in their buildings and therefore many of them decided to continue their services online and via social media. Life has become so different. Some people began to seek out people of faith and ask them to pray for them. There has never been a time like now where all over the world people are seeking answers to this virus. My prayer was and still is that many will find the answers in God and in the wisdom he brings. My heart is that many Christians across our world will have the courage to speak about their faith and see a great revival spread throughout the world. After a number of weeks of praying, we began to see a difference. Newspapers began to report that more people than ever before were attending church online, many of them said that they had never attended church before. The Guardian newspaper 's headline said, People in the UK turn to prayer as 1 in 4 tune into religious services. They said that a quarter of all adults had listened to or watched a religious service online. In their fear and panic, thousands were turning to God in prayer. I started a ngm prayer line, where people could email us prayer requests and from the first day of releasing this, prayer requests began to come in. This is all very encouraging, however, what happened next showed us that God is moving supernaturally in people's lives at this time.

I heard from a lady who I have known for many years but have never actually met. I only know her because she contacted me many years ago online. This lady would describe herself as someone who doesn't go to church, is not spiritual and has fought God for years. Yet just last weekend, God supernaturally visited her in her dreams. She contacted me to tell me that in one of her dreams she saw me in a waterfall and I was shouting to her, inviting her to come into the waterfall. She had a bucket in her hand and I was telling her to bring her bucket and get into the waterfall. She came closer to see the waterfall and when she did, she saw that the waterfall was not a waterfall of water, but was a waterfall of pure gold. She said it was cascading all over me and I was so full of joy that I couldn't contain it. When she saw it was pure gold it shocked her and she fell to her knees. The Lord spoke to her and said, "You can take a bucketload of my presence with you, but what I really want is for you to get into the waterfall. Do you see Nancy with a bucket? She replied, "No." The Lord said, "One day you will not have to fill your bucket but one day you will be in the waterfall just like Nancy." She woke up sobbing in the middle of the night! She had never felt good enough to be accepted by God.

When she contacted me she said, "Nancy, what is going on? I don't know what is happening to me." I said "Dawn, you have to know that this is supernatural. God is invading your dreams and is speaking to you. He wants you to get into the waterfall of his presence. He wants you to get to know him."

The next night she had another dream where she again saw me in the waterfall and this time I was telling her that God loved her and was waiting to forgive her and that all she needed to do was to trust him and get into the waterfall. She again woke up sobbing! I had put two verses of scripture into a message for her and she told me that those verses were saying the same things I had told her in the dream. When she read them, her hands became burning hot and she felt something like an electrical surge going through her body. She said, "I don't know what is going on. I can't concentrate on TV or anything." I wrote back saying, "Dawn, you have to know that this is supernatural and God is speaking so clearly to you and when you are ready here is a prayer that you can use." The next morning, she wrote to me again saying, "Early, just after the sun rose, in my garden when the birds were beginning to sing and chatter, I gave my heart to Jesus….."

I sent her a Passion Translation New Testament and she began to read it. She told me that she felt as though she had a blood transfusion. She was in the waterfall and was loving it. She told me she felt absolute peace, better than any spa day she has ever been on and that she cannot get enough of the Bible I sent her.

There have been a number of people from different areas of the UK who have invited their neighbours to learn more about God at this time. I saw on social media a man who held a short service in his street. To begin with as I watched, I wasn't sure how many would respond to his invitation to join him on the street for a short service. However, slowly but surely the doors opened and many came into the street, socially distancing of course, to hear the words he spoke and the songs that he played. It was a simple service, but it touched hearts. Many were visibly moved by the singing of the song Amazing Grace.

Now is the time to stand up and tell many of the love and power of God. There's a hunger in people right now like we have not seen for a long time. Who would ever have thought that a virus could open such a great door for the gospel? How wonderful and yet what a responsibility for us as Christians. Let's not hold back on telling people about a God who loves the world enough to send his beloved son to die for us. We may never get this opportunity again.

53

CELEBRATING 40 YEARS IN MINISTRY

I can hardly believe that I have now been in full time ministry for 40 years. I had arranged to have a 40th celebration on 6th June in Thornbury. The main purpose of this event was to celebrate and thank God for all he has done during those 40 years as we had travelled on our journey with him. I also wanted to thank others for the help they have given us and are continuing to give. I didn't want the event to be about Ray or myself, but instead to be about God and what he has done. However, because of coronavirus we have had to move the event to 10th October 2020. I really hope we can celebrate together then, but if not, then we will take the whole event online so that there is a way of celebrating and thanking God together. So many wonderful individuals have stood with us and believed in us and financially supported us along the journey and my heart is to take the time to say thank you! We hope to be able to do this in October one way or another.

As we couldn't celebrate the 40 years in June, I still felt it would be right to do something in June. So, on 1st June, the day when 40 years earlier Ray and I left Scotland, I celebrated in a few ways. In the morning, I spoke with Daniel and Veronica in California and then in the afternoon had a socially distanced meeting in ngm's garden with Aidan and Leanne. I wrote and sent a very personal letter to my two boys to mark the occasion. I felt this was important as this anniversary is as much about them as it is about Ray and myself. Daniel had travelled with us for 33 years and Aidan had travelled 23 years out of the 40. I wanted them both to know that they were important in the journey. They are amazing sons who carry our physical and our spiritual DNA. I thanked them for standing with their dad and I and for never rebelling against the vision. Instead they embraced the vision and even valued it as precious. Both of them had been in ngm at different times and they loved the vision and they still do. In fact, the vision still lives on in both Daniel and Aidan. Also, I wanted to thank Zoe, who together with her husband Tim has stood with us for the last 23 years. I ordered her a bouquet of flowers as a small way of saying thank you and asked for them to arrive at her home before 10am. What I didn't know was that Zoe, together with the Trustees and the rest of ngm, had ordered a bouquet of flowers for me. When Zoe's flowers arrived at her door and she realised that it was from the same florist that she had ordered my bouquet from, she immediately mistook them for being my bouquet and told them, "Oh no, you need to deliver these to Nancy Goudie." They then explained that these flowers were from Nancy Goudie. She was totally surprised and so was I when mine arrived! What a wonderful day of blessings!

At lunchtime Zoe came to my home and we had a socially distanced cream tea with a glass of prosecco in the garden. What I didn't realise was that she had asked several of our Trustees and also a number of family and friends to send a little message via video for me. I laughed, I cried and I rejoiced. They were very special and beautiful messages. I was really blessed by what each individual and couple said on these videos. Also, several people responded to an online offering that Zoe had arranged for the 40th. People marked the day by sowing a financial seed into our ngm bank account. What a blessing and such an answer to our prayers too! I also was blessed by three friends who gave me a personal gift to mark the occasion. They wanted me personally to feel the abundance of our Lord at this time. The generosity of everyone who gave to ngm and to me personally blew me away! I was overwhelmed. What a special day! Who would ever have thought?

54

LIVING IN THE NEW – EMBRACING THE FUTURE

It is now over 40 years since Ray and I left our home in Scotland to go on an amazing journey with God. If I had my time all over again, would I choose to stay in Scotland and reject the calling of a lifetime? No way! It's been 40 years of discovering more of our Lord and seeing so many wonderful and exciting things happen. It has been an adventure I would never have wanted to miss. Would I choose to do it all over again – you bet I would. The road has been littered with passion, peace and pain, mixed with much excitement, sheer bliss, joy, confusion and heartache. In one of the video messages I received on 1st June, Tim Eldridge said something as part of a greeting from him and his wife Sue that I identified with so much. He said, "Ministry is like an iceberg, people see the little bit that shows at the top and think how wonderful that is, but they don't see all the hard labour, the agony, the rejection and all the other things that are submerged. We understand all the sacrifices that you have made over four decades and the things that you have gone through that you probably wouldn't have chosen, but they have made you who you are. You are a strong woman and your ministry reflects that."

Ray and I have experienced so many wonderful and sometimes terrifying times, but I wouldn't have missed any of it for the world. What a journey! What a God! He called Ray and I out of Scotland, gave us a vision of seeing thousands of lives transformed all over the world and then as we followed him, we saw the vision become a reality. It's been nothing to do with us, but all to do with our God. All we needed to do was to do what he had called us to do and to go where he had called us to go and to say what he had asked us to say and this we have done willingly and gladly to the best of our ability.

I am praying God will grant me many more years so I can continue to serve him and see many more lives transformed. Ray and I always saw ourselves/ngm like a speedboat rather than the QE2. If the QE2 is required to change direction, it takes a while to do so. It eventually turns and changes direction. However, a speedboat can turn quickly and easily in any direction. We wanted to always be like a speedboat, able to turn quickly in any direction as the Spirit of God directs. As we did that throughout the years, God did so much that, to be honest not even half the stories have been told in this book. Our God is an outrageous giver, he has given life to so many through the small and at times seemingly insignificant work of ngm. So much has happened, so many untold stories, so many incredible miracles, so many times when we had to hold on and continue to trust, so many unanswered questions, but also so many acts of faith. There were many times when the storms raged and we felt so very small, we often felt overwhelmed with difficulties, but God somehow enabled us to stand in him and see the way forward. I cannot tell all the stories, but what I have related here of our failures and successes hopefully will encourage you to take the hand of God and walk with him into the future he has for you. There is no other way to walk other than holding on to his hand.

I want my life to continue to count and for every moment to be spent doing what the Lord tells me to do, going wherever he tells me to go and saying whatever he tells me to say, because in doing this there is no greater joy! He fills my heart and life every day with unspeakable joy and a peace that passes all understanding. Do I have moments of sadness and pain? Of course, I do, I miss Ray every day and still mourn the absence of my husband, but I am so grateful to God for his incredible presence with me. If God is with me, then I can face tomorrow and the truth is, you can too. Earlier this year I needed to get away for a week to rest, as I usually do after my Spiritual Health Weekends. I didn't know where to go, but eventually I managed to find a beautiful lodge at a very cheap price. It was a place I had been to many times with Ray. I knew I needed someone to come with me, but everyone I asked could not come for very genuine reasons. After asking five people and receiving negative replies each time, I have to say, I cried. I miss being able to organise a holiday with Ray; it's hard not having someone who can always go with you on holiday. I cried because it again brought back just how much I had lost. When Aidan heard that I was looking for someone to go with me to Lincolnshire he immediately said, "Mum, I'll go with you!" My kind and loving son took some time off his work to be able to go with me. Leanne was only able to join us for half of the week as she had to stay at ngm because she had classes to teach. We had a good and restful holiday together. The Lord answered my prayers and provided for me through my son. I have a kind and loving family.

I would love to live to see any grandchildren the Lord may give me; this was something that Ray longed for too, but never had a chance to see. I hope I get that chance if God blesses my children with children.

What happens now? I don't know what the future holds, but I do know who holds the future. One thing I know is that the best is always yet to come. Henry Nouwen said, "I know that I have to move from speaking about Jesus to letting him speak within me, from thinking about Jesus to letting him think within me, from acting for and with Jesus to letting him act through me. I know the only way for me to see the world is to see it through his eyes." This says exactly what has always been my aim and the goal that I pursue.

As I look back over the life that I have had, one song seems to say what I would want to say. It's called The Goodness of God.

The Goodness of God

I love You, Lord
Oh Your mercy never fails me
All my days, I've been held in Your hands
From the moment that I wake up
Until I lay my head
Oh, I will sing of the goodness of God

All my life You have been faithful
All my life You have been so, so good
With every breath that I am able
I will sing of the goodness of God

I love Your voice

You have led me through the fire
In darkest nights You are close like no other
I've known You as a Father
I've known You as a Friend
I have lived in the goodness of God

All my life You have been faithful,
All my life You have been so, so good
With every breath that I am able
I will sing of the goodness of God.

Your goodness is running after, it's running after me
Your goodness is running after, it's running after me
With my life laid down, I'm surrendered now
I give You everything
Your goodness is running after, it's running after me.
Your goodness is running after, it's running after me
Your goodness is running after, it's running after me
With my life laid down, I'm surrendered now
I give You everything
Your goodness is running after, it keeps running after me

All my life You have been faithful
All my life You have been so, so good
With every breath that I am able
I'm gonna sing of the goodness of God
I'm gonna sing, I'm gonna sing
All my life You have been faithful
All my life You have been so, so good
With every breath that I am able
I'm gonna sing of the goodness of God
I'm gonna sing of the goodness of God

Written by: Jenn Johnson, Jason Ingram, Ben Fielding, Ed Cash and Brian Johnson
© 2018 Bethel Music Publishing (ASCAP) / Fellow Ships Music (SESAC) / So Essential Tunes (SESAC) (admin. at EssentialMusicPublishing.com) /

SHOUT! Music Publishing (APRA) (adm. in the US and Canada at Capitol-CMGPublishing.com) / Alletrop Music (BMI) (Admin. by Music Services, Inc.)

That song truly does say it all. I could not have put it better myself. *All my life, you have been faithful. All my life you have been so, so good. With every breath that I am able, I'm gonna sing of the goodness of God.* I've had an amazing 40 years of serving Jesus, 36 of those years were with my wonderful husband. With every year that goes by, I will declare with my every breath that God is so, so good. I know as the years go by, that his goodness will continue to run after me. I don't know what I am going to face in the future, but I know whatever it is, I can face it with the Lord at my side. Without him, I can do nothing, but with him, I can do all things. The same is true for you!

I really hope you have enjoyed reading the stories within this book as much as I have enjoyed writing them. I can truly say as I look back on 40 miraculous years - who would ever have thought?

ABOUT THE AUTHOR

Nancy Goudie is a well-known speaker and author. She and her husband Ray formed the 80's band Heartbeat and went on to found New Generation Ministries and The Inspire Arts Trust based at Caedmon (their multi-million pound arts and music complex in Thornbury, Bristol, England). Nancy has written 17 books and recorded 6 meditation CDs as well as producing an annual Spiritual Health Magazine. She founded Nancy Goudie's Spiritual Health Weekends in the UK and in Spain in 4 and 5 star luxury hotels. These weekends are hugely popular and many hundreds of women have been transformed by the power of God through them. She is regularly on radio and has been on TV many times and has hosted her own TV chat show. She has developed her own podcast and also during the last number of months has developed a new online programme for men and women called Nancy Goudie's Spiritual Health Breakthrough Session. Nancy speaks at conferences, events and churches in many places across the world.

For more information on Nancy's ministry or to book her to come to your area, please visit www.nancygoudie.com or www.ngm.org.uk

Nancy Goudie's
Spiritual Health Weekends | UK

THREE EXCITING DAYS TO TRANSFORM YOUR SPIRITUAL WALK

Would you like to be pampered physically and toned up spiritually? Nancy Goudie's Spiritual Health Weekend could be just the thing you are looking for!

Nancy Goudie has been running these luxury, unique and sensational weekend conferences for the last 25 years at luxury four-star hotels in the UK. This blissful and revitalising weekend is for ladies of all ages. Come and enjoy the excellent food, the superb leisure facilities; *(spa, steam room, sauna, fitness room and luxury pool),* the life changing sessions from Nancy, the magnificent banquet and 5-star entertainment and the free pamper treatments, plus so much more. Each conference is usually booked well in advance, so please book early to avoid disappointment.

This refreshing escape will energise your body, mind and spirit. You will discover that you are treated as special from the moment you arrive until the moment you leave. Come and join us and you will find that you leave the weekend feeling like you are floating on air.

This is a women's conference like no other!

What people say:

"One of the best experiences! The moment you walk through that hotel door the cares of the world fall away. A protected place of rest – of being taken care of – made to feel special. A place of laughter and restoration. Would love to be able to take all my friends". **Delegate**

"The Spiritual Health Weekends are better than a holiday in Disneyland. – I just knew I had to be there this year" **SR**

Nancy Goudie's
Spiritual Health Weekends | SPAIN

How about spending a long weekend in the south of Spain in a 5 star luxury hotel, where you learn to cook Paella (optional), exercise on the beach (optional), eat out at a nice restaurant and lie in the sun but at the same time have worship and teaching and discover God in a deeper and more intimate way? The resort has four swimming pools, gorgeous rooms and apartments, a beautiful restaurant and a lovely sandy beach too. Every time we have held this weekend, the ladies have all said they would come back. They loved the resort, loved the company and loved the teaching. You will love this weekend in the sun so come and join us!

What people say:

"This is the second time I have been to Nancy Goudie's Spiritual Health Weekend in Spain and I absolutely loved it. I've been to Windsor and I've been to Preston but this is a new level altogether." **S.L Delegate**

FOR MORE INFORMATION AND
BOOKING DETAILS CONTACT:

Zoe Wickham at:

ngm, Caedmon Complex, Bristol Road, Thornbury, Bristol BS35 3JA
Tel: *01454 414880*
Email: *zoewickham@ngm.org.uk*
Or visit: *www.nancygoudie.com*

OTHER BOOKS AND PRODUCTS BY NANCY GOUDIE

Luv Esther - £3.00
This book takes you behind the scenes of the amazing luv esther musical. It's the story of how luv esther came about; how God provided more than half a million pounds and how God visited ngm with his deep intimacy. It is also a study on the life of Esther which can be used individually or in small groups.

"I thoroughly recommend this book to you"
Graham Kendrick

Treasures of Darkness - £3.00
This is a very naked and honest autobiographical account of a time when the world around Nancy started to collapse. Her husband, Ray, fell into a dark pit where he experienced ill health and burnout. At the same time God was taking their ministry, ngm, through a shift, which caused much pain and insecurity and led to many people eventually leaving. Pressures swept in like a storm leaving devastation, confusion and unanswered prayers. Nancy discovered that through this time there were 'treasures of darkness and riches hidden in a secret place' (Isaiah 45:3).

Spiritual Health Encounters - £6.99
This unique and creative book helps you to spend time in the secret place and will transform and deepen your intimacy with God. Each practical exercise takes you on an exciting, creative journey of mediation, hearing from heaven, writing a psalm and real encounters with God. It's great for individuals, small groups and for counsellors/disciplers to give to those who need to see a breakthrough.

This is a dynamic book that can really change lives! **Available on Amazon Kindle.**

The Beloved - £5.00
(hardback book)
This is a collection of real stories, poems, wise words, meditations and huge encouragement to know that you are God's beloved child. Any time you are feeling down, unloved, criticised or critical of yourself and life hits you hard, then pick up this book and flick through its pages. Each page is designed to bring you words of encouragement, hope and love.

Confident? - £5.00
(hardback book)
This book is for anyone who sometimes swings from being confident to feeling a failure. It's a book full of encouragement, wise words, poems, songs and stories to lift your spirit and get you back on your feet again, ready to face life once more. Through its pages you will feel accepted, really loved and realise afresh how amazing you are!

You are Special - £5.00
(hardback book)
In our culture of stress with so much pressure to look good and be famous, we often need to be reminded just how unique, precious, remarkable and extraordinary we are! No matter what colour our skin is, what size we are, what intelligence we display, what background we come from, the truth is each of us is an exceptional human being. In every page of this book you will discover the truth about yourself and realise afresh that you are deeply loved, special and accepted.

Oasis of Hope - £6.99
(hardback book)

There are times in our lives when we all need an oasis, a place where we can go and receive a thirst quenching drink for our souls. This book is such a place! A place where hope is renewed and faith can begin to grow. A place that will help refresh the reader physically, mentally, emotionally and spiritually. A place that gives us more of what we need to enable us to keep on going in our journey through life. It is designed to plant seeds of hope into the barren places of our hearts and encourage those seeds to grow and develop so that our faith will soar.

Oasis of Delight - £6.99
(hardback book)

There are times in our lives when we need an oasis, a place where we can go to receive a thirst quenching drink for our souls. This book is an exploration of what it means to live in the oasis of delight, tasting its fruit, relaxing and relishing in the lush surroundings; free to explore and enjoy the depths of his fulness of joy and his pleasures forevermore. It inspires us to enjoy the delightful fruit of intimacy with God whilst all the time pointing us towards the day when we will be in the ultimate garden of delight for eternity.

The Gift of Laughter - £6.00
(hardback book)

We live in an exhausting world often full of stress, concern and worry; one of the ways to help us navigate our way through life is laughter. Experts tell us that just 15 minutes of laughter can give the same benefit as two hours of sleep. It has been said that one good belly laugh burns off 3 to 4 calories and that laughing for only 15 seconds can add two days to your life span! Each of us has been created with the ability to laugh. We already have the language of laughter within us and it has no negative side effects! Use it and it could increase your quality and even quantity of life. If you are looking for tips, interesting quotes on laughter and many stories to help you laugh, then this is the book for you. These stories come from everyday situations – some are funny and some are laugh out loud funny! You can open this book at any page and you'll find something to either make you laugh and giggle or something to encourage or inspire you to laugh out loud! **Available on Amazon Kindle.**

Our Greatest Adventure – £8.99
This book tells a story of courage in the midst of pain, peace in the midst of sorrow and trust in the midst of confusion. It's a story of love and devotion in the midst of one of the biggest challenges Ray and Nancy Goudie have ever known. It's the story of God's faithfulness when Ray was diagnosed as having pancreatic cancer and of God's continued faithfulness and immense presence when Ray walked through the valley of the shadow of death and eventually fell asleep into the arms of Jesus. This is an honest, deep and raw story that will touch your emotions, making you laugh as well as cry. There are many funny and humorous moments amidst the pain and the heartache. It's a story that will fuel your faith in God and ignite your passion for his presence. This is a story that many have said had to be told. **Available on Amazon Kindle.**

The Best Is Yet To Come Journal - £6.50
This fantastic journal has a page of inspiration from Nancy and plenty of pages for your notes, drawings or whatever you wish. Printed with a luxury finish this is the ideal journal for you – grab your copy now.

ALL BOOKS ARE AVAILABLE DIRECT FROM NGM AT:

www.ngm.org.uk/shop, www.nancygoudie.com or through
www.amazon.co.uk

MEDITATION CDs

Peace Like a River - £8.00
If you have ever experienced stress, carried worries, fought fears or are just looking for an oasis in your busy life, then this CD is for you. This recording will take you to a place of tranquillity, where peace, love and grace are yours in abundance. Use this CD daily and you will find peace like a river flowing through your soul. **Available to download from iTunes and other online platforms.**

Smile - £8.00
If you are feeling the daily stresses of life, the busyness of work, the pressures of family or just need some soothing for your soul, then this is recording for you. **Available to download from iTunes and other online platforms.**

Meditations for the Beloved - £8.00
We all need to know we are loved and valued. This incredible music and mediation CD will take you to the secret place where you will know you are The Beloved; you will be overwhelmed with love, feel accepted and experience a peace that passes all understanding. **Available to download from iTunes and other online platforms.**

Speak…..Declare the Truth: Volume 1 - £8.00
Are you feeling overwhelmed? Are circumstances or people getting you down? Are you in need of encouragement? Do you need to know you are loved? Do you need to see a miracle of health or provision? Does everything seem impossible for you? Then I have news for you! The Bible says in 2 Peter 1:3 that God has already given you everything you need for life and godli-

ness. Not just some things, but everything you need. We need to start reading, believing and confessing the truth. This CD helps you to do just that!

What we speak has power and therefore when we confess the truth contained in the word of God, power is released and the word brings life. Speak life and truth into your circumstances and let's see God do a miracle! **Available to download from iTunes and other online platforms.**

Speak.....Declare the Truth: Volume 2 - £8.00
Do you know you are loved? Do you realise you are valued? Do you understand you are special? So many of us struggle with confidence, our self-image and our mental ability to believe we are worthy. We don't value ourselves and therefore we cannot see how anyone else will value us. Do you know God delights in you and celebrates you? Do you realise that he sings songs of joy and delight over you? Do you struggle with the ability to see a joyful future full of hope? God not only believes in you but he has wonderful plans and purposes for your life. Who are you listening to? Who are you believing? We need to listen to the truth of the word of God rather than listening to the lies of the enemy.

We need to believe the word of God rather than believing the enemy's lies. There is power in the spoken word, so read, believe and confess the truth and see your circumstances and your life change for the better. **Available to download from iTunes and other online platforms.**

ALL MEDITATION CDs ARE AVAILABLE DIRECT FROM NGM AT:

www.ngm.org.uk/shop, www.nancygoudie.com or through
www.amazon.co.uk

OTHER PRODUCTS

**Nancy Goudie's Spiritual Health Magazine -
£3.00** (annually)
Filled with stories, advice, tips and interesting articles – a
great glossy magazine to brighten up your day.

Bible Reading Planners – 50p
A superb way of systematically reading through the Bible in
one or two years.

Wholehearted - by Leanne Goudie - £5.00
Wholehearted is a 30-day interactive devotional written by
Leanne Goudie and packed full of encouragements, scriptures and space to journal. So many women go through life
struggling to embrace their God given identity and worth, so
Wholehearted was written to encourage and equip women in their everyday
lives.

Throughout, the book, there is space to journal and write, allowing you to
process anything that arises from reading the encouragement given each
day. This is your devotional and your space to process, so take it at your own
pace and enjoy the journey of living your life. Grab your copy now!

Secrets EP - £5.00
Secrets is the debut EP from Leanne Goudie
Leanne is a singer/songwriter. She has written these
songs herself and recorded them at Caedmon Complex
DNA Studio.

NEW GENERATION WORSHIP

Assured - £5.00

Assured is the debut EP from New Generation Worship featuring five fantastic new tracks. These new songs carry a fresh passion and prophetic edge. They all reflect a deep hunger for his presence which lies at the heart of the ngm community. **Available to download from iTunes and other online platforms.**

YOU CAN PURCHASE ALL OF THESE PRODUCTS DIRECT FROM NGM AT:

www.ngm.org.uk/shop, www.nancygoudie.com or through **www.amazon.co.uk**

GET IN TOUCH

Should you wish to contact Nancy then do write to her at:

ngm
Caedmon Complex
Bristol Road
Thornbury
Bristol, BS35 3JA
UK

Phone: 01454 414880
Email: nancy@nancygoudie.com
Website: www.nancygoudie.com

Follow Nancy on **Twitter** *(@NANCYGOUDIE)*

Join *'Nancy Goudie's Spiritual Health Weekends'* group on **Facebook**

Like Nancy Goudie's **Facebook** page